ELITE STUDENT EDITION

5 STEPS TO A 5™

AP Environmental Science

2024

ELITE STUDENT EDITION

5 STEPS TO A 5™

AP Environmental Science

2024

Courtney Mayer, MEd

McGraw Hill

New York   Chicago   San Francisco   Athens   London   Madrid
Mexico City   Milan   New Delhi   Singapore   Sydney   Toronto

1 2 3 4 5 6 7 8 9   LHS   28 27 26 25 24 23
1 2 3 4 5 6 7 8 9   LHS   28 27 26 25 24 23 (Elite Student Edition)

ISBN   978-1-265-29342-0
MHID   1-265-29342-2

e-ISBN   978-1-265-29459-5
e-MHID   1-265-29459-3

ISBN   978-1-265-29696-4 (Elite Student Edition)
MHID   1-265-29696-0

e-ISBN   978-1-265-29755-8 (Elite Student Edition)
e-MHID   1-265-29755-X

McGraw Hill, the McGraw Hill logo, *5 Steps to a 5*, and related trade dress are trademarks or registered trademarks of McGraw Hill and/or its affiliates in the United States and other countries and may not be used without written permission. All other trademarks are the property of their respective owners. McGraw Hill is not associated with any product or vendor mentioned in this book.

AP, Advanced Placement Program, and *College Board* are registered trademarks of the College Board, which was not involved in the production of, and does not endorse, this product.

McGraw Hill products are available at special quantity discounts to use as premiums and sales or for use in corporate training programs. To contact a representative, please visit the Contact Us pages at www.mhprofessional.com.

McGraw Hill is committed to making our products accessible to all learners. To learn more about the available support and accommodations we offer, please contact us at accessibility@mheducation.com. We also participate in the Access Text Network (www.accesstext.org), and ATN members may submit requests through ATN.

CONTENTS

STEP 5

Building Your Test-Taking Confidence

**ELITE
STUDENT
EDITION**

5 Minutes to a 5

PREFACE

Welcome to the *5 Steps to a 5 AP Environmental Science* (APES) review book! This book contains the information you need to be successful on the APES exam. In 2019, the College Board changed many things about the APES exam and course. I have written this book so that it is completely aligned to the curriculum framework that the College Board laid out. All the practice questions in the chapters, on the diagnostic exam, and on the two practice exams are written as closely to how they will be tested on the actual exam as possible.

Keep in mind that the test will be difficult, but with hard work and a plan in place, you will have a very good chance at earning college credit. This book will take you step-by-step through each topic and each type of question. There are different strategies on how you should approach your studying depending on when you start studying and how much time you have to devote to your studies spelled out in Chapter 2. Pick the strategy that works best for you and stick with it!

This book has all the major concepts, clear and easy-to-understand examples, and test questions that are written with the skills outlined by the College Board. There are other books out there with similar information about AP Environmental Science, but this one truly aligns to exactly the information you will be tested on. I have written the chapters to be conversational, which is exactly how I teach my students in class. After 15 years of teaching this course to thousands of students, I have learned the best ways to remember the concepts and have had feedback from my students on ways that help them. All of this is incorporated into the book. I have also pointed out throughout the chapters the way the information will be tested. For example, if a particular concept will be tested with your reading a short text, I tell you that; if it is tested using a graph or data table, I point that out as well. The fewer surprises you encounter when you sit down to take the test, the more successful you will be.

Make sure to not only take the two practice exams after you have reviewed all the concepts, but read the explanations, even on the questions you got right, to make sure you truly understand the concepts and why the answer was correct. The multiple-choice section constitutes 60 percent of your score and the free-response section 40 percent. Make sure you pay special attention to the types of free-response questions you will be given. Do not blow this part off, as it counts for almost half of the test. Read the details of how the free-response questions will be scored carefully and make sure to go into detail as you answer. Remember, the reader/grader can't call you and ask you questions about your answer. Practice this now, with this book and its examples, so you will do well on this part of the exam.

Let's get started. First, take the diagnostic exam and go through each answer and explanation. See which chapters and topics you need to work on most and where you just need to review. There are some topics that you will know better than others, and using the diagnostic exam with the "Analyzing Your Performance on the Diagnostic Exam" page, you can prioritize the chapters you have the most difficulty with. You might also want to form a study group with others from your class since studying with others helps many students. Good luck on the exam and happy studying!

ACKNOWLEDGMENTS

I would like to thank those who made this book possible: my husband, David, and my children, Caitlin, Colin, and daughter-in-law Rachel, all of whom allowed me to spend countless hours over the holidays working on it. I would also like to thank my parents, Dr. Michael Masser and Carolyn Elkins, for always supporting me. Thank you, Grace Freedson and Grace Freedson's Publishing Network, for offering so many writing opportunities over the years, including this book, and for always trusting me in my writing abilities. Thank you to my amazing science editor and friend, Elisa McCracken, for painstakingly going through every chapter and every question to make sure it was aligned to the new curriculum from the College Board and to my editor, Del Franz, for making all the changes that needed to be made to make this book a success.

ABOUT THE AUTHOR

Courtney Mayer taught science courses for 23 years, including AP Environmental Science for 15 years, in San Antonio, Texas. She is a College Board consultant for AP Environmental Science in the southwest. She has presented all over the United States and in China. Courtney is also a College Board consultant for Analytical Reading and Writing Strategies in Science and is on the writing committee for the Pre-AP Biology curriculum. Courtney was a reader and table leader at the AP Environmental Science reading where she scored free-response questions for thousands of students. She was honored in 2011 with the College Board's AP award for helping to promote and continue the mission set by the College Board.

Courtney recently retired as the Director of Advanced Academics in Northside ISD and is now the AP Environmental Science teacher for UT High School. Courtney has published 10 books, all around science topics, particularly AP Environmental Science.

Courtney graduated with a degree in Wildlife and Fishery Science from Texas A&M University in 1992, and she received her Master of Education in Administration from Lamar University.

INTRODUCTION: THE FIVE-STEP PROGRAM

The Basics

At this point, you are either in an AP Environmental Science class, planning on taking one, or already schooled in many biological and ecological sciences and believe you may be able to get AP college credit with extra focus on the environmental sciences. All are good reasons to take the AP Environmental Science Exam! Solid effort and review of the material and questions offered in the *5 Steps to a 5: AP Environmental Science* study guide will give you a leg up and help ensure your score is the best it can be with the time you have to study.

Organization of the Book

This book takes you on a journey of the five steps needed to get ready for the AP exam in environmental science. Each step will provide skills and approaches helpful in achieving a perfect 5.

First, you will be introduced to the five-step plan described in the book. Chapter 1 gives some background on the AP Environmental Science exam. Chapter 2 lays out three study plans based on the amount of time you have before the test. Chapter 3 has a diagnostic exam to give you an idea of how much you know already. In Chapter 4, various tips and different types of AP exam questions are presented.

Chapters 5 to 13 offer a broad overview of the information important in an AP Environmental Science course. Although this is meant as review, some information may be new to you depending on your previous classes, teachers' particular focus, and how up-to-date you are on global environmental concerns. A summary, key ideas, and keywords are presented at the beginning of each chapter. A rapid review, along with multiple-choice and free-response questions and answers, are also included.

Following the informational chapters, two practice exams are provided with both question types (i.e., multiple choice and free response) found on the AP Environmental Science exam. After going through the study guide, you will be able to test your knowledge level on questions similar to those asked on past AP Environmental Science exams. Should you find areas where your memory or understanding fog, check your answers with the explanations and note where you need to refresh. Go back to the subject chapters and review the information.

The Five-Step Program

Step 1: Set Up Your Study Program

The first step contains an overview of the AP Environmental Science exam and an outline of associated topics. It also offers a timeline to help with your exam review planning.

- **The School-Year Timeline:** An entire school year: September to May
- **The One-Semester Timeline:** One semester: January to May
- **The Six-Week Timeline:** Six weeks: Quick exam brushup

Step 2: Determine Your Test Readiness

This step offers a diagnostic exam for a "sneak peek" at your test readiness. Take your time with the questions and do your best. Remember, the diagnostic exam is intended to help you see how much you already know and how much preparation you need before you take the real exam.

Step 3: Develop Strategies for Success

Here the different question types are described with strategies for doing your best on the multiple-choice and free-response questions. You'll learn how to read and analyze the questions and whether or not to guess. How to organize your responses on the free-response questions is also presented.

Step 4: Review the Knowledge You Need to Score High

This step presents the bulk of the environmental science information you'll need to know to score well on the revised AP Environmental Science exam. Since teachers and classes in different geographical areas may focus on one topic more heavily than another, this material helps fill in your knowledge gaps. The topics covered in Chapters 5 to 13 parallel those presented in a year long AP class.

Step 5: Build Your Test-Taking Confidence

The final step in AP Environmental Science preparation gives you a chance to take a practice exam with advice on how to avoid common mistakes. Practice exam questions are not from actual AP Environmental Science exams but mirror test material and question format.

Introduction to the Graphics Used in This Book

To emphasize particular strategies, we use several icons throughout this book. An icon in the margin will alert you that you should pay particular attention to the accompanying text. We use these three icons:

This icon points out a very important concept or fact that you should not pass over.

This icon calls your attention to a strategy that you may want to try.

This icon indicates a tip that you might find useful.

STEP 1

Set Up Your Study Plan

CHAPTER 1

What You Need to Know About the AP Environmental Science Exam

IN THIS CHAPTER

Summary: Learn what's on the AP Environmental Science exam, how it is scored, and basic test-taking information.

Key Ideas

✪ Before taking the AP Environmental Science course, you should have at least one year of a life science (for example, biology) and one year of a physical science (for example, chemistry).

✪ Eighty multiple-choice questions account for 60 percent of your score on the AP Environmental Science exam; three free-response (essay) questions account for the remaining 40 percent.

✪ You will receive a score of 1 to 5 on the AP exam. Most colleges will award credit for a score of 3, 4, or 5.

✪ There is no guessing penalty; if you don't know an answer to a multiple-choice question, you should try to eliminate incorrect answer choices and then guess.

The Advanced Placement (AP) Exams

The Advanced Placement Program (AP) is designed to allow high school students to earn credit for college-level courses by showing they have mastered the subject matter through their performance on an AP exam. Started in 1955, the program now encompasses dozens of AP exams across a range of disciplines. A complete list of the 38 AP courses offered and exams given is available at AP Central on the College Board website (https://apcentral .collegeboard.org/courses).

Who Creates the AP Environmental Science Course and Exam?

The College Board (www.collegeboard.com) is responsible for creating and administering the AP exams. For the AP Environmental Science course and exam, it is guided by members of the AP Environmental Science Development Committee, which is composed of leading educators in environmental science at both the high-school and college levels. AP environmental science teachers around the country follow a basic course curriculum that covers everything that will be on the AP exam. The AP course is designed to be the equivalent of a one-semester introductory environmental science college course. It includes biology, geology, chemistry, Earth science, and geography and fulfills a laboratory science requirement.

All questions developed for the exam go through a rigorous review process to ensure that they are accurate, fair, and valid. As part of this process the questions are tested on actual students. In fact, some of the questions you will encounter are actually questions that are being tested for use on a future AP exam and do not count on your test score. But since there is no way of knowing which questions these are, you should do your best on all questions.

Why Take the AP Environmental Science Exam?

The most obvious reason to take an AP exam is that you can earn college credit while you are still in high school, but there are other reasons as well. By taking an introductory college course in high school, you satisfy a prerequisite for many more advanced courses. This means you can jump right into more advanced courses in your field of study in college. Furthermore, since you are taking a college-level course in high school for free, you save a bundle of money over what it would cost to take the course in college. If you are taking several AP courses, you may even be able to finish college early. But even if you don't do well enough on the AP exam to earn college credit, you will still impress college admission officials. Your college application will show you have experienced a college-level course, are serious about school, and are not afraid of hard work.

Since you have bought this book, you are probably already enrolled in the AP Environmental Science course at your school. It is not a requirement that everyone enrolled in the course take the AP Environmental Science exam, but you should. Of course, doing well on the test is the only way to get college credit. Even if you think you will not do well enough to pass the test, have confidence in yourself; you may do better than you expect. And if you don't get a good score, you don't have to report it to the colleges you are planning to apply to.

Most students taking the AP Environmental Science exam are also taking biology, geology, chemistry, or other related science classes. An interesting thing about environmental science is that many subjects merge when studying the environment. Nature contains many interconnected components and concepts. In fact, most environmental jobs in the real world call for a general knowledge of all these areas when a job application is being considered.

Frequently Asked Questions About the AP Environmental Science Exam

Are There Any Prerequisites for the AP Environmental Science Course?

Students who take AP Environmental Science should have already completed one year of life science and one year of physical science (for example, one year of biology and one year of chemistry). Students should also have at least a year of algebra because of the quantitative analysis that is required in the course.

Is There a Lab Requirement?

Yes. It is required that the students spend at least 25 percent of instructional time engaged in laboratory inquiry or fieldwork investigations.

What Is the AP Classroom?

The AP Classroom is the name given to the online platform designed to the used by teachers and students during the AP course. It includes an online library of real AP exam questions from previous tests. Questions for every unit provide feedback, allowing you to check on your progress. The sign-up process includes entering a code provided by your teacher that is unique to your class so your teacher can monitor your progress, give you online assignments, and create unit tests. To start the sign-up process, go to www.collegeboard.com/apstudents.

What Type of Questions Are on the AP Environmental Science Exam and How Long Is It?

The exam actually consists of two separate tests: Section 1 and Section II. The first section of the exam includes 80 multiple-choice questions and accounts for 60 percent of your total score. You have 90 minutes to complete this section of the test. Part II of the exam consists of three free-response questions and accounts for 40 percent of your final score. You have 70 minutes for this section. In total, the exam is 2 hours and 40 minutes.

What Can I Expect Regarding the Multiple-Choice Questions?

The chart below shows what is on the test and the amount of your total score each part comprises.

Unit 1:	The Living World: Ecosystems	6–8%
Unit 2:	The Living World: Biodiversity	6–8%
Unit 3:	Populations	10–15%
Unit 4:	Earth Systems and Resources	10–15%
Unit 5:	Land and Water Use	10–15%
Unit 6:	Energy Resources and Consumption	10–15%
Unit 7:	Atmospheric Pollution	7–10%
Unit 8:	Aquatic and Terrestrial Pollution	7–10%
Unit 9:	Global Change	15–20%

Source: The College Board

The multiple-choice section includes both individual and set-based questions. The set-based questions will have two or three multiple-choice questions relating to a chart, graph, map, etc., that you are given. This visual representation of data is called a "stimulus" by the test creators. There will be three to four question sets based on quantitative data (tables, charts, graphs) and three to four question sets based on qualitative information (models, representations, maps). You can also expect two sets of questions that will include text-based sources.

What Can I Expect Regarding the Free-Response Questions?

There are three free-response or essay questions and each of them is worth 10 points. In the first essay question you will be asked to design an investigation. In the second question, you will be asked to analyze an environmental problem and propose a solution. For the third, you will have to use calculations to propose a specific solution to an environmental problem.

Each free-response question typically has multiple parts. Be sure to answer all parts of each question and label your answer to each part. If you are asked to "propose two realistic solutions to reduce greenhouse gas emissions," you should be sure to give exactly two realistic solutions. Giving only one solution, no matter how comprehensive, will not earn you full credit. And, more important, giving three solutions, when only asked to give two, will not earn you any extra credit. Stick to exactly what you are asked to do.

How Is the Exam Graded?

The multiple-choice questions are graded by a computer, but the essay questions are graded by humans. At the AP Reading in June, the free-response questions are read by environmental science college faculty and expert AP teachers at the high-school level. A group of readers are assigned to each question; the three essay questions you write will be evaluated by three teams of teachers. Readers are carefully trained in their question and their work is monitored throughout the reading for fairness and consistency. Scores on the free-response questions are weighted and combined with the results of the multiple-choice section of the exam that was scored by computer. The raw score is converted into a score of 1–5; this is your final score on the AP Environmental Science exam. In July, you will receive your AP score for the exam you took in May.

What Does the Score Mean?

Your AP score can be interpreted as follows:

AP SCORE	RECOMMENDATIONS	COLLEGE GRADE EQUIVALENT
5	Extremely well qualified	A
4	Well qualified	A–, B+, B
3	Qualified	B–, C+, C
2	Possibly qualified	n/a
1	No recommendation	n/a

Source: The College Board

Colleges and universities are responsible for setting their own policy of what score you will need on the AP exam to receive credit. Most colleges and universities will award credit for a score of 3 or higher; however, elite colleges often require a score of 4 or better. Check the AP credit policy of each college or university you are applying to. A search engine to do this is available at the College Board website: go to apstudent.org/creditpolicies.

How Do I Sign Up for the Exam?

The deadline for registration for the exam is in October or November. Signing up is easy; your name and personal data is taken from the information you input when you registered for the AP Classroom. Schools receive personalized registration labels for each student taking the exam; you will no longer need to bubble in your personal information. The cost to students to take the exam in 2020 was $94. Students who sign up late pay an additional $40. If you cancel your registration to take the exam, that will also cost $40.

Is There a Guessing Penalty on the Exam?

No. In times past there was a guessing penalty; a fraction of a point was subtracted for each incorrect answer but not for an unanswered question. But this is no longer the case. Points are given for each correct answer and no points are subtracted for a wrong answer. For that reason, if you don't know an answer, you should try to eliminate as many answer choices as possible and then guess. If you are running out of time, you should randomly guess the answers. You have a 25 percent chance of getting an answer correct simply by guessing. Never leave an answer blank.

Is a Calculator Allowed?

A four-function, scientific, or graphing calculator is allowed on both sections of the exam. But only certain types and brands of calculators are allowed. Check the College Board website for a list of approved calculators at https://apstudents.collegeboard.org/exam-policies-guidelines/calculator-policies. Alternatively, just search for "approved calculators" on the website.

No calculator will be allowed that has the option to communicate with the world outside the exam room. Therefore, the calculator on your cell phone will not be allowed. You must have your own calculator; you will not be allowed to share calculators with a friend. Be sure your calculator is fully charged before the test.

A calculator will be a big help on questions that ask for a specific answer and on the third free-response question where you will have to use calculations to propose a solution to an environmental problem. But just because you *can* use a calculator, doesn't mean you *should*. You won't find it helpful on most of the questions on the exam—only when a specific calculation is asked for.

What Should I Bring to the Test?

1. Two sharpened No. 2 pencils with erasers for all your responses on your multiple-choice answer sheet. Be sure the eraser will erase pencil marks completely without smudging.
2. Two pens with black or dark-blue ink for writing your essays in the exam booklet.
3. A watch will allow you to pace yourself by keeping track of the time in case the exam room does not have a clock or the exam room's clock is not correct. Make sure your watch does not have Internet access, does not have an alarm, and does not beep.
4. An approved calculator. (You can actually bring two of these. If yours suddenly quits working for some reason, you'll have a backup.)
5. If you don't attend the school where you're taking the exam, you must bring a current government-issued or school-issued photo ID.

What Should I Not Bring to the Exam Room?

1. Most types of electronic equipment (phones, smartwatches, laptops, cameras, recording devices, etc.) are prohibited. Approved calculators are the only exception.
2. Scratch paper; instead, you can write on blank areas of the exam booklet. Do *not* write anything on the exam answer sheet except to bubble in the answers.
3. Food or drink.

CHAPTER 2

How to Plan Your Time

IN THIS CHAPTER

Summary: The right preparation plan for you depends on your study habits, your own strengths and weaknesses, and the amount of time you have to prepare for the test. Take the diagnostic test in the next chapter to assess your strengths and weaknesses and get started.

Key Ideas

✪ Create a study plan that best suits your needs. It should take into account your strengths and weaknesses, your study habits, and the amount of time you have to prepare for the AP Environmental Science exam.

✪ The first step in creating your study plan is to take the diagnostic test in the next chapter; it will help identify where you need to prioritize your review.

✪ Your study plan will depend on when you start your test preparation. You can choose a full school-year, a one-semester, or a six-week timeline for your plan.

Your Personalized Study Plan for the AP Environmental Science Exam

Your study plan will be unique to your needs—your strengths and weaknesses and the amount of time you have to review. It's up to you to decide how you want to use this book to study for the AP Environmental Science exam. This book is designed for flexibility; you can work through it in order or skip around however you want. In fact, no two students who purchase this book will probably use it in exactly the same way.

The first step in developing your plan is to take the diagnostic test in the next chapter. This practice exam closely mirrors the multiple-choice section of the actual exam. The diagnostic test lets you experience what the multiple-choice section is like and also tells you what you are reasonably good at and what things you need to practice. Identify your weakness and focus on these first.

Also helpful in identifying strengths and weaknesses are the chapter summary and the key terms and ideas that begin each content review chapter. Use these to test yourself to determine if you need to carefully review the chapter or if your knowledge will allow you to skip it and move on to chapters that you need to study more completely.

Three Timelines for Preparing for the AP Environmental Science Exam

Besides your strengths and weaknesses, another factor to consider is the amount of time you have to prepare for the test. This includes not only how long you have before the exam, but also the amount of time you have to devote to the review effort. For example, for students who are taking more than one AP course and have to divide their study time among many demands, it is especially important to prioritize the areas they need to review.

Below are three timelines for study plans based on how long you have before the test. Decide on a timeline for your study plan and get started.

The School-Year Timeline

Choose this timeline if you like taking your time going through the material. Following this plan will allow you to practice your skills and develop your confidence gradually. You should go through the chapters in the book as you go through the units of your course. Take the diagnostic exam during Winter break, the first practice exam during spring break, and the final practice exam a week before the actual exam. You will be able to see your progress!

This book is filled with explanatory material and practice exercises. Beginning to work through the chapters at the beginning of the school year will allow you to get to all the material in the book and maximize your preparation for the exam.

The One-Semester Timeline

Starting in the middle of the school year should give you ample time to review and prepare for the exam. Begin by taking the diagnostic test in the next chapter; this will give you an idea of what the test is like. You'll get a sense of how hard the test will be for you, how much time you need to devote to practice, and which type of questions or tasks you most need to work on. Then skip around in this book, prioritizing the chapters that you most need to review or that you find most difficult. Take the first practice exam during spring break and the final practice exam a week or a few days before you take the actual test.

The Six-Week Timeline

OK, maybe you procrastinated a bit too long. But this might not be a problem if you are doing well in your AP Environmental Science class. In fact, preparation for the exam is included in most AP classes, so you may be better prepared for the exam than you realize.

Start by taking the diagnostic test in the next chapter to find out what the actual test will be like and to identify the chapters you most need to review. With limited time, it is especially important to prioritize wisely the areas you need to review. If you found the practice test difficult, try to devote as much time as possible to reviewing the chapters you found most difficult, paying special attention to the practice problems in these chapters. Save time to take the practice exams at the back of this book; take the final one a few days before you take the actual test. Even if you did well on the diagnostic test, you should take both practice exams; taking them will give you experience in pacing yourself within the time limits of the exam.

When to Take the Practice Exams

Most students should take the diagnostic test in Chapter 3 when they begin test preparation. Taking the test will show you what the actual exam will be like and, based on your performance, you can identify your strong points as well as the weaknesses you'll need to focus on. Take the first practice exam at the end of this book during spring break or midway through your test preparation to measure your progress and see if your priorities should change. Take the final practice exam a week, or perhaps only a few days, before the actual test.

The practice tests are perhaps the most important part of this book. Taking them will accomplish all of the following:

- Give you practice with all the different types of questions you'll encounter on the AP Environmental Science exam.
- Allow you to measure your progress and identify areas you need to focus on in your test preparation.
- Allow you to practice pacing yourself with the time limits imposed on the test.

Below are some things to remember as you plan your test-prep effort, regardless of when you start and how long you plan to practice:

- Establish a specific calendar of review so you stay on schedule and check off tasks as you complete them.
- Use your mobile phone to time yourself every time you take a timed test.
- Take advantage of the practice tests in this book. They are your friends.
- Don't stay up the night before the test trying to do some last-minute cramming; this may be counterproductive.

Good luck!

STEP **2**

Determine Your Test Readiness

CHAPTER 3

Take a Diagnostic Exam

IN THIS CHAPTER

Summary: In the following pages you will find a diagnostic exam that is modeled after the multiple-choice section of the actual AP exam. Take it as you begin your review for the AP Environmental Science Test. Use it to prioritize which chapters you will need to review for the actual exam.

Key Idea

✪ Practice the kind of multiple-choice questions you will be asked on the real exam.
✪ Check your work against the answers and explanations provided.
✪ Determine your areas of strength and weakness.
✪ Earmark the concepts to which you must give special attention.

How to Take the Exam

When you take the diagnostic exam, try to reproduce the actual testing environment as closely as possible. Find a quiet place where you will not be interrupted. Do not listen to music or watch a movie while taking the exam! Set the timer on your cell phone for 90 minutes. If you didn't finish, note how far you have gotten so you can learn to pace yourself, but then take the extra time to complete all the questions so you can find your areas of weakness. One more thing: tear out the answer sheet provided and fill in the correct ovals with a No. 2 pencil. The AP Environmental Science Exam is a paper-and-pencil test.

After Taking the Diagnostic Exam

Following the exam, you'll find not only the answers to the test questions, but also explanations for each answer. Don't just read the explanations for the questions you missed; you also need to understand the explanations for the questions you got right but weren't sure of. In fact, it's a good idea to read through the explanations for all the questions. Finally, complete the chapter-by-chapter analysis of your test results by filling in the boxes for the questions you missed. Then you have it—the chapters you most need to review.

AP Environmental Science Diagnostic Exam

ANSWER SHEET

1 Ⓐ Ⓑ Ⓒ Ⓓ	31 Ⓐ Ⓑ Ⓒ Ⓓ	61 Ⓐ Ⓑ Ⓒ Ⓓ
2 Ⓐ Ⓑ Ⓒ Ⓓ	32 Ⓐ Ⓑ Ⓒ Ⓓ	62 Ⓐ Ⓑ Ⓒ Ⓓ
3 Ⓐ Ⓑ Ⓒ Ⓓ	33 Ⓐ Ⓑ Ⓒ Ⓓ	63 Ⓐ Ⓑ Ⓒ Ⓓ
4 Ⓐ Ⓑ Ⓒ Ⓓ	34 Ⓐ Ⓑ Ⓒ Ⓓ	64 Ⓐ Ⓑ Ⓒ Ⓓ
5 Ⓐ Ⓑ Ⓒ Ⓓ	35 Ⓐ Ⓑ Ⓒ Ⓓ	65 Ⓐ Ⓑ Ⓒ Ⓓ
6 Ⓐ Ⓑ Ⓒ Ⓓ	36 Ⓐ Ⓑ Ⓒ Ⓓ	66 Ⓐ Ⓑ Ⓒ Ⓓ
7 Ⓐ Ⓑ Ⓒ Ⓓ	37 Ⓐ Ⓑ Ⓒ Ⓓ	67 Ⓐ Ⓑ Ⓒ Ⓓ
8 Ⓐ Ⓑ Ⓒ Ⓓ	38 Ⓐ Ⓑ Ⓒ Ⓓ	68 Ⓐ Ⓑ Ⓒ Ⓓ
9 Ⓐ Ⓑ Ⓒ Ⓓ	39 Ⓐ Ⓑ Ⓒ Ⓓ	69 Ⓐ Ⓑ Ⓒ Ⓓ
10 Ⓐ Ⓑ Ⓒ Ⓓ	40 Ⓐ Ⓑ Ⓒ Ⓓ	70 Ⓐ Ⓑ Ⓒ Ⓓ
11 Ⓐ Ⓑ Ⓒ Ⓓ	41 Ⓐ Ⓑ Ⓒ Ⓓ	71 Ⓐ Ⓑ Ⓒ Ⓓ
12 Ⓐ Ⓑ Ⓒ Ⓓ	42 Ⓐ Ⓑ Ⓒ Ⓓ	72 Ⓐ Ⓑ Ⓒ Ⓓ
13 Ⓐ Ⓑ Ⓒ Ⓓ	43 Ⓐ Ⓑ Ⓒ Ⓓ	73 Ⓐ Ⓑ Ⓒ Ⓓ
14 Ⓐ Ⓑ Ⓒ Ⓓ	44 Ⓐ Ⓑ Ⓒ Ⓓ	74 Ⓐ Ⓑ Ⓒ Ⓓ
15 Ⓐ Ⓑ Ⓒ Ⓓ	45 Ⓐ Ⓑ Ⓒ Ⓓ	75 Ⓐ Ⓑ Ⓒ Ⓓ
16 Ⓐ Ⓑ Ⓒ Ⓓ	46 Ⓐ Ⓑ Ⓒ Ⓓ	76 Ⓐ Ⓑ Ⓒ Ⓓ
17 Ⓐ Ⓑ Ⓒ Ⓓ	47 Ⓐ Ⓑ Ⓒ Ⓓ	77 Ⓐ Ⓑ Ⓒ Ⓓ
18 Ⓐ Ⓑ Ⓒ Ⓓ	48 Ⓐ Ⓑ Ⓒ Ⓓ	78 Ⓐ Ⓑ Ⓒ Ⓓ
19 Ⓐ Ⓑ Ⓒ Ⓓ	49 Ⓐ Ⓑ Ⓒ Ⓓ	79 Ⓐ Ⓑ Ⓒ Ⓓ
20 Ⓐ Ⓑ Ⓒ Ⓓ	50 Ⓐ Ⓑ Ⓒ Ⓓ	80 Ⓐ Ⓑ Ⓒ Ⓓ
21 Ⓐ Ⓑ Ⓒ Ⓓ	51 Ⓐ Ⓑ Ⓒ Ⓓ	
22 Ⓐ Ⓑ Ⓒ Ⓓ	52 Ⓐ Ⓑ Ⓒ Ⓓ	
23 Ⓐ Ⓑ Ⓒ Ⓓ	53 Ⓐ Ⓑ Ⓒ Ⓓ	
24 Ⓐ Ⓑ Ⓒ Ⓓ	54 Ⓐ Ⓑ Ⓒ Ⓓ	
25 Ⓐ Ⓑ Ⓒ Ⓓ	55 Ⓐ Ⓑ Ⓒ Ⓓ	
26 Ⓐ Ⓑ Ⓒ Ⓓ	56 Ⓐ Ⓑ Ⓒ Ⓓ	
27 Ⓐ Ⓑ Ⓒ Ⓓ	57 Ⓐ Ⓑ Ⓒ Ⓓ	
28 Ⓐ Ⓑ Ⓒ Ⓓ	58 Ⓐ Ⓑ Ⓒ Ⓓ	
29 Ⓐ Ⓑ Ⓒ Ⓓ	59 Ⓐ Ⓑ Ⓒ Ⓓ	
30 Ⓐ Ⓑ Ⓒ Ⓓ	60 Ⓐ Ⓑ Ⓒ Ⓓ	

AP Environmental Science Diagnostic Exam

SECTION I: Multiple-Choice Questions
Time—90 minutes

Directions: For the multiple-choice questions that follow, select the best answer and fill in the appropriate letter on the answer sheet.

1. The graph below shows the total number of endangered species per year.

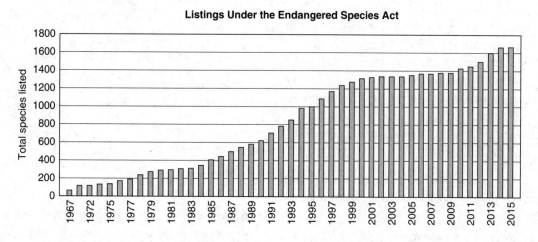

Listings Under the Endangered Species Act

Which of the following solutions could lead to a decrease of species on the endangered species list for future years?

(A) Introduce species to environments to compete for resources.
(B) Decriminalize poaching.
(C) Provide wildlife habitat corridors.
(D) Build roads and human habitation in wildlife areas.

2. The diagram below shows a convergent plate boundary.

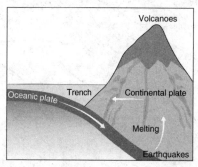

Convergent Plate Boundary

What is causing the formation of the volcano near the convergent plate boundary you see in the picture above?

(A) The two continental plates are coming together and forming mountains.
(B) The ocean plate is subducting below the continental plate, melting, and rising to form a volcano.
(C) As the magma from the mantle rises, and the lithosphere is moving over a stationary hot spot, a line of volcanic islands is forming.
(D) Land is being formed at a divergent plate boundary as magma rises.

3. "Loud noises from cities are becoming a huge problem for animal species. The sound of vehicles and construction are causing changes to animals' migratory routes, as well as causing problems to how they interact within their own species. This noise can have devastating effects to our biodiversity."

Which of the following statements would most likely support the author's claim?

(A) Vehicles and construction in cities are producing photochemical smog.
(B) Species need to learn to adapt to the sounds coming from cities.
(C) Urban sprawl is leading to environmental problems.
(D) Noise pollution is caused by transportation and construction.

4. Which of the following changes would most likely occur if the rat was removed from the food web?

A Food Web

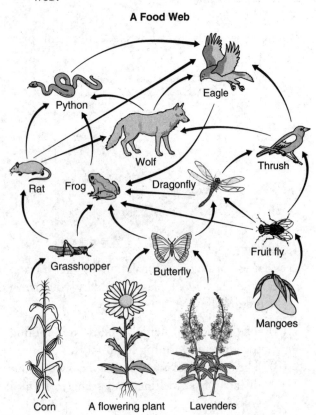

(A) Increase in grasshoppers and a decrease in pythons
(B) Decrease in frogs and a decrease in eagles
(C) Increase in eagles and an increase in thrush
(D) Increase in lavenders and an increase in corn

5. If the producers in an ecosystem convert 2,000 kCal of energy stored in organic compounds, which of the following would most likely be the amount of energy available to the secondary consumers?

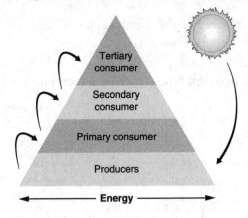

(A) 2,000
(B) 200
(C) 20
(D) 2

6. Soil erosion costs the world billions of dollars every year. Reasons for this economic cost include the number of pollutants washing into rivers and the loss of farmland due to erosion. A group of students decides to set up an experiment to see if they can reduce the amount of soil that is eroded after a rainfall.

Which of the following would the students discover as a benefit of reducing soil erosion?

(A) Soil filters and purifies water when protected from erosion.
(B) Soil can help reduce the effects of ozone depletion.
(C) Less soil erosion can help increase runoff and decrease infiltration.
(D) Clear-cutting can reduce the impacts of soil erosion.

7. People that live in the northern part of the United States can reduce their energy cost by lowering their thermostat by 2° in the winter. This reduces their energy costs by about 8 percent in many homes. If the family was paying $150 per month, how much will their bill be if they lower the thermostat by the 2°?

(A) $12
(B) $187.50
(C) $37.5
(D) $138

8. Which of the following is true about persistent organic pollutants (POPs)?

    (A) POPs break down easily in the environment.
    (B) POPs are found naturally on Earth.
    (C) POPs can travel very long distances through the food chain.
    (D) POPs cause nervous system damage.

9. Which of the following is a nonpoint source pollutant that might affect the air quality of a major city?

    (A) Automobile exhaust
    (B) Mercury from a coal burning power plant
    (C) A camper's campfire
    (D) Fertilizer runoff from a CAFO

10. Which of the following best describes an environmental disadvantage of aquaculture?

    (A) Aquaculture leads to overfishing.
    (B) Aquaculture can generate wastewater and contaminate waterways.
    (C) Aquaculture can be cost prohibitive.
    (D) Aquaculture helps build resistance to disease in wild populations of fish.

11. A country has a growth rate of 3 percent. How many years will it take for the population to double?

    (A) 3 years
    (B) 23 years
    (C) 30 years
    (D) 210 years

12. A country is going through the demographic transition and has lowered its total fertility rate (TFR) from 6.0 to 3.2 in 50 years. Which of the following could have affected the decline in TFR?

    (A) The government put in place strict laws on who could receive access to family planning.
    (B) Women have married at younger ages.
    (C) Good nutrition and medical attention are not accessible for many.
    (D) Women have gained more access to education.

13. Which of the following would be the most effective solution for reducing ozone depletion?

    (A) Encourage the manufacturers to utilize alternative chemicals.
    (B) Utilize chlorofluorocarbons in industrial processes.
    (C) Eat lower on the food chain so methane is reduced from cattle farming.
    (D) Ensure landfills are capped and gases can't be released into the atmosphere.

14. The graph below would be best used to compare to which of the following environmental concerns?

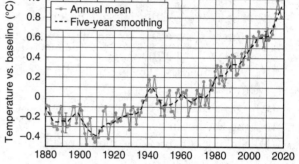

Global Average Temperature

    (A) Depletion of the stratospheric ozone levels
    (B) Increase of tropospheric ozone levels
    (C) Rising sea levels from melting ice sheets
    (D) Decreases in insect-borne vector diseases

15. One island is 30 km away from the mainland and another is 10 km away. They are both virtually the same size. Which of the following would be correct about the number of species living on the islands?

    (A) The numbers would be generally the same and would include species from the mainland.
    (B) There would be fewer species on the island farther away and more species on the island closer to the mainland.
    (C) There would be more species on the island farther away and fewer species on the island closer to the mainland.
    (D) The numbers would be generally the same but neither island would have species from the mainland.

16. Based on the diagram below, which of the following best describes what happens during a thermal inversion?

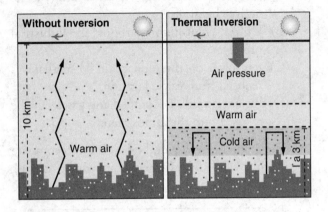

(A) The air temperature is cooler near the Earth's surface than above so pollution is trapped close to the Earth.
(B) Warm air rises, allowing pollution to escape to space.
(C) Warm air rises, trapping pollution close to the Earth's surface.
(D) Sinking air pressure allows pollutants to escape to space.

17. Coyotes eat rabbits as one of their main sources of food. Which of the following would be true of coyotes?

(A) Coyotes are herbivores.
(B) Ten percent of the energy from the rabbit will go to the coyote when he eats the rabbit.
(C) The coyote and the rabbit are in a mutualistic symbiotic relationship.
(D) If you removed the coyote from the food web, rabbits would decline in numbers.

18. Michelle likes to take a walk and enjoy nature. It calms her down, allows her to think about the next day, and she is able to get exercise while doing it. Which ecosystem service is Michelle benefiting most from?

(A) Provisioning
(B) Regulating
(C) Cultural
(D) Supporting

19. A student is on a walk and decides to test some of the soil he finds. After testing he discovers it is 10 percent sand, 60 percent silt, and 30 percent clay. Which of the following soil types would the student classify the soil as?

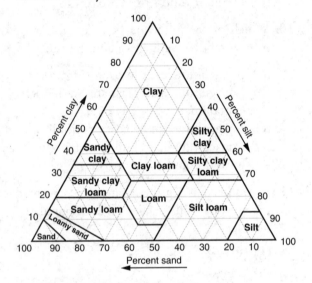

(A) Silty clay loam
(B) Clay loam
(C) Sandy clay loam
(D) Clay

20. The image below shows the different layers of the atmosphere.

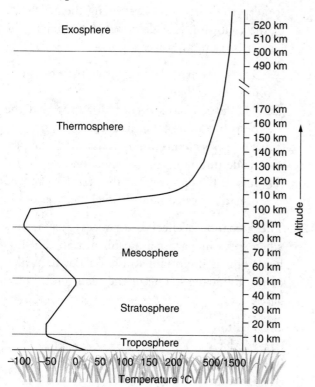

What layer is where chlorofluorocarbons have destroyed ozone?

(A) Troposphere
(B) Stratosphere
(C) Mesosphere
(D) Thermosphere

21. The diagram below shows a typical nuclear power plant.

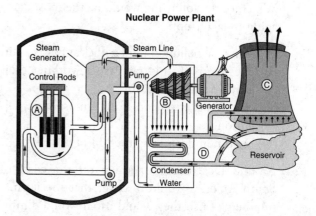

Which letter corresponds to the part of the plant where steam is used to turn a turbine?

(A) A
(B) B
(C) C
(D) D

22. Which of the following best describes why tidal energy is a renewable energy source?

(A) There is only a certain amount of tidal energy that can't easily be captured once it is used.
(B) Tidal energy is only available in certain places on Earth; therefore, it is considered nonrenewable.
(C) Each day, as the tides go in and out, tidal energy can be captured; it doesn't run out and can be replaced.
(D) Tidal energy can damage ecosystems so it is nonrenewable.

23. Lake trout like cold, oxygen-rich waters due to their bodies' need for high amounts of oxygen. Which of the following would be the most damaging to lake trout?

    (A) Thermal pollution from a nuclear power plant
    (B) Persistent organic pollutants working their way up the food chain
    (C) A thermal inversion from atmospheric pollution
    (D) Acid rain decreasing the pH of the lake

24. Around December, fishermen off the coast of South America would discover that the normal numbers of fish they would catch would diminish every three to seven years. Which of the following is the best explanation of why this was happening?

    (A) Individual sport fishing was occurring in the region.
    (B) Fallout from local coal-burning power plants was generating acid rain.
    (C) Warmer waters were causing the fish to move to colder waters.
    (D) Large predators such as sharks were frequenting the region.

25. The diagram below shows how the Earth is tilted on its axis.

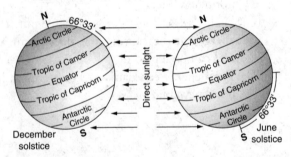

    Which best explains why the Arctic Circle would have the lowest solar radiation per unit area in December?

    (A) During December, the Arctic Circle receives the most direct sunlight.
    (B) During December, the Arctic Circle has the longest days of the year.
    (C) The Antarctic Circle is in the Southern Hemisphere so it is tilted toward the sun in December.
    (D) During December, the Arctic Circle is tilted away from the sun so it receives the lowest solar radiation compared to anywhere else on Earth.

26. A farmer wants to discover why every year he has to put more and more pesticides on his crops to keep the pests from destroying them. Which of the following best describes the problem the farmer is trying to solve?

    (A) The pests are breeding faster than ever due to climate change.
    (B) The farmer has switched to a crop that the pests like more than his previous crop.
    (C) The pests are becoming resistant to the pesticide through artificial selection.
    (D) It is an El Niño year and the pests have moved due to increased rainfall along the coasts.

27. The greenhouse effect is a process that occurs when gases in Earth's atmosphere trap the sun's heat. This is important to life on Earth. Which of the following is one of the main greenhouse gases?

    (A) Helium
    (B) Methane
    (C) Radon
    (D) Lithium

28. The carbon cycle is shown in the diagram below.

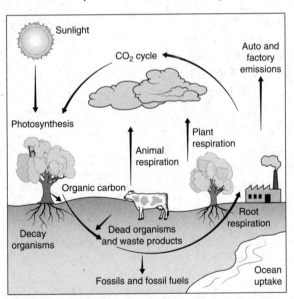

    Which of the following is a place where carbon is added to the atmosphere?

    (A) Photosynthesis
    (B) Fossils and fossil fuels found underground
    (C) Ocean uptake
    (D) Animal respiration

29. A scientist is interested in seeing how high the levels of DDT are in a population of bald eagles she has living near her wetland. Which of the following would be a testable hypothesis she could use for her investigation?

(A) Because DDT is fat soluble, it will bioaccumulate in living organisms and will be found in the tissues of the bald eagles.

(B) Because DDT was banned and removed from the market, it will not be found in the tissues of the bald eagles.

(C) Because DDT is only found in primary consumers, it will not be found in the tissues of the bald eagles.

(D) Because DDT is found in the atmosphere and soaks into the feathers as the birds fly, it will be found in the tissues of the bald eagles.

30. A gas station wants to prevent the fumes from escaping into the atmosphere as people pump gas into their vehicles. Which of the following devices would the gas station want to install?

(A) Catalytic converter
(B) Scrubber
(C) Vapor recovery nozzle
(D) Electrostatic precipitator

31. Which of the following is a benefit of using wind energy?

(A) Steam generated from wind energy is used to turn a turbine and generate energy.

(B) Wind turbines can be placed on land that is being used for farming or ranching to multipurpose the land.

(C) The carbon dioxide produced from wind energy can be captured and used for carbon sequestration.

(D) The energy created from the wind turbines can be used in hydrogen fuel cell technology.

32. In 2018/2019, Japan's greenhouse gas emissions fell to a record low. The country's greenhouse gas (GHG) emissions have declined from 1,291 $MtCO_2$ in 2017/18 to 1,244 $MtCO_2$ in 2018/19. What percent decrease has Japan seen in its GHG emissions?

(A) 3.6%
(B) 4,700%
(C) 47%
(D) 3.8%

33. The data table below shows how many animals are born every day.

ANIMAL	HOW MANY ARE BORN EACH DAY
Humboldt penguins	40
Rabbits (UK)	1,900,000
Chickens	62,000,000
Bees (UK)	370,000,000
Nematodes	600,000,000,000,000,000,000

Which of the following is most likely an animal that is an r-strategist?

(A) Humboldt penguins
(B) Rabbits
(C) Chickens
(D) Nematodes

34. Based on the data in graph below, if a city wanted to start a recycling advertisement campaign to encourage people to recycle materials generated before they ended up in the local landfill, what would be the material the city would spend the least time convincing people to recycle?

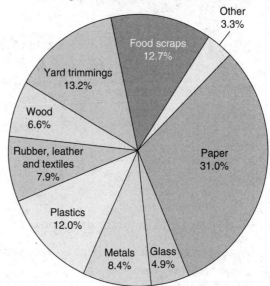

Percentage of Materials Sent to Local Landfills

(A) Paper
(B) Yard trimmings
(C) Plastics
(D) Glass

35. The graph below shows the number of spruce trees per hectare of land over the years of glacial retreat in Glacier Bay, Alaska.

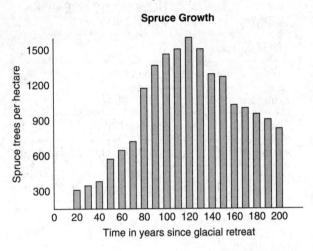

Based on the graph, when was the total biomass of spruce trees the greatest?

(A) 20 years since glacial retreat
(B) 80 years since glacial retreat
(C) 120 years since glacial retreat
(D) 200 years since glacial retreat

Use the graph below to answer questions 36–37.

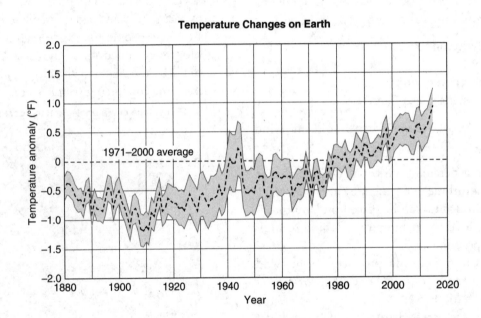

36. What is the trend shown in the graph?

(A) Use of chlorofluorocarbons is destroying the stratospheric ozone layer
(B) Global temperatures have increased over the past 140 years.
(C) The negative feedback loop in the Arctic is impacting the temperatures on Earth.
(D) The circulation patterns in the Hadley cells have caused Earth's temperatures to lower over time.

37. Which of the following would be the best way to slow the trend that is seen in the graph?

(A) Limit the addition of greenhouse gases in the atmosphere.
(B) Discourage the use of nonrenewable energy sources.
(C) Limit the process of secondary success in land environments.
(D) Encourage people to eat higher on the food chain.

38. Stratospheric ozone depletion has led to increased UV rays reaching the Earth's surface. Which of the following would help to stop the depletion of stratospheric ozone?

    (A) Limit the addition of greenhouse gases in the atmosphere.
    (B) Limit the use of fossil fuels for energy production.
    (C) Reduce methane gas release from landfills.
    (D) Stop using chlorofluorocarbons in industry and household products.

39. A scientist is trying to determine the best way to help farmers limit the number of pests on crops while lowering the environmental effects of pesticides. He sets up an experiment using predator bugs that eat the pests and collects the following data.

WEEK	NUMBER OF PREDATOR BUGS	NUMBER OF PEST SPECIES
1	2,000	1,000
2	2,500	700
3	3,500	300
4	5,000	20

What method of pest management is the scientist incorporating?

    (A) Using organophosphates on crops to lower pest numbers
    (B) Using persistent organophosphates on crops to lower pest numbers
    (C) Using integrated pest management to lower pest numbers
    (D) Using terracing methods to lower pest numbers

40. Which of the following activities are humans doing that are bleaching coral reefs due to ocean acidification?

    (A) Dumping untreated sewage into the open ocean
    (B) Leaking oil from tanker boats
    (C) Dumping plastic, forming the Pacific garbage gyre
    (D) Burning fossil fuels and increasing atmospheric carbon dioxide

41. A population is growing exponentially and eventually overshoots its carrying capacity. Which of the following would be an impact of this overshoot?

    (A) Starvation and disease will increase.
    (B) Resources will increase to support the population.
    (C) Carbon levels in the atmosphere will increase globally.
    (D) Competition will decrease as the population explodes.

42. Japan's age-structure diagram is pictured below. What type of growth does the diagram demonstrate?

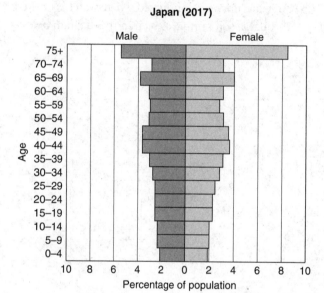

Japan (2017)

    (A) Rapid growth
    (B) Slow growth
    (C) Stable growth
    (D) Declining growth

43. Which of the following is the best example of the tragedy of the commons?

    (A) Timber companies paying private tree farmers for timber.
    (B) Farmers in arid climates overdrawing on water resources.
    (C) Farmers negotiating usage of grazing land.
    (D) Licensing sports fishermen being given regulations and limits.

44. Overfishing is a concern for many countries and it has lowered the biodiversity in aquatic systems. Which of the following could a country implement to solve this environmental problem?

(A) Give tax incentives to the fisherman who brings in the largest catch of the day.

(B) Extend the fishing season.

(C) Ban the use of purse seines, long-line fishing, and trawling nets that can take thousands of fish at a time.

(D) Remove all restrictions on different fishing methods.

45. An experiment is conducted where water is poured through a soil sample as seen in the diagram below.

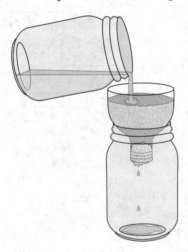

Then 100 ml of water is added and after 1 hour 95 ml is found in the bottom of the jar. Which of the following is most likely the type of soil being tested?

(A) Sand

(B) Silt

(C) Loam

(D) Clay

46. A scientist has been asked to find out why sulfur dioxide emissions are down 73 percent from 2006 to 2015. He discovers that coal-fired electricity generation is down 32 percent in that time, but this is a much larger reduction. Which of the following is most likely the device being used on power plants that are lowering the SO_2 emissions the greatest?

(A) Vapor recovery nozzle

(B) Catalytic converter

(C) Fluidized bed combustion and gas scrubbing

(D) Electrostatic precipitators

47. Use the graph below to answer the following question.

Percentage of Population Using Solid Fuels as the Main Cooking Fuel
The percentage of households in each region that rely on solid fuels (wood, crop residues, dung, charcoal or coal) as the main cooking fuel. The use of solid fuels for cooking can lead to very low indoor air quality and illnesses such as pneumonia, stroke, heart disease, or lung cancer.

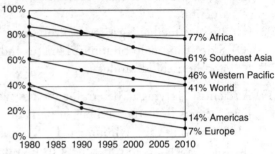

Which of the following conclusions can you draw from the graph above?

(A) People living in Africa are 77 percent more likely to suffer from diseases like pneumonia, stroke, and lung cancer than people living in high-income countries.

(B) Indoor air quality has risen in the past 30 years.

(C) Fewer people suffer from diseases like pneumonia, stroke, and lung cancer in the Americas than they do in Europe.

(D) Southeast Asia has not taken any steps in the past 30 years to lower indoor air pollution.

48. Nitrous oxides are considered trace gases and compose less than a tenth of 1 percent of the atmosphere. Why would scientists be concerned about the global climate impact of these trace gases?

(A) Nitrous oxides cause brain damage in children.

(B) The global warming potential (GWP) of nitrous oxide is 310, so it has a GWP of 300 times more than carbon dioxide, which has a GWP of 1.

(C) Nitrous oxides come from the production of Styrofoam and refrigerants, substances used all over the Earth that lead to stratospheric ozone depletion.

(D) Nitrous oxides rise on air currents and destroy stratospheric ozone.

49. The graph below shows the energy output in kWh for a local solar energy system. Use the graph to determine which of the following statements is true.

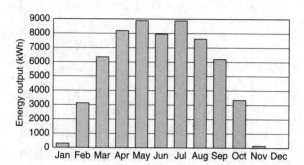

(A) Solar energy is available all year in amounts needed to supply cities with renewable energy.

(B) The output of this energy system is the highest during the month of June.

(C) Solar energy should not be used to support local energy demands due to the low output in the winter months.

(D) This energy system can produce over 7,000 kWh per month April through August, making it a good supplement for local energy output.

50. The chart below has the ecological footprint for five different people and is measured in the number of hectares (10,000 square meters) of land required to support the activity.

	FOOD	CARBON EMISSIONS	HOUSING	GOODS AND SERVICES	TOTAL
Person 1	1.8	2.9	2.4	1.6	8.7
Person 2	3.2	3	1.6	1.2	9
Person 3	1.4	2.7	2.2	2.0	8.3
Person 4	2.7	3	1.5	2.9	10.1
Person 5	2.8	3	3.4	1.9	11.1

If person 4 wanted to lower his ecological footprint to be more like person 1, what two activities should he change?

(A) He should increase his use of fossil fuels and food.

(B) He should decrease his housing and increase his goods and services.

(C) He should eat lower on the food chain and purchase fewer goods and services.

(D) He should increase his housing and increase his goods and services.

Use the graph below to answer questions 51–52.

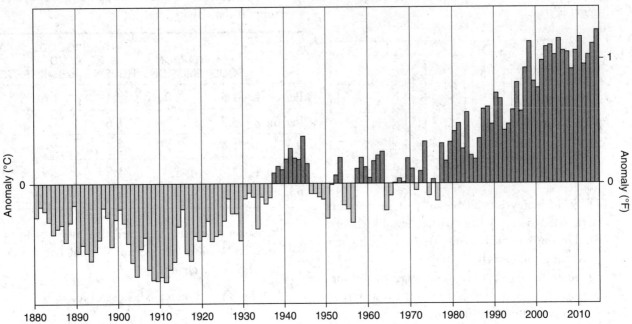

Global Land and Ocean Temperature Anomalies, January–December

Source: National Oceanic and Atmospheric Administration

51. The graph above shows the trend in global temperatures from 1880 to 2010. Which of the following could be a likely consequence of the temperature changes in this graph?

(A) Sea levels will rise, flooding coastal areas.
(B) Permafrost will freeze and not allow as long a growing season.
(C) Sea ice will freeze, lowering the salt content of the surrounding oceans.
(D) Specialist species will flourish.

52. Which of the following most likely caused the trend you see in the data above?

(A) Increased use of fossil fuels
(B) A shift to eating lower on the food web
(C) Increased use of lead gasoline in developing countries
(D) Biomagnification up the food web of persistent organic pollutants (POPs)

53. The picture below shows what happens when a body of water becomes eutrophic.

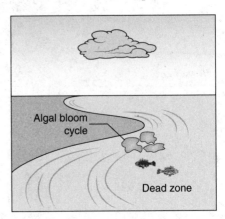

Which of the following would be the cause of what is seen in the illustration above?

(A) Increased use of fossil fuels for energy production
(B) Increased use of fertilizers from agriculture
(C) Increased thermal pollution from nuclear power plants
(D) Increased acid deposition from coal burning power plants

54. A scientist is taking water samples of a nearby lake. He takes the pH of the lake water and discovers it has a pH of 6.5. Which of the following activities will the scientist most likely conclude is causing the change in lake pH?

   (A) The release of chlorofluorocarbons in the nearby town
   (B) The escape of endocrine disruptors into the lake
   (C) Limestone rock that is leaching into the lake
   (D) A high concentration of motor vehicles and coal-burning power plants in the vicinity of the lake

55. The LD_{50} for table salt in humans is approximately 12,357 mg/kg. If a person weighs 200 lbs. and 1 kg = 2.2 lbs., how many grams of salt would it take to reach the LD_{50} for a human?

   (A) 1,123.4 grams
   (B) 1,123,363.6 grams
   (C) 561.7 grams
   (D) 22.47 grams

56. Burning biomass would be one way to move from our dependence on fossil fuels and also decrease the waste stream. Which of the following correctly describes a concern of using biomass on a large scale?

   (A) Earthquakes can result from the heated water pumped into the Earth.
   (B) Temperature inversions can result from the heat from the fires.
   (C) Deforestation and habitat destruction can result.
   (D) Helium can be released into the atmosphere.

57. The Goliath frog is the largest living frog on Earth, growing to 13 inches (33 centimeters) in length and weighing up to 7 pounds. The females lay several hundred eggs at one time with very few making it to adulthood. Adult frogs can live up to 15 years in the wild. Which of the following best characterizes this type of animal?

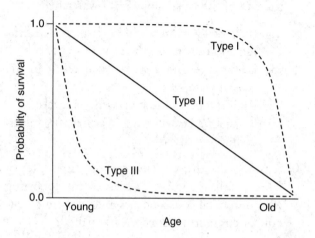

   (A) Goliath frogs are k-selected species, displaying a Type III survivorship curve.
   (B) Goliath frogs are r-selected species, displaying a Type I survivorship curve.
   (C) Goliath frogs are k-selected species, displaying a Type II survivorship curve.
   (D) Goliath frogs are r-selected species, displaying a Type III survivorship curve.

58. Which of the following would have the best success of surviving stress from environmental problems?

   (A) Populations with high genetic biodiversity
   (B) Populations with low genetic biodiversity
   (C) Populations with k-strategists
   (D) A population with low species richness

59. The largest watershed in the United States is the Mississippi River watershed. Pollution from farm fertilizers, soil erosion, and wastewater from sewage treatment plants are causing problems with the coastal waters at the end of this watershed. Which of the following would be an environmental concern for the estuary system at the end of the Mississippi River watershed?

(A) Increased fertilizers will bring increased fishing and tourism to the area.

(B) Low oxygen, or hypoxia, will result in the coastal waters.

(C) Runoff will lead to increased sea levels.

(D) Sewage waters will bring in estuary organisms containing disease.

60. A timber company is clear-cutting large acres of land to sell as lumber. Which of the following environmental consequences and economic benefits of clearcutting are correctly paired?

(A) Clear-cutting leads to soil erosion but provides the most profits.

(B) Clear-cutting leads to lower soil temperatures but provides the most profits.

(C) Clear-cutting leads to soil erosion but is costly to lumber companies.

(D) Clear-cutting leads to higher soil temperatures but is costly to lumber companies.

61. Surface mining removes the plants from an area leaving it vulnerable to erosion. Which of the following would be a way to remediate the loss of soil by mining?

(A) Take the slag and tailings to a certified landfill for removal.

(B) Use the overburden as agricultural filler.

(C) Reestablish the vegetation and assess and evaluate frequently.

(D) Grind up the overburden into a fine powder and spread on the area evenly.

62. The diagram below shows the rain shadow effect. Which of the following correctly identifies the factors behind this phenomenon?

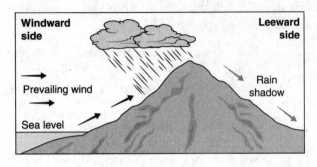

(A) As the air mass moves to higher elevations, it expands and warms. This warm air holds more moisture so clouds form and it rains. The air mass then moves over the mountain and there is less rainfall.

(B) As the air mass moves to higher elevations, it expands and cools. This cool air doesn't hold as much moisture so clouds form and it rains. The air mass then moves over the mountain and causes catastrophic flooding concerns.

(C) As the air mass moves to lower elevations, it expands and cools. This cool air holds more moisture so clouds form and it rains. The air mass then moves over the mountain and there is more rainfall, ending droughts when they occur.

(D) As the air mass moves to higher elevations, it cools. This cool air doesn't hold as much moisture so clouds form and it rains. The air mass then moves over the mountain and there is less rainfall.

63. Giant pandas eat bamboo and live in a few mountain ranges in south central China in Sichuan, Shaanxi, and Gansu provinces. The koala, a marsupial, lives in eastern Australia and eats eucalyptus trees. Pigeons and doves are distributed everywhere on Earth, except for the driest areas, and eat seeds, fruits, insects, and worms. Based on the descriptions above, what can we determine about these animals?

(A) Giant pandas and koalas are specialists and pigeons and doves are also specialists.
(B) Giant pandas and koalas are generalists and pigeons and doves are specialists.
(C) Giant pandas and koalas are specialists and pigeons and doves are generalists.
(D) Giant pandas and koalas are generalists and pigeons and doves are also generalists.

64. If the graph below shows the numbers of lionfish found in the Western Atlantic Ocean, Caribbean Sea, and Gulf of Mexico, what could we conclude from the data?

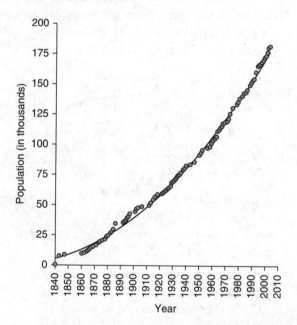

(A) Lionfish are an invasive species that has not yet reached its carrying capacity.
(B) Lionfish are an endangered species that should be federally protected.
(C) Lionfish live in coastal regions all over the globe.
(D) Lionfish have predators that were hunted to extinction, allowing their unprecedented growth to occur.

65. A farmer wants to increase the number of crops he produces. To do this he uses a tiller to turn over the land and prepare the ground for sowing while breaking up the soil and removing weeds. Which of the following environmental problems might the farmer encounter because of his tilling practice?

(A) Compaction of soil not allowing water to infiltrate
(B) Erosion of soil and water eutrophication
(C) Terracing leading to flooding
(D) Acid deposition from a lowered pH

Use the graph below to answer questions 66–68.

Projected Total Fertility Rate by World Region

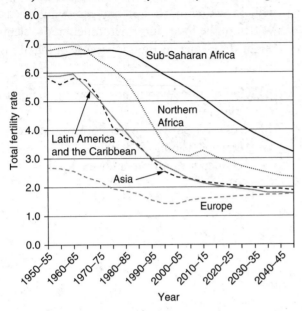

66. Which of the following can we conclude from the graph above?

    (A) Sub-Saharan Africa is at replacement level fertility in 2010.
    (B) In 1990, Northern Africa was a developed country with access for women to education and jobs.
    (C) Europe has had a low total fertility rate since 2000.
    (D) People in Latin America have more land per person than people in Europe.

67. Which of the following age-structure diagrams would most likely describe sub-Saharan Africa in 1970?

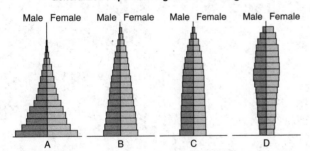

    (A) A
    (B) B
    (C) C
    (D) D

68. Which of the following environmental problems would a scientist expect to see in Northern Africa in 1960?

    (A) Habitat loss from deforestation to provide for the growing populations
    (B) Thermal pollution from nuclear power plants
    (C) Large-scale flooding from a rain shadow effect
    (D) The greenhouse effect

69. Methane is a greenhouse gas that contributes to climate change. Which of the following correctly describes methane's contribution to climate change?

    (A) Methane increases acid deposition.
    (B) Methane increases the albedo effect in polar regions.
    (C) Methane gas has the ability to trap infrared energy from the sun.
    (D) Methane gas is an endocrine disruptor in many species.

70. The graphic below shows the water (hydrologic) cycle. If we use asphalt and concrete to cover natural surfaces, which of the following would be the most likely impact on the water cycle?

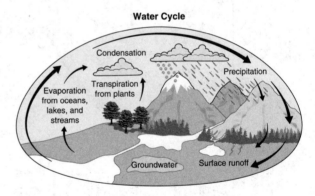

    (A) There would be less precipitation.
    (B) Evaporation would decrease.
    (C) Surface runoff would decrease.
    (D) Less water would infiltrate into the groundwater.

71. Sea urchins belong to the phylum Echinodermata, the same group as sea stars, sand dollars, and sea cucumbers. Many saltwater aquarium enthusiasts like to introduce sea urchins into their tanks. However, adult sea urchins have a very narrow range of salt concentration. Salinity levels that are too low or too high will result in reabsorption of gametes or death.

Which of the following best identifies the author's claim?

(A) If you love salt water aquariums you should introduce sea urchins.
(B) Sea urchins have a narrow ecological tolerance for salinity.
(C) Sea urchins need warm water to survive.
(D) Sea stars, sand dollars, and sea cucumbers are fragile specialist species.

72. Many environmentalists propose removing dams from rivers because of their environmental impact. What environmental disadvantage would occur by removing dams?

(A) Air pollution could occur if we revert back to burning fossil fuels to generate energy.
(B) Sediment could build up behind where the dam used to be.
(C) Estuary systems below the dam could dry up after dam removal.
(D) The energy that had been created before the dam was removed would need to be stored for future use.

73. Use the graph below to answer the following question.

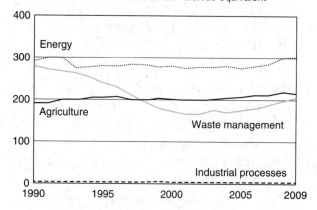

U.S. Methane Emissions by Source, 1990–2009
Million metric tons carbon dioxide equivalent

Which of the following can you derive from the graph above?

(A) The largest source of methane emissions is from industrial processes.
(B) In the past 20 years, methane emissions from energy has steadily increased.
(C) In 2009, methane emissions reached nearly 300 million metric tons carbon dioxide equivalency.
(D) Agriculture, which includes concentrated feeding operations, has increased from less than 200 million metric tons carbon dioxide equivalence to 210 million metric tons carbon dioxide equivalence.

74. Which of the would result from the plate boundary seen below?

Divergent Plate Boundary

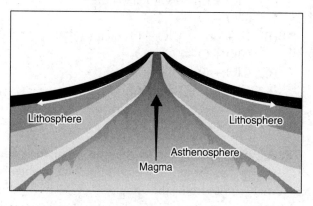

(A) Mountains would be formed.
(B) Island arcs would be formed.
(C) Sea-floor spreading would occur.
(D) Hot spots would occur.

75. A country had a birth rate of 20 individuals per every 1,000 persons and a death rate of 8 individuals per every 1,000 persons in 2019. In 1960 the same county had a birth rate of 40 individuals per every 1,000 persons and a death rate of 17 individuals per every 1,000 persons. What best describes what has happened in this country in the past 70 years?

    (A) The country is going through the demographic transition and there is less infant mortality, better living conditions, and more women are educated.
    (B) In 2019 the country is shrinking due to less births than deaths.
    (C) Density-dependent factors are at work in this country.
    (D) The growth rate of this country has increased.

76. A company produces power from coal and during the process captures the excess heat that would have been wasted. The company then uses this heat to boil water, create steam, or heat buildings. What process is the company implementing?

    (A) Hydrogen fuel cell technology
    (B) Passive solar generation
    (C) Cogeneration
    (D) Renewable energy transformation

77. The depletion of the stratospheric ozone layer is threatening the health of life on Earth. Which of the following chemical equations best explains the reaction that occurs in the stratosphere that breaks down ozone molecules?

    (A) $ClO + O_3 \rightarrow ClO + O_3$ then
        $ClO + O_2 \rightarrow Cl + O_3$
    (B) $Cl + O_3 \rightarrow ClO + O_2$ then
        $ClO + O \rightarrow Cl + O_2$
    (C) $ClO + O \rightarrow Cl + O_2$ then
        $Cl + O_3 \rightarrow ClO + O_2$
    (D) $ClO_2 + O \rightarrow Cl + O_2$ then
        $Cl + O_3 \rightarrow ClO_2 + O$

78. As we continue our reliance on fossil fuels for energy, we expand the environmental problems that come from this practice. Which of the following correctly describes an environmental problem of burning fossil fuels?

    (A) Fracking is used to obtain oil and gas but leads to groundwater contamination and releases volatile organic compounds during the production process.
    (B) Storage of lithium batteries used in fossil fuel production can leak and contaminate groundwater.
    (C) Damming of rivers prevents migration of fish species like salmon.
    (D) Storage of the radioactive waste produced from fossil fuel production can lead to radiation exposure and cancers.

79. "As transportation networks expand and urban areas grow, noise from sources such as vehicle engines is spreading into remote places. Human-caused noise has consequences for wildlife, entire ecosystems and people. It reduces the ability to hear natural sounds, which can mean the difference between life and death for many animals, and degrade the calming effect that we feel when we spend time in wild places."

    —From "How Noise Pollution Is Wreaking Havoc on U.S. Wildlife," by Rachel Buxton in *The Nation*, July 18, 2017.

    Which of the following best identifies the author's claim?

    (A) Limiting energy production near wild areas will help prevent noise pollution.
    (B) Noise pollution is a bigger problem in the northeastern United States than anywhere else.
    (C) Animals are migrating across large areas to escape the consequences of noise pollution.
    (D) Humans are causing noise pollution that is impacting animals and human relaxation.

80. Oceans are warming due to climate change, which is having a devastating impact on wildlife. Which of the following would be a consequence of our oceans warming?

    (A) Arctic species are moving farther north.
    (B) Coastal ecosystems are becoming shallower, allowing more light to penetrate farther into the waters.
    (C) Aquatic animals are being impacted by noise pollution from surrounding cities.
    (D) Coral bleaching is occurring, which is damaging reef systems.

STOP. End of Part I.

› Answer Key and Explanations

1. **C**—Building wildlife habitat corridors can allow animals to have a place to live, find food, and migrate, which will lower the impact of human habitation.

2. **B**—As the ocean plate subducts, or is forced below the continental plate, the ocean plate melts and rises. Have you ever watched a lava lamp work? The wax (lava) is down on the bottom of the lamp where the heat source (light bulb) is found. As the heat melts the wax, the wax begins to rise up through the liquid to the top—this is like what is happening on our planet. As the ocean plate melts because of the heat in our Earth, it begins to rise, forming a volcano.

3. **D**—The author states that vehicles and construction are causing noise pollution that is harming species.

4. **A**—Rats eat grasshoppers, so removing rats would cause grasshoppers to increase. But rats are a food source for pythons, so removing the prey would decrease the predators (pythons).

5. **C**—According to the 10 percent rule, a plant (which in this case has 2,000 kCal) will be eaten by a primary consumer, giving the primary consumer 200 kCal. When a secondary consumer eats the primary consumer it only gets 10 percent of that energy, or in this case 20 kCal.

6. **A**—Soil erosion can be caused by water and wind taking soil away. It is very important to stop soil erosion if possible because of the importance of soil for plants, the ability soil has to clean and filter water, and the concern that when soil erodes it can damage the local waterways.

7. **D**—$150 × $.08 = $12 less, so $150 − 12 = $138

8. **C**—Because animals migrate long distances in the water or in wind, and because these chemicals can travel in wind and water long distances, there are POPs in almost all parts of our planet. These chemicals are passed from one species to the other in the food chain (biomagnification).

9. **A**—The car's exhaust is nonpoint source pollution. You can't point to one particular thing. You can't point with your finger to all the cars on the road. As you read the question think about it like this: is that a single thing or a bunch of things? If it is a single thing, it is most likely point; many things is most likely nonpoint.

10. **B**—The environmental problem of aquiculture is that large numbers of fish can produce huge quantities of waste (fish poop, excess fish food, etc.), which can pollute the river, lake, or ocean.

11. **B**—70/3 = 23 years

12. **D**—If girls and women have access to education, the TFR of a country will go down because women usually postpone having children until they educate themselves and possibly go into the workforce.

13. **A**—The main way we have tried to stop the problem of ozone depletion is to stop using ozone-depleting substances. The Montreal Protocol (1987) and the Vienna Convention (1985) were treaties to control the release of these substances.

14. **C**—Currently, we are in a warming trend, which has impacted the environment and human health, including rising sea levels. Rising sea levels can flood coastal communities and leave ocean organisms too deep to photosynthesize.

15. **B**—The theory states that islands closer to the mainland (where the animals/plants have moved from) and/or larger islands will have more species than islands that are farther away or smaller. The size of the island in theory matters because larger islands can support more and different species while smaller ones would be more limited.

16. **A**—A thermal inversion is a weather condition when warm, less dense air moves over dense, colder air. Because of the thermal weather condition and the dense air, pollution, particularly smog and particulates, get trapped near the ground and can't "escape" to space.

17. **B**—The 10 percent rule is the idea that as usable energy moves up the pyramid much of it is "lost" to the laws of thermodynamics. The first law of thermodynamics states that energy cannot be created or destroyed, but the second law states that it can be transferred or transformed. So according

to the 10 percent rule, a plant or primary producer will only transfer 10 percent of the energy to the primary consumer that eats it, let's say a rabbit. This rabbit then goes about his day hopping around, heating his body, etc., and he uses up 90 percent of the energy he received from the plant. Next, when a coyote comes around and eats the rabbit, we assume the coyote only gets about 10 percent of the energy from the rabbit because the rabbit "used up" 90 percent doing what rabbits do.

18. **C**—Cultural: These are not "things" we benefit from but rather interactions with nature, such as taking a walk or enjoying what you see or art that comes from looking at nature, etc.

19. **A**—To do this, you start with the sand and find the percentage along the bottom of the triangle, in this case 10 percent, and follow the line that goes up and to the left for sand. Then, you move to the right side of the triangle and find the line for silt, in this case 60 percent. Follow this line down and to the left until it hits the line you had drawn for sand. They should cross. Then, where they cross, if you draw a straight line to the left, where you find clay, you should be at the 30 percent line, which is your percentage of clay. Where these three lines intersected is the type of soil you have. In this case, silty clay loam.

20. **B**—The stratosphere contains the ozone that chlorofluorocarbons have destroyed as they break down ozone into O_2.

21. **B**—This is where steam is pumped through a pipe that is focused on the giant turbine at extremely high pressures, causing the turbine to spin. This spinning is connected to an electrical generator that generates electricity.

22. **C**—Renewable energy resources are resources that can be replaced over a relatively short time scale. These include things like solar, wind, hydroelectric, geothermal, and biomass resources. Tidal is a type of hydroelectric power source.

23. **A**—Thermal pollution is often from a nuclear power plant where large amounts of heated water are being dumped into a body of water. The heated water doesn't have to have any pollutants in it, but just being warm can cause problems. This is because warm water can't hold as much oxygen as cold water. The oxygen diffuses out of the water and into the air. If organisms, such as fish, that need dissolved oxygen in the water can't get it, they might die.

24. **C**—In the Pacific Ocean, every three to seven years on average, warmer surface waters known as the El Niño–Southern Oscillation (ENSO) occur. Upwellings from the seabed in normal years bring nutrients up to the surface for the plankton to feed on; the plankton is food for the marine life up the food chain. In an El Niño year, that upwelling does not occur so the plankton is reduced and in turn, so are the fish stocks.

25. **D**—The amount of sunlight varies seasonally. The equator gets sun year-round, but as you move up or down to the poles you get less and less direct sunlight. The Arctic Circle is near the pole and during December it is pointed away from the sun.

26. **C**—One problem with many of these pesticides is that the organism that it is designed to kill builds up resistance over time. Pesticides are designed to prevent crop damage and increase crop profits. But if pesticide resistance becomes a problem, the pesticide will no longer work (or work as well) and the farmer/homeowner will have to either apply more pesticide, use stronger doses, or switch to a new type.

27. **B**

GAS	SOURCES	GWP	ATMOSPHERIC LIFETIME
Carbon dioxide	Decomposition, respiration, burning fossil fuels, deforestation	1	50–200 years
Methane	Burning of fossil fuels, livestock, landfills, decomposition, burning biomass, natural wetlands	21	12 years
Nitrous oxide	Soils, livestock manure, biomass or fossil fuel combustion, wastewater management	310	120 years
Chlorofluorocarbons	Refrigerants, aerosols, aircraft halons, solvents	12,000–16,000	20–100 years

28. **D**—As seen in the illustration, animal respiration puts carbon into the atmosphere. The rest are all examples of removing carbon from the atmosphere.

29. **A**—DDT can bioaccumulate in the fatty tissues of animals. This is because they don't break down and "accumulate" there. In addition, because animals eat other animals, these chemicals can magnify up the food chain.

30. **C**—Vapor recovery nozzles are put on gasoline pumps to capture the fumes that are produced.

31. **B**—Wind energy is a type of power that is clean, free, and can be used in areas where the land is being used for other things, such as ranching or growing crops.

32. **A**—$1,244 \, MtCO_2 - 1,291 \, MtCO_2 / 1,291 \, MtCO_2 \times 100\% = -3.6\%$

33. **D**—Since the nematodes have 600,000,000,000,000,000,000 babies a day, we can assume this means they have very little parental care with so many offspring, a characteristic of an r-selected species.

34. **D**—Glass is only 4.9 percent of the material generated, the lowest of all materials. The city would want to promote materials that are of greater quantities.

35. **C**—At 120 years since glacial retreat, there were over 1,500 trees per hectare, which is the greatest biomass of spruce trees on the graph.

36. **B**—The Earth has had many different changes in temperature over its history. There are times when it has been much warmer and times when it has been much colder. Currently, we are in a warming trend due to global climate change.

37. **A**—Greenhouse gases from transportation, electricity production, industry, businesses and homes, agriculture, and reduction of forested land have caused temperatures to rise causing global climate change.

38. **D**—Humans produced chemicals such as chlorofluorocarbons (CFCs). Although they are heavier than air, the air currents and mixing processes of the atmosphere have carried them into the stratosphere. These CFC molecules are hit by the sun's UV energy, which breaks up the CFCs and releases chlorine atoms. The chlorine atoms then react with the O_3 molecules breaking up the O_3 and taking one oxygen atom to form chlorine monoxide and O_2. This process reduces the amount of ozone found in the stratosphere.

39. **C**—IPM is killing or preventing the bugs without using as much pesticide. IPM can include biological methods like predator bugs that a farmer buys to eat the pests (biocontrol).

40. **D**—The ocean absorbs carbon dioxide from the atmosphere. The carbon dioxide reacts with the ocean water creating carbonic acid. The oceans absorb almost a quarter of global CO_2 emissions we create from burning fossil fuels and deforestation. As the CO_2 enters the ocean, it causes the ocean to become more acidic (lower pH). This acidity doesn't allow animals like clams and mussels to make protective shells, due to the loss of calcium carbonate. It can impact corals since they also make protective shells.

41. **A**—The species can continue to reproduce until it goes beyond what the area can support, then the species begins to starve, is impacted by disease, etc.

42. **D**—Declining/negative growth countries: countries like Japan, Germany, Bulgaria, and Russia are considered negative or declining growth countries because there are fewer children than middle-aged adults. In these countries, mom and dad may only be having one child, so when mom and dad die the family (and country) get smaller.

43. **B**—The tragedy of the commons is that individuals tend to overexploit shared resources until the resource becomes unavailable to all.

44. **C**—Overfishing is commercial fishing in which large quantities of fish are caught faster than the species can breed and replace itself. By banning this you would stop the loss of biodiversity.

45. **A**—Permeability is the ability of a material to allow liquid to flow through it. So sand has a high permeability, since water flows easily through it. Since 95 ml of the 100 ml went through, it is most likely sand.

46. **C**—Sulfur dioxide can be removed by gas scrubbing or by using fluidized bed combustion in coal-fired power plants.

47. **B**—Indoor air quality has risen in the past 30 years. The lines on the graph are all trending down showing that the percentage of people using solid fuel for cooking is decreasing. Since the percentage is going down, indoor air quality has gone up.

48. **B**—Nitrous oxide has a GWP 310 times that of carbon dioxide as seen in the chart below.

GAS	SOURCES	GWP	ATMOSPHERIC LIFETIME
Carbon dioxide	Decomposition, respiration, burning fossil fuels, deforestation	1	50–200 years
Methane	Burning of fossil fuels, livestock, landfills, decomposition, burning biomass, natural wetlands	21	12 years
Nitrous oxide	Soils, livestock manure, biomass or fossil fuel combustion, wastewater management	310	120 years
Chlorofluorocarbons	Refrigerants, aerosols, aircraft halons, solvents	12,000–16,000	20–100 years

49. **D**—During the months of April, May, June, July, and August, according to the graph, the solar energy system produces over 7,000 kWh, making it a good energy source to supplement local energy needs.

50. **C**—Person 4 has the highest ecological footprint when it comes to food and goods and services. Eating lower on the food chain will lower the ecological footprint as would purchasing less "stuff" since that is where person 4's ecological footprint is highest.

51. **A**—One of the consequences of increased temperatures is a rise in sea levels, which can flood coastal communities.

52. **A**—Increased levels of carbon dioxide and nitrogen oxides from burning fossil fuels is leading to increased global temperatures.

53. **B**—*Eutrophication* is the term used to describe a body of water that has an abundance of nutrients (fertilizers like nitrogen and phosphorus) that have run off from the land; these nutrients "fertilize" the algae that live in the water. This is caused by agriculture runoff, runoff from fertilizers, and wastewater runoff from CAFOs. This can cause the water to become so thick and green with algae that no light can penetrate through the water. It can also cause dead zones due to the lack of oxygen in the water.

54. **D**—Coal-burning power plants, vehicles, manufacturing, and even volcanoes release nitrogen oxides (NO_x) and sulfur oxides (SO_2) into the atmosphere. When these chemicals mix with atmospheric water (like rain, snow, fog, and hail) or dust, they can become acid rain and fall to the Earth. Because this is acidic (low pH), it lowers the pH of bodies of water near where the acid rain falls.

55. **A**—$200 \text{ lb} \times \dfrac{1 \text{ kg}}{2.2 \text{ lb}} \times \dfrac{12{,}357 \text{ mg}}{1 \text{ kg}} \times \dfrac{1 \text{ g}}{1{,}000 \text{ mg}}$

$= 1{,}123.4 \text{ gram}$

56. **C**—Burning biomass is burning wood and similar products. If we did this on a large scale, we could have some concerns of deforestation and habitat destruction to obtain these large wood supplies.

57. **D**—Since very few frogs make it to adulthood, they would have a Type III survivorship curve. Think of frog eggs—most get eaten, dry out, and never hatch at all. Then, tadpoles are also a major food source for many species, so lots of young frogs are also killed. However, a few make it to old age and become adult frogs. This survivorship curve is characteristic of an r-selected species.

58. **A**—Genetic diversity refers to the diversity within a species. These genetic differences often determine if the organism can withstand different environmental pressures. Genetic diversity is important because it helps maintain the health of a population.

59. **B**—Centered at the end of the Mississippi River system, the zone is one of the largest areas of oxygen-depleted coastal waters in the world. Low oxygen, or hypoxia, can be caused by pollution from farm fertilizer, soil erosion, and discharge from sewage treatment plants.

60. **A**—Clear-cutting has many environmental consequences even though, from an economic standpoint, it is a benefit since it is cheaper than other methods. Since trees have roots that hold in the soil, when we clear cut large areas of land we expose this soil, leaving it vulnerable to erosion and/or flooding.

61. **C**—Mining removes plant life, opens the soil up to erosion and runoff, and harms habitats. By reestablishing the vegetation and assessing and evaluating the replanted area frequently, you would help to "fix" the problems that were caused from the mining.

62. **D**—In the diagram, we see the ocean on the left, which provides a lot of moisture to the area. A lot of rain falls on the windward side of the mountain because as the air mass moves to higher elevations, it expands and cools. This cool air doesn't hold as much moisture so clouds form and it rains. The air mass, which has lost most of its moisture then moves over the mountains, where there is less rainfall.

63. **C**—Giant pandas and koalas are specialists that require particular habitats and food while pigeons and doves are generalists that can live almost anywhere and eat almost anything.

64. **A**—The graph shows that lionfish are growing exponentially, so we can assume they might be invasive and that they have not yet reached their carrying capacity. Invasive species tend to be generalists and r-selected species and they become invasive because of a lack of competition, no predators, and abundant resources.

65. **B**—Tilling the soil leaves it vulnerable to erosion and if the eroded soil has fertilizers in it, it could cause eutrophication of the body of water. In addition, the farmer may add more fertilizers to combat the loss of soil, compounding the problem.

66. **C**—The graph shows that in 2000 and the years since, Europe has had a very low total fertility rate (TFR), well below replacement level.

67. **A**—Sub-Saharan Africa had a rapid growth in 1970; the first graph typifies rapid growth countries. These are countries with a lot of infants, babies, and children who can be expected to grow up and have even more children. Some examples of countries today with an age structure like this are Kenya, Nigeria, and Saudi Arabia.

68. **A**—In 1960 in Northern Africa the TFR was near 7. With a fertility rate that high it can be expected that population growth would put demands on forests to provide fuel for cooking and human habitation. Deforestation would have been occurring, leading to habitat loss.

69. **C**—Methane is a greenhouse gas that traps heat and leads to the greenhouse effect, raising temperatures on the Earth.

70. **D**—If natural land is covered with asphalt and concrete, more water would run off the land and less would infiltrate in to fill up aquifers.

71. **B**—All organisms have a range of conditions that they can survive in. Ecological tolerances are things like temperature, salinity, sunlight, flow rate, availability of water, etc., and can apply to species or to individuals. The author states that sea urchin have a narrow ecological tolerance for salinity.

72. **A**—The benefit of hydroelectric power is that it doesn't produce any air pollution or greenhouse gases since nothing is burned. If you took down the dam, you would need to turn to other types of energy sources. If you had to replace the power produced by the dam by burning fossil fuels, you would create air pollution and further global warming.

73. **D**—The graph shows an increase in agriculture methane release from below 200 to 210 million metric tons. Animals produce a lot of methane and carbon dioxide, two things that lead to climate change.

74. **C**—The plate boundaries are divergent when the plates move apart, resulting in seafloor spreading, rift valleys, volcanoes, and earthquakes. Along these boundaries, earthquakes are common and magma (molten rock) rises from the Earth's mantle to the surface. Once this magma solidifies, the result is new oceanic crust.

75. **A**—The birth rates have dropped in half from 40/1,000 to 20/1,000 and the death rates have dropped from 17/1,000 to 8/1,000. This indicates

that the country is moving through demographic transition, lowering birth rates and death rates and lowering infant mortality. More women are becoming educated and there are generally better living conditions.

76. **C**—When an energy source is used to generate both heat and electricity, it is a combined heat and power (CHP) system or cogeneration.

77. **B**—The chemical equation, which you need to know and memorize, looks like this: $Cl+O_3 \rightarrow ClO + O_2$. Next, if the ClO molecule finds a free oxygen atom, the oxygen atom will steal the O from the ClO to become O_2, which releases the Cl atom back into the stratosphere to destroy more ozone. The second equation looks like this: $ClO + O \rightarrow Cl + O_2$.

78. **A**—Fracking is forcing liquid at very high pressures down into the rock to cause the oil or gas to be released. This can lead to groundwater contamination because the water that is used to

release the oil or natural gas can contain contaminates that then run off into waterways. In addition, this process releases volatile organic compounds during the natural gas production process.

79. **D**—The article states that humans are causing noise pollution that is impacting animals and human relaxation. Noise pollution, the author states, reduces the ability of animals to hear natural sounds and degrades the calming effect that we feel when we spend time in wild places.

80. **D**—Our oceans are getting warmer because of climate change from greenhouse gases. Corals need zooxanthellae, an algae that lives in the tissues of the coral and captures sunlight and converts into it energy for the coral animals. When the water is warmer, the zooxanthellae come under stress and can die or leave their coral host, causing the coral to die and turn white, a process known as coral bleaching.

Analyzing Your Performance on the Diagnostic Test

The exercise below will help you quickly and easily identify the chapters in Step 4 that you most need to review for the AP Environmental Science multiple-choice exam. Revise your study plan so that you prioritize the chapters with which you had the most difficulty.

Look at your answer sheet and mark all the questions you missed. Then shade in, highlight, or mark an X in the boxes below that correspond to the question numbers that you missed. For what concepts did you miss the most questions? This is where you want to spend the most time as you review!

Chapter 1: The Living World: Ecosystems

4	5	17	28	70

Chapter 2: The Living World: Biodiversity

15	18	35	58	71

Chapter 3: Populations

11	12	33	41	42	45	57
63	66	67	75			

Chapter 4: Earth Systems and Resources

2	6	19	20	24	25	59
62	74					

Chapter 5: Land and Water Use

10	26	39	43	44	50	60
61	65	73				

Chapter 6: Energy Resources and Consumption

7	21	22	31	32	49	56
72	76	78				

Chapter 7: Atmospheric Pollution

3	16	30	46	47	54	79

Chapter 8: Aquatic and Terrestrial Pollution

8	9	23	29	34	53	55

Chapter 9: Global Change

1	13	14	27	36	37	38
40	48	51	52	64	68	69
77	80					

STEP **3**

Develop Strategies
for Success

CHAPTER **4**   How to Approach Each
Question Type

CHAPTER 4

How to Approach Each Question Type

IN THIS CHAPTER

Summary: Become familiar with the multiple-choice and free-response questions on the exam and learn tips and strategies that will allow you to score your best. Pace yourself and know when to skip a question that you can come back to later.

Key Ideas

✪ On multiple-choice questions, you don't lose any points for wrong answers. You should fill in an answer bubble for every question.

✪ On multiple-choice questions, don't "overthink" the test. Use common sense because that will usually get you the right answer.

✪ Free-response answers must be in essay form. Outline form is not acceptable.

✪ Free-response questions are multipart questions—be *sure* to answer each part of the question or you will not be able to get the maximum possible number of points for that question.

✪ The free-response questions are graded using a positive-scoring system, so wrong information is ignored.

Multiple-Choice Questions

You will have 90 minutes to answer 80 multiple-choice questions, which works out to about 67 seconds per question. However, some questions will take longer than others, so make sure you are watching the time and pacing yourself. The multiple-choice section accounts for 60 percent of your final AP score.

Here are some helpful tips and strategies:

- ***Don't leave questions blank***. The AP Environmental Science exam used to take off a fraction of a point for each wrong answer. This is no longer the case. You should answer each multiple-choice question. If you don't know the answer, try to eliminate options that you know aren't correct and then make your best guess. If there are only seconds left and you're not done, you should just take random guesses. There is a 25 percent chance you'll get the right answer.

- ***All questions are weighted equally***. It doesn't matter which questions you get correct, just that you get enough questions right. So, don't spend too much time on one question. If a question is taking a long time, make your best guess and move on. Mark the question in your test booklet and go back to it later if you have time.

- ***There is no logic to the order of questions***. The test doesn't start out with the easy ones and go on to the hard ones. You may get the hardest question first. That's why it's important not to waste time on any one question. Again, if a question is taking a long time, make your best guess and move on.

- ***Don't overthink the test***. If you encounter a question that you immediately know the answer to, don't ponder it, just fill in the bubble on the answer sheet and move on. Just because the question seems easy doesn't mean it is a trick question. Some of the test questions will be easy ones.

- ***Be careful about changing answers***. If you answered a question already and come back to it later on, resist the urge to change it. Make sure that you have a real reason to change it. Oftentimes you are overthinking the question and your first answer is correct. Only change your answer if you can justify your reasons for making the switch.

- ***Check your calculations***. The math on the AP Environmental Science exam isn't all that difficult and you are allowed a simple calculator. That said, it would be unfortunate to lose points because of a silly calculation error. Make sure to work carefully and check your math. Remember, the test writers know all the possible answers you could get using the numbers given, so memorize those formulas so you get the correct solution!

- ***Make sure there are no stray marks on your answer sheet***. When you erase, make sure the wrong answer is completely erased. It may seem clear which answer you intended to mark to anyone reading it, but remember that your answer sheet is not read by humans. When more than one answer to a question is perceived, the answer is counted incorrect, no matter how much darker one of the answer bubbles is.

› Free-Response Questions

You will be given 70 minutes to write your answers to three broad questions on the free-response section of the exam That works out to about 23 minutes per question. It is important that your answers to these questions display solid reasoning and analytical skills. Expect to have to use data or information from your laboratory experiences as you answer some of these questions. The free-response section of the test accounts for 40 percent of your final AP score.

Answers for the free-response questions must be in essay form. Outline form is not acceptable. Be sure you answer all parts of a question and label your answer as to what part it is. If the question asks for a calculation, you *must* show your work.

It is important that you read each question completely before you begin to write so you are sure what you are being asked to do. Take a moment to plan your answer, and then write all your answers on the pages following the questions in the booklet.

Question 1 will require you to design an investigation and will be worth 10 points. Question 2 will require you to analyze an environmental problem and propose a solution. It is also worth 10 points. For Question 3, you'll have to analyze an environmental problem and propose a solution, as in Question 2, but you'll be required to do calculations. It's also worth 10 points.

Some important strategies and tips to keep in mind as you write your essays:

- It is very important that you read the question carefully to make sure you understand exactly what you are being asked and what you have to do in your answer.

- There are three questions in the free-response section. However, it isn't really three questions—it is more like 15 questions since each free-response question will have four, five, six, or more parts to it. For example, question 1 will be divided into parts (a), (b), (c), and so on, and each of these parts may be broken down further and labeled (i), (ii), etc. Make sure you label carefully each section you are answering. Label it exactly as it is labeled in the question. For example, label 1a, then write your answer. Then label 1b, and so on. Do not take all the parts and create one giant super essay. This could possibly make you lose points because the grader will not know which part of the question you are responding to. Instead, label and respond; then label the next section and respond again.

- Do not leave any part of a free-response question blank. If you aren't sure of the answer, skip it for now and answer the rest of the question. Sometimes this will jump-start your thinking, causing you to remember the part you didn't know. If you still don't know, then put down your best, most thoughtful guess. Wrong answers are ignored but you just might get a point or two when you didn't think you knew it. If you leave it blank, you will definitely get no points.

- The free-response section is graded using a "positive scoring" system. You do not lose points for saying things that are incorrect. If you are asked for one cause of eutrophication and you are unsure of your answer, give your best possible guess. A good guess is better than a blank response.

- However, just as you do not lose credit for wrong answers, you will not gain credit for doing more than is asked for. For example, if the question asks for two results of global warming and you are sure you have good answers, you will not get extra credit if you give three. Don't waste time giving a more complete answer than what is being asked for.

- Finally, you should know the verbs that the test writers will use and how you should respond to each verb:
  - **Calculate**—This means to do math and arrive at a final answer, including using algebra, substituting numbers, and making sure you correctly label your units. Also, you *must* show your work! No work means no points. Even if you can do the calculation in your head, you must show on paper how you got to the answer. The test graders can't look into your head.
  - **Describe**—Give relevant information on a particular topic.
  - **Explain**—Give the reasons for a particular environmental problem and tell how or why the problem happened, using evidence to support your claim.
  - **Identify**—Give information about a particular topic but you won't have to explain in detail.

- **Justify**—Provide evidence to support or defend a claim and give the reasons for this justification.
- **Make a claim**—Provide a reason based on evidence or knowledge.
- **Propose a solution**—Give a solution to an environmental problem using things you learned in the class.

Science Practices

Finally, you should know that you will be assessed using seven different science practices with varying weights on each part of the exam. Use the points below from the College Board to know what you will be asked to do.

- Practice 1—Concept Explanation will be 30–38% of the multiple-choice section and 13–20% of the free-response section.
- Practice 2—Visual Representations will be 12–19% of the multiple-choice section and 6–10% of the free-response section.
- Practice 3—Text Analysis will be 6–8% of the multiple-choice section and none of the free-response section.
- Practice 4—Scientific Experiments will be 2–4% of the multiple-choice section and 10–14% of the free-response section.
- Practice 5—Data Analysis will be 12–19% of the multiple-choice section and 6–10% of the free-response section.
- Practice 6—Mathematical Routines will be 6–9% of the multiple-choice section and 20% of the free-response section.
- Practice 7—Environmental Solutions will be 17–23% of the multiple-choice section and 26–34% of the free-response section.

STEP 4

Review the Knowledge You Need to Score High

CHAPTER 5

The Living World: Ecosystems

IN THIS CHAPTER

Summary: This chapter sets the foundation for all future chapters by showing the relationships and interactions with the living world.

Key Ideas

✪ Ecosystems are the result of biotic and abiotic interactions.

✪ Energy can be converted from one form to another.

Key Terms

- 10 percent rule
- Biome
- Carbon cycle
- Commensalism
- Competition
- Desert
- Ecosystem
- Food chains
- Food web
- Freshwater biomes
- Gross Productivity
- Hydrologic cycle
- Mutualism
- Net Productivity
- Nitrogen cycle

- Parasitism
- Phosphorus cycle
- Predator-prey
- Primary productivity
- Saltwater biomes
- Savanna
- Shrubland
- Taiga
- Temperate grassland
- Temperate rainforest
- Temperate seasonal forests
- Trophic levels
- Tropical rainforests
- Tundra

This chapter will cover about 6 to 8 percent of your AP Environmental Science Exam, or about 5 to 6 questions out of the 80 multiple-choice questions. It will be mostly a review of concepts you learned in previous years of school. This includes topics like predator-prey, biomes, nutrient and water cycles, food chains/webs, and energy flow. Most of it will be a review but there will be some new concepts.

Introduction to Ecosystems

There are many types of relationships in environmental science. **Predator-prey** relationships are when a predator, such as a lion, eats his prey, such as a gazelle. These two organisms must exist together and each organism relies on the other. For example, Figure 5.1 shows the relationship between the lynx and the hare. The lynx would not survive without his food source, the hare. However, the lynx keeps the hare numbers in check so they don't reach high numbers and begin to starve for lack of food resources for the prey. A healthy predator-prey relationship is important in the environment.

Symbiosis is the relationship between two species that have a close and long-term interaction with one another. There are many types of symbiosis: mutualism, commensalism, and parasitism. Let's begin with mutualism.

In **mutualism** both species benefit from the relationship. The example you are probably most familiar with is the clownfish and anemone. Thank you, Disney®, for Finding Nemo! In this common example, the anemone has stinging tentacles that allow it to sting and eat its prey . . . usually small fish like the clownfish. However, the clownfish has a slimy mucus that protects her from the anemone. The clownfish benefits by eating the algae and left over fish from the anemone and the anemone benefits by getting more oxygen to its tentacles as the clownfish swims through it.

Commensalism is another relationship between species when one organism benefits and the other neither benefits nor is harmed. One example you might be familiar with is the remora and the shark. The remora uses the shark for both food and for transportation. It eats food that is left over from the shark and also has a sucking disk that allows her to adhere to the body of the shark and get a free ride. The shark is not helped or harmed.

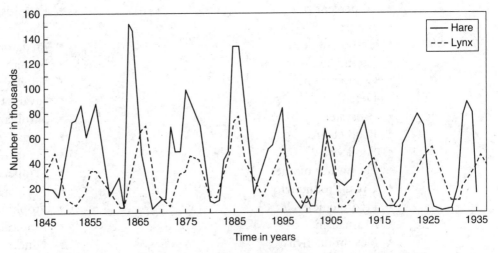

Figure 5.1   The relationship between the lynx and the hare.

Another example is the cattle egrets and cattle. The cattle egrets eat the insects that the cattle disturb as the cattle forage. The cattle are not helped or harmed but the cattle egrets benefit.

Parasitism is the final example of symbiosis. In this relationship, one species benefits while the other is harmed. The common examples here are fleas, mosquitoes, and tapeworms. All of these organisms feed off a host and benefit while the host is harmed, some more than others.

Another type of relationship is **competition,** when two or more species (or between members of the same species) are all competing for the same, usually limited, resource. These limited resources are often food, water, or territory. **Intraspecific competition** is competition between members of the same species and **interspecific competition** is between members of different species. Oftentimes species will learn to coexist by living in different parts of the same habitat, sharing food, or eating at different times of the day, which is known as resource partitioning.

Terrestrial Biomes

A **biome** is the world's major communities of plants and animals and can be made up of many different ecosystems. An **ecosystem** is the living and nonliving parts of an environment and many ecosystems may make up a biome.

Climate is the normal conditions of temperature, humidity, atmospheric pressure, wind, rainfall, etc. that define an area for a long period of time. Biomes are defined by the type of climate that is found in the biome.

The main terrestrial (land) biomes and their characteristics are:

- **Taiga**—A coniferous forest (pine trees), with permafrost soil, usually found between the tundra and temperate forests. This is the world's largest land biome.
- **Temperate rainforest**—Found on the coast and consists of both coniferous and broadleaf trees. This biome is characterized by a lot of rain.
- **Temperate seasonal forests**—These forests have all four seasons and are characterized by trees that are green in the spring and summer and turn bright colors of yellow, orange, and red in the fall, losing their leaves in the winter. This biome has warm, wet summers and cold winters.
- **Tropical rainforests**—These forests are found near the equator and stay warm all year-long. They are characterized by extreme amounts of rainfall all year. More than half of the world's species live in this biome.
- **Shrubland**—This biome is typically found near coasts and have hot, dry summers and cool, moist winters. Shrubland consists of shrubs and short trees with grasses. Some plants are adapted to little rainfall, such as cacti.
- **Temperate grassland**—This biome has many different types of grasses and very few trees due to the low levels of rainfall. The climate varies during the seasons from very cold to very warm.
- **Savanna**—This biome is a grassland with widely scattered trees found in tropical regions usually between the desert and rainforest. Wildfires are common and there is a wet and dry season.
- **Desert**—This biome covers about 20% of the land on our planet and is characterized by less than 50 cm a year of rain. Trees are usually absent and there is little vegetation.
- **Tundra**—This is an extremely cold climate characterized by no trees, little precipitation, short growing seasons for plants and grasses, and poor nutrients.

Aquatic Biomes

Aquatic biomes can be broken down into freshwater and marine. The types of resources found in these biomes depend on many things, including location, temperature, sunlight, and salinity.

- **Freshwater biomes**—These include streams, rivers, lakes, and ponds. These provide humans with water and food and could be considered the most important of all the biomes.
- **Marine biomes**—These include oceans, coral reefs, kelp forests, marshland (salt marshes), estuaries, mangrove forests, and tidepools. Marine biomes cover about 75% of Earth's surface and are important in climate control, providing much of the world's oxygen and also acting as a huge carbon dioxide sink.

You will need to learn about the different cycles in nature. The APES exam will focus on four cycles: the carbon, nitrogen, phosphorus, and hydrologic (water) cycles. For each of these, you will need to be able to look at the cycle in a visual representation or model and answer questions about the cycle. This means you must be familiar with the model/picture but also familiar with the details of each cycle.

Carbon Cycle

As seen in Figure 5.2, carbon is found in the land, water, and atmosphere. A carbon sink is where carbon is stored, for example in plants, the ocean, and soil. Carbon sources include

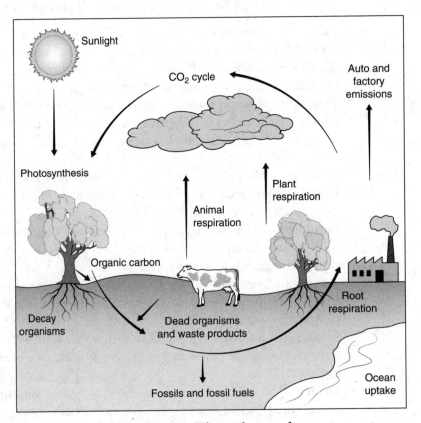

Figure 5.2   The carbon cycle.

forest fires, respiration, and burning of fossil fuels. As carbon moves through the carbon cycle it moves between sources and sinks, which can take very long periods of time or be rather quick.

Photosynthesis and cellular respiration are how carbon cycles in living things and is known as short-term cycling. When living organisms die and get buried deep underground, we see the long-term cycling and storage of carbon. This long-term storage has been interrupted by humans with the burning of fossil fuels. This takes carbon that has been stored for millions of years and puts it back into the atmosphere.

Nitrogen Cycle

Like carbon, nitrogen cycles between sources and sinks (Figure 5.3). Seventy-eight percent of our atmosphere is composed of nitrogen, which makes it the primary sink, but other sinks include living organisms, sedimentary rocks, and sediments. Denitrifying microorganisms are fixers of nitrogen, making them a major source of nitrogen because they push nitrogen back into the atmosphere. This form of nitrogen is unusable by plants. Another type of microorganism, known as nitrifying microorganisms, fix nitrogen into a useable form for plants. The steps of the nitrogen cycle can be easily memorized by a mnemonic device known as FixNAAD ANPAN. Let's put this into a chart so this will make more sense (Table 5.1).

As you can see from the chart, the nitrogen cycle relies heavily on bacteria to cycle it between land, water, and the atmosphere. It is a relatively fast cycle.

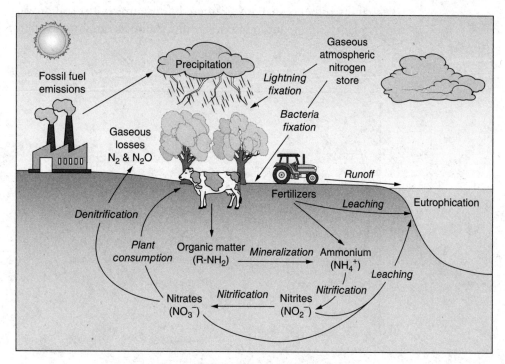

Figure 5.3   The nitrogen cycle.

Table 5.1   The Steps of the Nitrogen Cycle

PROCESS	PRODUCT	EXPLANATION
Fix—Nitrogen Fixation	**A**—Ammonia	During nitrogen fixation, N_2 from the atmosphere is converted by nitrogen-fixing microorganisms into ammonia.
N—Nitrification	**N**—Nitrites/Nitrates	During nitrification, bacteria convert ammonia into nitrites and then nitrates.
A—Assimilation	**P**—Proteins (DNA/Amino Acids)	During assimilation, nitrates are then converted into plant proteins, and nucleic acids that animals can then get from the plant tissues.
A—Ammonification	**A**—Ammonia	Ammonification is the process where decomposers take plant and animal cells and return the nitrogen back to the soil in the form of ammonia.
D—Denitrification	**N**—Nitrogen Gas	Bacteria convert nitrogen in the soil back to an atmospheric form.

Phosphorus Cycle

The phosphorus cycle is a slow cycle and it does not have an atmospheric form; phosphorus is only found on the land and in the water (Figure 5.4). The major sinks for phosphorus are rocks and sediments that are weathered. Once it is in the soil or water it can be easily taken up by plants, fungi, and microorganisms. Animals obtain phosphorus by eating plants and

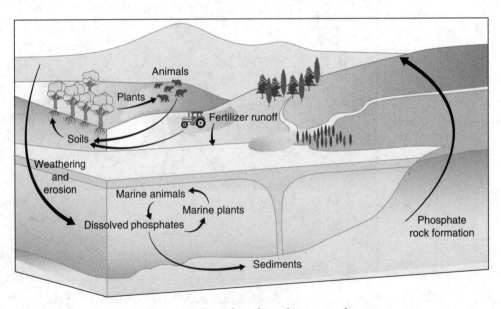

Figure 5.4   The phosphorus cycle.

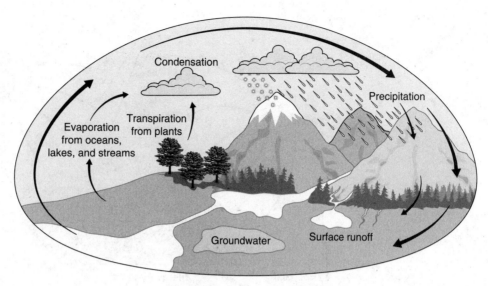

Figure 5.5　The water cycle.

it is returned to the soil or water when they die. Phosphorus is used as a building block for DNA, RNA, and ATP. Phosphorus is often considered a limiting factor in the environment because there is very little available and because it is not very water soluble.

Hydrologic Cycle (Water)

The water cycle is the process in which water moves from the atmosphere to the oceans/lakes/rivers to the land (Figure 5.5). The major steps include evaporation, condensation, runoff, precipitation, transpiration, and infiltration. Water on our planet is found in three phases: solid (ice or snow), liquid (rainfall or water in lakes), and gas (in the atmosphere). The majority of water on our planet is found in the oceans, which cover approximately 70% of the Earth.

Primary Productivity

Primary productivity is the rate at which food energy is generated by photosynthesis. It is measured in units of energy per unit area per unit time. Since energy cannot be created or destroyed, and since the sun is the source of energy for our planet, we can study the two parts of primary productivity (gross productivity and net productivity) to see how productive a particular area is. In some areas productivity changes with the seasons, like the wet and dry seasons of the tropics or the spring or fall seasons in the United States. We also consider the primary productivity of bodies of water by looking at the photosynthesizers found there. The primary productivity in water is dependent on how clear the water is and how deep the red and blue light can penetrate. Primary productivity is important because it is the process that forms the foundation of food webs in most ecosystems.

Gross productivity is the total rate of photosynthesis in an area, or the full amount of food produced by the producers.

Net productivity is the difference between gross productivity and the energy lost by producers for respiration.

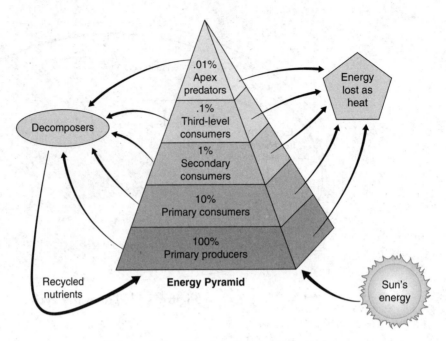

Figure 5.6   Trophic levels and energy.

Trophic Levels

Once again, all energy comes from the sun but it can be converted from one form to another. Plants take energy from the sun in the process of photosynthesis and convert that energy into usable forms (Figure 5.6). Animals eat that plant or another animal and get their energy from the food they eat. The cycles we studied earlier are how matter moves around the planet. These cycles demonstrate the law of conservation of matter.

The **first trophic level** are the plants, or primary producers. These are then eaten by primary consumers (the second trophic level) and so forth up the pyramid.

Energy Flow and the 10 Percent Rule

The 10 percent rule is the idea that as usable energy moves up the pyramid much of it is "lost." The first law of thermodynamics states that energy cannot be created or destroyed, but the second law states that it can be transferred or transformed. So according to the 10 percent rule, a plant or primary producer will only transfer 10 percent of the energy to the primary consumer that eats it, let's say a rabbit. This rabbit then goes about his day hopping around, heating his body, etc., and he uses up 90 percent of the energy he received from the plant. Next, when a coyote comes around and eats the rabbit, we assume the coyote only gets about 10 percent of the energy from the rabbit because the rabbit "used up" 90 percent doing what rabbits do. This also explains why the shape is a pyramid because energy is "lost" as it goes up to each higher level.

Food Chains and Food Webs

A food chain is a visual representation of how organisms depend on one another for a source of food with arrows pointing from the organism that is being eaten to the organism that eats it and receives the energy from it (Figure 5.7).

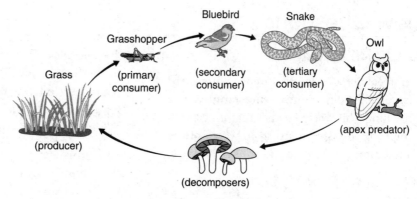

Figure 5.7   Food chain.

A food web is a visual representation of many food chains put together and is more like real life because it shows the complexity of feeding relationships in the system (Figure 5.8). In other words, most animals don't have just one thing they eat, but rather multiple options for any given meal.

The important thing as you look at a diagram of a food chain or food web is to understand the relationships that occur and be able to predict what might happen if a particular animal or plant were to be removed from the food web/chain.

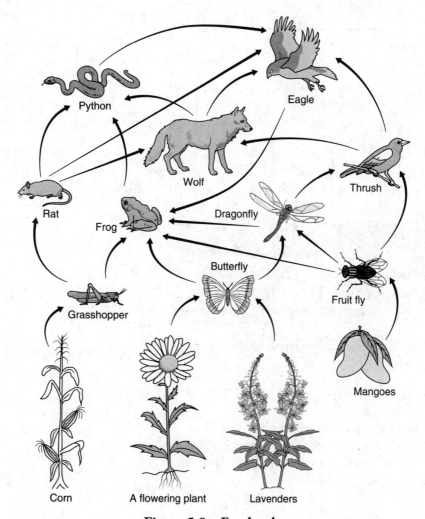

Figure 5.8   Food web.

› Review Questions

Multiple-Choice Questions

1. An evergreen plant is found in an environment with extremely cold winter temperatures. The plant has long, thin waxy needles that it keeps all year long. The soil is permafrost. In which of the following biomes is the plant most likely found?

   (A) Taiga
   (B) Desert
   (C) Tundra
   (D) Grassland

2. What is the process where bacteria take nitrogen from the atmosphere and convert it to a form that is usable by plants (primarily ammonia)?

   (A) Nitrogen fixation
   (B) Nitrification
   (C) Ammonification
   (D) Denitrification

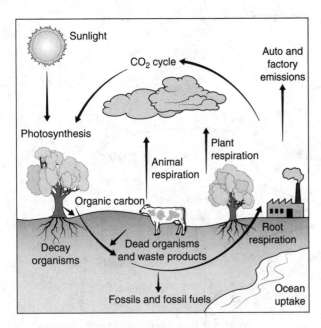

3. Which of the following is true and seen in the image above?

   (A) Carbon does not have an atmospheric component.
   (B) The majority of our atmosphere is carbon.
   (C) Carbon is found only anthropogenically.
   (D) Carbon cycles between photosynthesis and cellular respiration.

4. The burdock plant produces spiny seeds that cling to the fur of animals or clothing of humans. The plants rely on this method of seed dispersal for reproduction, while the animals are unaffected. Which of the following is this an example of?

   (A) Mutualism
   (B) Commensalism
   (C) Parasitism
   (D) Predator-prey

5. If the producers in an ecosystem convert 15,000 kCal of energy stored in organic compounds, which of the following would most likely be the amount of energy available to the tertiary consumers?

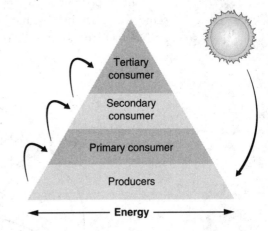

   (A) 15,000
   (B) 1,500
   (C) 150
   (D) 15

6. According to the graph below, what best describes the relationship between what is happening in 1885 with the lynx and hare?

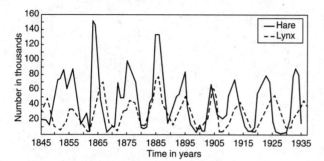

(A) The lynx numbers are higher than the hare numbers because of predation.

(B) The environment experienced a severe drought limiting the number of plants the hares were able to graze on.

(C) There is a mutualistic relationship between hare and lynx.

(D) There were more hares in the area than lynx because of healthy predator-prey relationships.

7. Which of the following changes would most likely occur if the wolf were removed from the food web below?

A Food Web

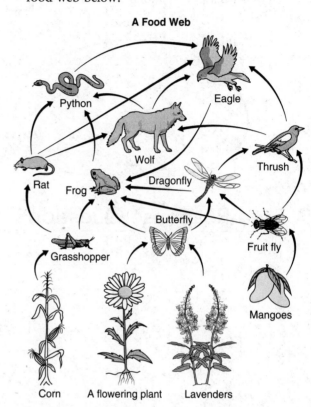

(A)	increase in eagles	increase in pythons
(B)	increase in frogs	decrease in eagles
(C)	decrease in eagles	increase in thrush
(D)	increase in lavenders	decrease in corn

8. Which of the following is true of gross primary productivity?

(A) Gross primary productivity is the total rate of photosynthesis in an area, or the full amount of food produced by the producers.

(B) Gross primary productivity is the difference between net productivity and the energy lost by producers for respiration.

(C) Gross primary productivity is the energy captured by producers added to the energy used by primary and secondary consumers over time.

(D) Gross primary productivity is the total amount of energy lost by both producers and consumers through respiration over time.

9. Which letter correctly identifies the process of the water cycle that would most be impacted by a city with asphalt parking lots and buildings?

(A) A
(B) B
(C) C
(D) D

Water Cycle

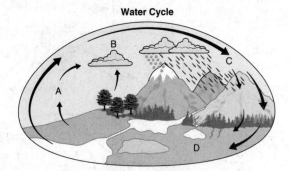

› Free-Response Question

A Food Web

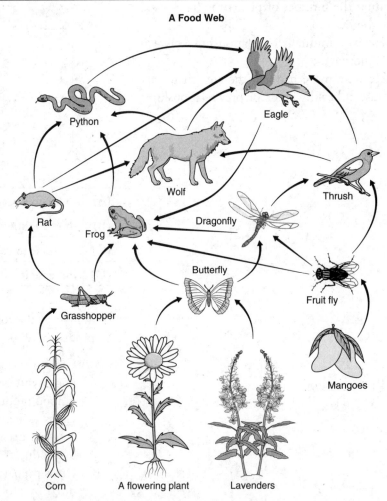

10. Refer to the diagram above to answer all parts of the question.

(A) **Identify** one primary producer in the food web above.

(B) **Identify** one primary consumer in the food web above.

(C) **Identify** one predator-prey relationship in the food web above.

(D) If the corn plant has 12,000 kCal available, **identify** the kCal available for the grasshopper, the rat, and the python and then **explain** why these organisms would have the amount you identified.

› Answers and Explanations

1. A—The taiga is a coniferous forest (pine trees), with permafrost soil, usually found between the tundra and temperate forests. It is also the world's largest land biome.

2. A—During nitrogen fixation, N_2 from the atmosphere is converted by nitrogen-fixing microorganisms into ammonia.

3. D—Photosynthesis and cellular respiration are how carbon cycles in living things and is known as short-term cycling.

4. B—Commensalism is a relationship between species where one organism benefits and the other neither benefits nor is harmed. In this case the burdock plant has its seeds dispersed for reproduction but the animal is not affected.

5. D—According to the 10 percent rule, a plant (which in this case has 15,000 kCal) will be eaten by a primary consumer, giving the primary consumer 1,500 kCal. When a secondary consumer eats the primary consumer, it only gets 10 percent of that energy (or in this case 150 kCal). Finally when a tertiary consumer eats the secondary consumer, it gets 10 percent or 15 kCal.

6. D—The graph shows the relationship between the lynx and the hare. The lynx would not survive without his food source, the hare. However, the lynx keeps the hare numbers in check so they don't reach high numbers and begin to starve for lack of food resources for the prey. A healthy predator-prey relationship is important in the environment.

7. C—If the wolf were removed, the eagle would decrease because he preys on the wolf and some of his food source would be removed. At the same time, there would be an increase in thrush birds since the wolves prey on thrush birds and without wolves their numbers would go up.

8. A—Gross productivity is the total rate of photosynthesis in an area, or the full amount of food produced by the producers.

9. D—If you built a city with parking lots and buildings, less water would be able to infiltrate into the ground and more would run off since asphalt and concrete are impermeable.

10. (A) One point for identifying either corn, flowering plant, lavenders, or mangoes.
(B) One point for identifying either grasshopper, butterfly, or fruit fly.
(C) One point for identifying a predator-prey relationship in the food web. There are many but some are python and rat, python and frog, eagle and wolf, eagle and frog, etc.
(D) One point for identifying the grasshopper as 1,200 kCal, one point for identifying the rat as 120 kCal, and one point for identifying that the python would get 12 kCal. Then one point for explaining that according to the 10 percent rule:

A plant or primary producer has 100 percent of the energy from the sun. But once a primary consumer eats that plant, he only gets 10 percent of the original energy from the producer so, in this case, the grasshopper will get 1,200 kcal. Then as the grasshopper goes about his day hopping around, heating his body, etc., he uses up 90 percent of the energy he received from the plant, leaving only 120 kCal for the rat. Next the python will only get 12 kCal because he only gets 10 percent of the energy from the rat.

› Rapid Review

- Predator-prey—One eats, one gets eaten.
- Mutualism—Both species benefit by being in the relationship. Example: clownfish and anemone.
- Commensalism—One species benefits and the other is unaffected. Example: remora and shark.
- Parasitism—One species benefits and one species is harmed. Example: fleas on a dog.

- Competition—Two species competing for the same resources. There are two types:
  - Intraspecific competition is competition between members of the same species.
  - Interspecific competition is competition between members of different species.
- Biome—Major communities of plants and animals.
- Ecosystem—Living and nonliving parts of an environment.
- Taiga—Lengthy cold, wet winters with lots of coniferous trees.
- Temperate rainforest—Coniferous and broadleaf trees with lots of rain.
- Temperate seasonal forests—Four seasons with warm, wet summers and cold winters.
- Tropical rainforests—Greatest diversity of species with rain all year and warm all year.
- Shrubland—Hot, dry summers and cool, moist winters; found near coasts with short trees and grasses.
- Temperate grassland—Lots of grasses, low rainfall.
- Savanna—Grassland with a wet season and a dry season; wildfires are common.
- Desert—Dry with little vegetation.
- Tundra—Extremely cold, no trees, little rain.
- Freshwater biomes—Examples: rivers, lakes, streams, ponds.
- Saltwater biomes—Examples: oceans, coral reefs, kelp forests, marshlands, estuaries, mangrove forests, tidepools.
- Carbon cycle—How carbon cycles in the environment. It includes both photosynthesis and cellular respiration, which is how carbon is stored in the short term. Also included are dead organisms buried for millions of years, which is long-term storage of carbon.
- Nitrogen cycle—Nitrogen makes up 78 percent of our atmosphere. Bacteria are important in the nitrogen cycle. FixNAAD/ANPAN is a mnemonic way to remember the steps (see chart in this chapter).
- Phosphorus cycle—Phosphorus cycles in the environment but it is a slow cycle with no atmospheric form. It is found in rocks and sediments.
- Hydrologic cycle—Otherwise known as the water cycle and includes evaporation, condensation, runoff, precipitation, and transpiration.
- Primary productivity—The rate at which food energy is generated by photosynthesis. It is measured in units of energy per unit area per unit time.
- Gross productivity—The total rate of photosynthesis in an area, or the full amount of food produced by the producers.
- Net productivity—The difference between gross productivity and the energy lost by producers for respiration.
- Trophic levels—Made up of producers, primary consumers, secondary consumers, and decomposers and shows that each level has less energy available.
- The 10 percent rule—90 percent of energy is used by the organism and only 10 percent moves up the pyramid because the organism below it used up the energy to heat its body and move, etc. The shape is a pyramid because energy is "lost" as it goes up to each higher level.
- Food chains—Visual representation of how one organism is food source for another.
- Food webs—Visual representation that is more like real life with multiple food source options for each animal.

CHAPTER 6

The Living World: Biodiversity

IN THIS CHAPTER

Summary: Biodiversity is all the variety of life on Earth. If we lose one part of the biodiversity on our planet, other species, and entire ecosystems can be affected. Each species, no matter how large or how small, has an important role to play and species depend on each other for their own survival. There are both natural and human causes that can impact ecosystems and organisms must adapt to these causes.

Key Idea

✪ Ecosystems have structure and diversity that change over time.

Key Terms

- Adaptations
- Climax community
- Cultural service
- Ecological tolerance
- Generalists
- Genetic diversity
- Habitat diversity
- Indicator species
- Island biogeography
- Keystone species

- Pioneer members
- Population bottleneck
- Primary succession
- Provisioning service
- Regulating service
- Secondary succession
- Specialists
- Species diversity
- Species richness
- Supporting service

This chapter will be 6 to 8 percent of your AP Environmental Science exam, or about 5 to 6 questions out of the 80 multiple-choice questions. We will focus on biodiversity, things the environment does for humans, island biogeography, tolerance, impacts on ecosystems, how organisms adapt to their environment, and how environments change over time.

Introduction to Biodiversity

There are three types of biodiversity: genetic, species, and habitat:

- **Genetic diversity** refers to the diversity within a species. Think of humans. Unless you are an identical twin, you are different from every other person on the planet. Each person has unique features such as eye color, skin color, hair color, height, and so on. These genetic differences also contribute to different environmental pressures, which affect organisms in different ways. Some organisms can withstand a particular environmental pressure while others will die. Genetic diversity is important because it helps maintain the health of a population.
- **Species diversity** is the number of species and abundance of each species that live in a particular community. Species diversity helps to contribute to the health of an ecosystem because each species has an important role in this heath.
- **Habitat diversity** is the different habitats found in a certain region. Since a habitat is a home to plants and animals, how diverse a habitat is can tell us about the health of the area.

Genetic diversity is a way for populations to adapt to changing environments and allows for the population to better respond to environmental stress. With more **variation**, it is more likely that some individuals in a population will possess variations of alleles that are suited for the environment and it is more likely that these individuals will survive and reproduce.

A population that has been reduced for a generation or more, usually due to an environmental event like a drought or flood, is a **population bottleneck.** This reduces genetic variation and can lead to a loss of biodiversity. Ecosystems with many different species are more likely to recover from an environmental event than ecosystems with fewer species.

Specialists are organisms that require particular habitats, food, and so on. An example of a specialist species would be a koala, who can only eat eucalyptus. If the habitat where koalas live is damaged and their specific food source is gone, this could be particularly devastating to the population of koalas.

Generalists are the opposite. They can live in many different places and eat many different things. Generalists are less likely to be impacted by an environmental event. For example, think of a cockroach, who can live almost anywhere and eat almost anything.

Species richness is the number of species per sample. The more species present in a sample, the "richer" the sample. It is a count of the species, not the abundance or number of individuals of each species present. It gives as much weight to those species that have very few individuals as to those that have many individuals. Thus, one cactus has as much influence on the richness of an area as 1,000 dandelions.

Ecosystem Services

Think about the many different ways that you as a human benefit from healthy ecosystems. These are tangible items like food, money, medicine, and more. Human activities can damage these services both economically and ecologically.

Scientists break these services into four categories:

- Provisioning—Services like food and clean water.
- Regulating—Services like plants cleaning the air, bees pollinating flowers, plants holding soil in place to prevent erosion, or the regulation of climate by natural processes.
- Cultural—Services that are not tangible things that benefit us but rather interactions with nature, such as taking a walk and enjoying what you see or art that comes from looking at nature, and so on.
- Supporting—These are harder to understand but are the ecosystem services that support all other others, such as producing oxygen, water cycling, and so on.

Island Biogeography

Figure 6.1 is an example of a mainland with several small islands located different distances away from the mainland. You can see that each island is a different size. Island biogeography is the study of the species and distribution that would occur on each of these islands. The theory states that islands closer to the mainland (where the animals/plants have moved from) and/or larger islands will have more species than islands farther away or smaller. The size of the island in theory matters because larger islands can support more and different species while smaller ones would be more limited.

I do an activity in my class where I use masking tape to tape "islands" on the floor of different sizes and different locations from the "mainland" where my students stand. I then give them lots of different supplies such as cotton balls, toothpicks, paper clips, rubber balls, rubber bands, etc. I then have my students stand on the "mainland" and try to get as many objects to land (by throwing them) onto the "islands." Can you picture this? I'm sure you can understand that the islands that are smaller and farther away will have less items land on them than larger or closer ones. This helps to explain island biogeography to my class. A real-life example would be why are there more birds on the island of New Guinea than the island of Bali? Well, New Guinea is 50 times the size of Bali!

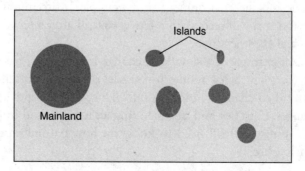

Figure 6.1   Island biogeography.

The other thing you will be tested on is how island biogeography has impacted evolution. Because an island is a special kind of environment, isolated and where species can't move easily, species on islands react to environmental pressures differently than species on continents. Islands have limited resources like food and habitats. Islands also often have specialists living on them. These species have adapted to become a specialist because of the unique characteristics on islands such as limited food or habitat resources. Because specialists are more likely to be impacted by human and/or natural events, such as the introduction of a nonnative (invasive) species, they could become threatened.

Ecological Tolerance

All organisms have a range of conditions that they can survive in. Consider a goldfish in a bowl. If you put that bowl out in the sun in Texas in the middle of the summer, it will not only be cruel, but will result in a dead goldfish. Why? Well, because a goldfish has an ecological tolerance for temperature and the water temperature in the bowl has gone above that.

Other ecological tolerances in addition to temperature are salinity, sunlight, flow rate, and availability of water. These tolerances can apply to species or to individuals.

So far, everything you have seen will be tested as either a concept explanation or a visual representation. In other words, you will either have to read the question and be asked to explain an environmental concept, process, or model or analyze a visual like a food web or biogeochemical cycle.

On the exam, any questions relating to ecological tolerance will be in a text-analysis form where you will read a short passage, answer questions regarding the passage, and identify the author's claim.

In the next section, natural disruptions to ecosystems, adaptation, and ecological succession will all be tested as some sort of data analysis. This might involve reading a graph, data table, or chart or perhaps looking at a picture or map and explaining what is seen and so on. Make sure you can look for patterns, trends, or relationships and draw conclusions.

Natural Disruptions to Ecosystems

Ecosystems can be impacted by natural factors such as fire, climate change, sea level rising, and more. These disruptions may be short/fast as in a fire, or slow/long over thousands or millions of years such as natural impacts of climate change. This factor will determine the impact on the environment. For example, a fire might have a large impact immediately, but the area will recover in a few years and after a few decades you might not even know a fire had even occurred.

An example of a slow/long change is climate. It has changed many times over millions of years, which has resulted in sea levels rising and falling over this time span. Sea levels respond to changes in ice on our planet and as land ice melts sea levels rise. All of these changes, both fast and slow can impact habitats and impact wildlife.

Terms you will need to know on how natural changes have occurred during Earth's timeline are:

- Periodic—This is a change that occurs at regular intervals, for example, the tides that comes in every day at a predictable time.

- Episodic—This means it happens in irregular intervals. It repeats but irregularly, for example, El Niño and La Niña.
- Random—This is something that is totally random and can't be guaranteed to repeat. It might happen once or multiple times, for example, a meteor striking the Earth.

Adaptations

We have discussed both short- and long-term changes as well as both natural and human-caused changes. In order for organisms to survive these changes they have to be able to adapt. This is done by incremental changes at the population level.

The different ways organisms can adapt are biological (structural) adaptation and behavioral adaptation. Keep in mind these genetic adaptations do not happen over a lifetime or even over a few generations but rather take thousands of years and multiple generations before they are found in a species. Organisms that can't adapt to both short- and long-term environmental changes may not survive.

Ecological Succession

There are two ways that habitats or communities change over time. One is primary succession and the other is secondary succession.

Primary succession occurs when an area has barren rock with no soil; for example, a new volcanic island (Figure 6.2). First, lichens will come in and begin to break down the rock. After small amounts of soil are formed, small annual plants followed by grasses and perennial plants will arrive. More soil will now form because these "pioneer" plants break down the rock and form soil. Larger plants, grasses, and fast-growing trees like conifers will then grow. Finally, after hundreds of years hardwood trees will be established in the area.

Secondary succession is a much faster process and occurs after a disturbance of some kind (Figure 6.3). This could be a fire, flood, or human activity like farming. Because soil is already well established, plants can return faster than without soil.

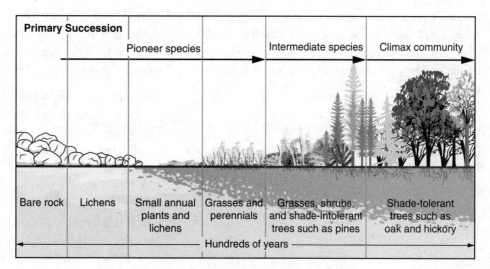

Figure 6.2 Primary succession.

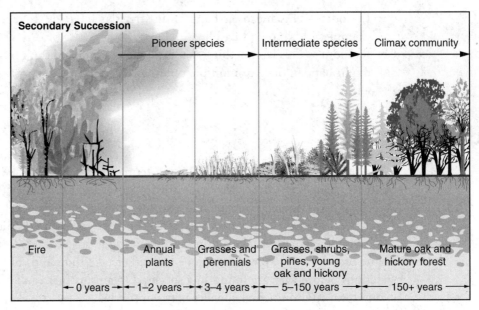

Figure 6.3 Secondary succession.

You will also be tested on the following terms, so make sure you know what each is describing:

- Keystone species—Species that many other species depend on. If this species is removed the ecosystem would be drastically impacted. Some common examples of keystone species are otters, prairie dogs, and bison.
- Indicator species—A species that "indicates" an environmental condition and is used to diagnose the health of the ecosystem. Some common examples of indicator species are plants, lichens, and many amphibians like frogs.
- Pioneer species—The first species into a disturbed area undergoing succession.

› Review Questions

Multiple-Choice Questions

1. A family goes to a protected National Park for a hike. They take in the beauty of the surroundings and are inspired by what they see. Which of the following ecosystem services is the family enjoying?

   (A) Provisioning
   (B) Regulating
   (C) Cultural
   (D) Supporting

2. One island is 50 km away from the mainland and another is 10 km away. Both are virtually the same size. Which of the following would be correct about the number of species living on the islands?

   (A) The numbers would be generally the same and would include species from the mainland.
   (B) There would be fewer species on the island farther away and more species on the island closer to the mainland.
   (C) There would be more species on the island farther away and fewer species on the island closer to the mainland.
   (D) The numbers would be generally the same but neither island would have species from the mainland.

3. Oftentimes, in the hot summer temperatures, lakes and rivers will become so warm and the dissolved oxygen levels fall so low that there are major fish deaths. This usually occurs to large fish and will often be seen in the morning after oxygen levels plummet overnight. Large fish are more susceptible to low oxygen turnovers than small fish and small fish are often seen at the surface of the water gulping for air.

Which of the following best identifies the author's claim?

(A) The author claims that the kills of large fish are from not enough dissolved oxygen in the water.
(B) The author claims that large fish are unable to breathe air from the surface.
(C) The author claims that small fish consume the excess dissolved oxygen.
(D) The author claims that small fish don't require oxygen to survive but large fish do.

4. The picture below shows where climate change is impacting coastal communities. Which of the following would be best supported by the map?

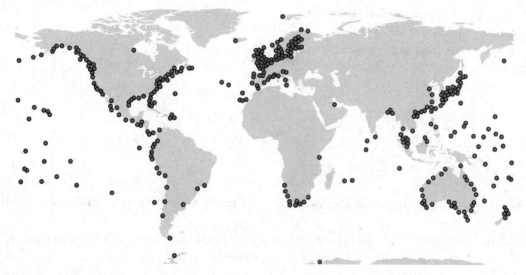

(A) Wildlife near coastal areas will be impacted.
(B) Iceland will have extensive habitat loss.
(C) Invasive species will become a larger concern in Asia.
(D) Island nations will need to switch to renewable energy.

5. Looking at the graph below you can see that many plant species move into an area over time. Which of the following claims would be best supported by the graph?

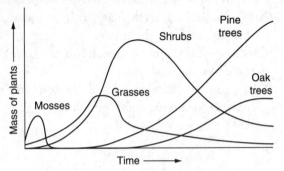

(A) Shrubs are pioneer plants and arrive first into a disturbed ecosystem.
(B) Oak trees are pioneer species.
(C) Mosses are known as climax species.
(D) Mosses are pioneers and trees are climax communities.

6. The raccoon is an animal who lives in all areas of the United States. They eat a wide variety of food sources, including human garbage. Which of the following best describes a raccoon?

(A) Raccoons are predators.
(B) Raccoons are generalists.
(C) Raccoons are specialists.
(D) Raccoons are keystone species.

› Free-Response Question

7. (A) **Identify** one regulating service provided by ecosystems and for that service **describe** how this benefits humans.
  (B) **Define** a keystone species and **describe** how a lion could be considered a keystone species.
  (C) **Define** primary succession and **explain** how primary succession can lead to soil formation on a newly formed volcanic landscape.

› Answers and Explanations

1. C—Cultural ecosystem services are not "things" we benefit from but rather interactions with nature, such as taking a walk and enjoying what you see or art that comes from looking at nature, and so on.

2. B—The theory states that islands closer to the mainland (where the animals/plants have moved from) and/or larger islands will have more species than islands farther away or smaller. The size of the island in theory matters because larger islands can support more and different species while smaller ones would be more limited.

3. A—The author is stating that large fish need greater amounts of oxygen and during the summer months will die because of less oxygen due to heat.

4. A—The graph shows that coastal communities are being affected by climate change, so any wildlife near the coasts could be impacted.

5. D—Pioneer species are the first species into a disturbed area undergoing succession and climax communities are the last. According to the graph, the first things that moved into the area were the mosses and over time came the trees, or climax community.

6. B—Generalists are animals who can eat anything and live in many different places.

7. (A) One point for identifying it is a regulating service and one point for describing how this benefits humans. Things like plants cleaning the air, bees pollinating flowers, plants holding soil in place to prevent erosion, or the regulation of climate by natural processes are regulating services. Describing how this benefits humans will depend on what you choose to write about. For example, bees pollinating plants and flowers provides food and beauty to humans.

(B) One point for defining a keystone species and one point for explaining why the lion can be considered a keystone species. A keystone species is a species that many other species depend on. If this species is removed the ecosystem would be drastically impacted. Lions help balance large ecosystems by consuming a wide variety of prey species.

(C) One point for defining primary succession and one point for explaining how primary succession works. Primary succession occurs in an area that has barren rock with no soil, a new volcanic island for example. First, lichens take hold and begin to break down the rock. After small amounts of soil are formed, small annual plants followed by grasses and perennial plants arrive. More soil is created because these "pioneer" plants break down the rock and form soil. When enough soil has been created, larger plants, grasses, and fast-growing trees like conifers will grow. Finally, after hundreds of years, a climax community of hardwood trees will be established in the area.

〉 Rapid Review

- Genetic diversity—Diversity within a species. Example: unless you are a twin you look different than all other humans on the planet.

- Species diversity—Number of species and abundance in a community. Example: the bears, rabbits, toads, ferns, and oak trees in an area.

- Habitat diversity—How many different habitats are in a region. Example: tropical rainforest, tropical dry forest, grasslands.

- Population bottleneck—A population that has been reduced because of an environmental event. Ecosystems with many different species are more likely to recover from an environmental event than ecosystems with fewer species.

- Species richness—The number of species per sample. The more species present in a sample, the "richer" the sample.

- Provisioning service—Ecosystem services that give humans what they need to survive, like food and clean water.

- Regulating service—Ecosystem services that indirectly benefit humans, such as plants cleaning the air and bees pollinating plants.

- Cultural service—Ecosystem services that provide humans beauty, art, and enjoyment.

- Supporting service—Ecosystem services such as producing oxygen, water cycling, and other services that support human life.

- Island biogeography—Study of the species and distribution that would occur on islands. There are usually more species on islands closer to the mainland (more migration from the mainland) and larger islands that can hold more species.

- Specialists—Organisms that require specific habitats, food, etc., like a koala.

- Generalists—Organisms that can live in many places and eat many things, like a cockroach.

- Ecological tolerance—The total range of conditions organisms can live in. Each species has its own ecological tolerance before it dies.

- Adaptations—Biological and behavioral ways organisms adapt over time to survive.

- Primary succession—Bare rock, such as after a volcanic eruption, over time becomes a climax community. Moss or lichen usually inhabit first, break down rock to make soil, and afterward larger and larger plants move in. This is a slow process.

- Secondary succession—After a fire or flood destroys the habitat, but the soil remains. Over time it becomes a climax community as new plants begin move in. This is faster than primary succession.

- Keystone species—Species that many other species depend on.

- Indicator species—Species that indicate an environmental problem.

- Pioneer members—First members into an area after a fire, etc.

- Climax community—The stable stage of the environment after a disruption.

CHAPTER 7

Populations

IN THIS CHAPTER

Summary: Populations in ecosystems change over time in response to factors in their environment and populations are limited by availability of resources and space. This chapter is all about populations, both populations in nature and human populations.

Key Ideas

✪ Populations change over time in reaction to a variety of factors.
✪ Human populations change in reaction to a variety of factors, including social and cultural factors.

Key Terms

- Age-structure diagrams
- Biotic potential
- Carrying capacity
- Demographic transition
- Density-dependent factors
- Density-independent factors
- Generalist
- Infant mortality rate
- K-selected species

- Population overshoot
- R-selected species
- Rule of 70
- Specialist
- Total fertility rate
- Type I survivorship curve
- Type II survivorship curve
- Type III survivorship curve

This subject will account for about 10 to 12 percent of your AP Environmental Science exam, or about 8 to 10 questions out of the 80 multiple-choice questions. Make sure you can discuss trends in population data and can read and interpret different population graphs.

Generalist and Specialist Species

Generalists, defined in Chapter 6, are going to be able to survive in habitats that change often. If the food availability of the area changes, a generalist can just change his diet and will most likely survive. Generalist species are more adaptable than specialist species.

A specialist species will have a difficult time with changing habitat conditions. In fact, a specialist will likely become endangered in an area if habitat conditions change because specialists are less likely to adapt to the new environment. They require very specific conditions and specific food requirements to survive and when these conditions or requirements change they suffer or die.

k-Selected and r-Selected Species

I always taught my students that this was an easy one! For "k" just remember kangaroo and for "r" remember roach. If you can remember that, you can answer any questions about this. However, keep in mind this topic will be taught as a data analysis, so you will have to describe patterns or trends in data.

What do we know about kangaroos? Well, they are large animals, they have a pouch, they hop around carrying their baby for 11 to 18 months . . . that's huge parental care! Usually a kangaroo only has one baby at a time, or maybe twins, and they don't have a baby until they are a few years old. They are herbivores who live in only one place in the world (Australia) and can live 12 to 18 years on average.

What are the characteristics of **k-selected species**?

- Large size
- Few offspring per year
- Live in stable environments in certain places
- Specialized diets
- Spend a lot of time and energy caring for their offspring
- Long life spans
- Reproduce more than once in their lifetime
- Can be impacted by invasive species or environmental changes

What about roaches? Roaches are small and live only a few months. They lay lots of eggs (sometimes 16 at a time), they can lay eggs about 14 times during their life, and they can lay eggs when they are only three to five months old. When a cockroach lays eggs they leave them and never return to care for the young. They can live almost anywhere on the planet and eat almost anything, but they only live about six months.

What are the characteristics of **r-selected species**?

- Small
- Many offspring
- Don't take care of their offspring (or very little care)
- Mature early
- Short life spans
- Live almost anywhere

- Eat almost anything
- Not as impacted by invasive species or environmental changes

Now, can you see how just remembering "r" for roach and "k" for kangaroo helps remember the characteristics of r-selected and k-selected species? It is an easy way to remember these two concepts!

Biotic potential is the maximum number of offspring a species could have if conditions were perfect. If we think about the roach and kangaroo examples from above, the roaches would have a high biotic potential and the kangaroos would have a low biotic potential. In other words, if conditions for a roach were perfect, one could produce a lot of babies before it died. On the other hand, a kangaroo, even under perfect conditions, would only produce a few babies in its lifetime.

When you plot biotic potential on a graph, it would look like the letter J and is known as exponential growth (Figure 7.1). Below is an example of exponential growth on a graph. This section will be tested using data analysis so make sure you can recognize different graphs like the ones below.

Survivorship Curves

Figure 7.2 demonstrates the three **survivorship curves**.

Humans are the example most often used for Type I. If you look at Type I, you can see that almost 100 percent of humans survive childhood and most humans survive many years. Type I are often k-selected species.

Songbirds are an example of a Type II. In other words, the death rate for this species is constant during their entire lifetime. Some die young, others in middle age, and some live a long time. Type II are often k-selected species.

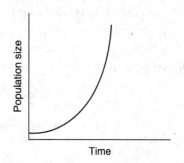

Figure 7.1 Exponential growth.

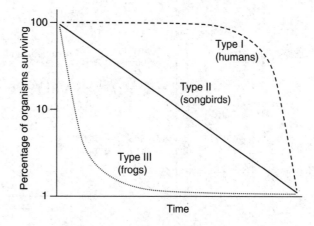

Figure 7.2 Survivorship curves.

The final type, Type III, can be characterized by frogs. Very few frogs make it to adulthood. Think of frog eggs—most get eaten, dry out and never mature, or never hatch at all. Then, tadpoles are also a major food source for many species so lots of young frogs are also killed. However, a few make it to old age and become adult frogs. Type III are often r-selected species.

Carrying Capacity

Carrying capacity is the number of organisms an ecosystem can support over time. This is often shown in a graph depicted in Figure 7.3. The dotted line shows the carrying capacity and the solid line shows the growth of a particular species. As the species increases in number, it will sometimes overshoot the carrying capacity. This is usually because the species has continued to reproduce beyond what the area can support. However, there can be a lag before we begin to see the die-off because it takes a while before the species begins to starve, is impacted by disease, and so on. A reproductive time lag is the time it takes for the birth rates to decline and the death rates to increase in response to the amount of resources in the area.

The population could crash completely if the ecosystem can't recover. But usually, there will be small die-off and then the population will hover around the carrying capacity.

Population Growth and Resource Availability

Populations are limited by the amount of resources available. When resources, things like food and shelter, are available and plentiful, populations can grow. When resources are scarce, populations will exhibit a dieback and decrease in size. This dieback is due to species dying or species being unable to reproduce or having a decreased rate of reproduction.

One way you might be tested on population growth and resource availability, other than carrying capacity, is by a formula that you will have to solve. This will usually involve calculating the percent change. The formula for percent change is shown below.

$$\text{Percent change} = \frac{\text{New value} - \text{Old value}}{\text{Old value}} \times 100$$

If the result is positive, it is an increase.
If the result is negative, it is a decrease.

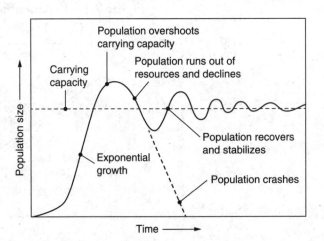

Figure 7.3 Population changes and carrying capacity.

Let's look at a money example. Let's say you had $100 and spent $50. What is the percent change of your money?

You would solve it like this:

$$\frac{\$50 - \$100}{\$100} \times 100 = -50\%$$

Your answer is negative 50 percent, or in other words, you have 50% less than what you started with. However, in an AP Environmental Science class you might be asked about the percent change of a population of cactus or blackbirds, etc. Regardless, you solve it the same way.

Age-Structure Diagrams

You will be asked to look at an age-structure diagram like the four shown in Figure 7.4 and answer questions about it. Let's look at each one separately, but first let's see how we read one.

The size of the population (in either total numbers or percentage) is along the x-axis. Males are on the left side and females on the right and infants/children are along the bottom of the pyramid while elderly are on the top. Each age group is represented by a bar that is usually five years each.

Rapid growth countries: These are countries with a lot of infants, babies, and children. These countries grow very quickly because these children will grow up and have even more children since they are close to reproductive age. Some examples of countries with an age structure like this are Kenya, Nigeria, and Saudi Arabia. See Figure 7.4A.

Slow growth countries: These are countries with more a more column-shaped pyramid with steeper sides. There are more older people in this population than in a rapid growth country because conditions in this country (health care, food, etc.) are usually more advanced. There are still more children than adults but not as great a difference as in a rapidly growing country. See Figure 7.4B.

Zero/stable growth countries: These countries have about the same number of middle-aged people as children so they are considered stable or having a zero growth rate. In other words, for example, a family would have two children and when mom and dad die, the two children replace mom and dad and the population remains stable. This would be like Japan, Italy, and Greece. See Figure 7.4C.

Declining/negative-growth countries: Countries like Germany, Bulgaria, and Russia are considered negative or declining growth countries because there are fewer children than middle-aged adults. In these countries, mom and dad may only be having one child so when mom and dad die, the family (and country) gets smaller. See Figure 7.4D.

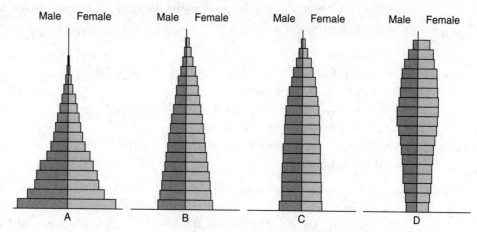

Figure 7.4 Age-structure diagrams.

Sometimes the AP exam will only have three pyramids, essentially combining slow and zero into the same one. Don't let this confuse you. Just make sure you look at the pyramid structure and answer the questions accordingly.

Total Fertility Rate

This is another topic that will be tested using data for you to interpret. This could be in the form of data tables or graphs. You will need to understand things like total fertility rate and replacement levels and then look at the data and answer questions.

The definition of **total fertility rate (TFR)** is the total number of children born, or likely to be born, to a woman in her lifetime if she were subject to the prevailing rate of age-specific fertility in the population. In other words, what is the age in the country that girls normally have their first child? Do they wait until they are in their 30s to start having kids? Or do they have them in their early teens? What educational opportunities are available in the country and specifically to the women in the country? Is there good, reliable birth control in the country and is it acceptable to use birth control? What impact does the government have in the country when it comes to women, family planning, etc.? All of these things can determine the total fertility rate of a country.

In a country that has a TFR of 2.0 or close to that, the country is considered in **replacement level fertility** because the two children will replace the parents when they die and the country has a population growth rate that is relatively stable.

Infant mortality rates are also important to understand when it comes to the country's total fertility rate. A country where there is not good health care and/or nutrition will have high infant mortality rates. Infant mortality rates are expressed as the number of infants that die before they reach their first birthday out of every 1,000 births in that country. This rate is often an indicator of the health of the country. In most cases, when infant mortality rates are high, the TFR is also usually high. I know this seems to contradict itself. You might be asking yourself, "If a lot of babies die, how can the total fertility rate be high?" Well, population scientists have discovered that in developing nations, when lots of babies die, moms have even more babies to ensure at least a few make it to adulthood. So, when lots of babies die, the population usually increases dramatically.

Human Population Dynamics

Human populations can be growing or declining. There are many factors that can impact this, including:

- Birth rate
- Death rate
- Infant mortality rate
- Access to reliable birth control/family planning
- Nutrition and food availability
- Education, particularly for women and girls
- Age of marriage

Thomas Malthus wrote an essay in 1798 in which he stated that humans were growing exponentially, but that food on our planet grew in a linear fashion. He developed the Malthusian Theory of Population Growth in which he proposed that if left unchecked, populations (specifically the human population) will outgrow their resources, particularly food. In other words, humans will grow beyond the Earth's carrying capacity. Of course,

Malthus could not predict in the late 1700s that we would be able to grow food more efficiently and more abundantly with the invention of fertilizers and more. Nor could he have known that we would have the capability to ship food around the world to where it is needed. However, the question still exists of what is the carrying capacity for humans on Earth and could it ever be reached?

Density-dependent factors are things that affect a population as its density increases. For example, diseases are transmitted from human to human; if you live in a place with a lot of people you are more likely to get the disease (let's say the flu) than if you live in the middle of nowhere on a farm with very little interaction with other humans. Other density-dependent factors are air pollution and access to clean water.

Density-independent factors are things such as severe storms, droughts, heat waves, and fires that can influence populations regardless of their density. For example, a drought can hit a tiny town or a large city.

Finally, you will almost certainly be asked to solve a problem using the rule of 70. This is simply done. The formula is:

$$\text{number of years to double} = \frac{70}{\text{annual percentage growth rate}}$$

You might be given the annual percentage growth rate and asked to solve for how many years it takes for the population to double. Or you might be given the number of years it takes for the population to double and asked to determine the annual percentage growth rate. Regardless, just manipulate the formula algebraically and solve for the missing value. Do not change the number given to a decimal; use the percent as a whole number in the calculation. So, if you are told the annual percentage growth rate is 4 percent, then you just take 70 and divide it by 4, so it will take 17.5 years to double.

Demographic Transition

The **demographic transition model** is another way to look at populations (Figure 7.5). Similar to age-structure diagrams, these are broken up into four stages: preindustrial, transitional, industrial, and postindustrial. The model demonstrates how countries change as they develop economically. Let's break down each.

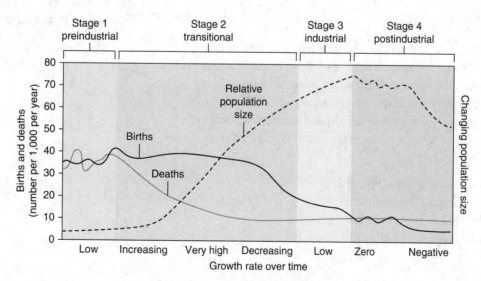

Figure 7.5   The demographic transition.

Preindustrial countries have high birth rates and high death rates so the country has a low growth rate. This stage applied to most of the world before the Industrial Revolution. Even though birth rates are very high, with death rates just as high the country is stable and not growing.

Transitional countries are the ones you will most likely be asked about on the exam because these are countries where birth rates stay high but death rates begin to drop due to increases in health, food availability, and medicine. Infants begin to survive into childhood but because there are still so many births the country's population begins to explode. In addition, because education and birth control for women is limited, the TFR will remain high and the population will grow exponentially. The least developed countries today are in the transitional stage of the demographic transition.

Industrial countries have birth rates that begin to drop due to access to reliable birth control, family planning, women getting educations and jobs and are similar to most developing countries today. With birth rates dropping, the population begins to slow, but not as quickly as you might think due to population momentum.

Population momentum is the idea that even though birth rates have fallen, since there are already so many people in reproductive ages, it takes many decades for the population to finally stabilize.

In **postindustrial** countries economies are strong, citizens are highly educated, medical care is advanced, and women have access to many employment opportunities. In this final stage, both birth rates and death rates continue to fall until death rates exceed birth rates and thus the population begins to decrease.

› Review Questions

Multiple-Choice Questions

1. A country has a growth rate of 4%. How many years will it take for the population to double?

   (A) 17.5 years
   (B) 1,750 years
   (C) 175 years
   (D) 280 years

2. A country has begun to get access to health care for women and children and there is better access to food resources and clean water. However, it is still very expensive to get access to reliable birth control so most women do not use it. What stage of the demographic transition is this country most likely in?

   (A) Stage 1—preindustrial
   (B) Stage 2—transitional
   (C) Stage 3—industrial
   (D) Stage 4—postindustrial

3. Which of the following would be an r-selected species with very little parental care?

   (A) Fish with 9,000 eggs per season
   (B) Bird with five eggs per clutch
   (C) Bat with one pup per season
   (D) Dog with eight pups per year

4. Which of the following characteristics is most closely associated with the age-structure diagram below?

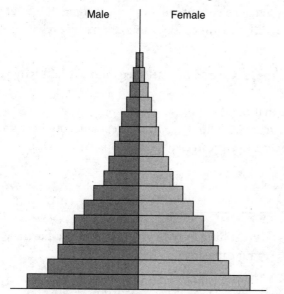

Male   Female

(A) People in this country have access to good, reliable birth control.
(B) People in this country have high levels of education
(C) People in this country have one child or fewer per couple
(D) People in this country have a high total fertility rate

5. Sparrows are a type of small passerine bird that shows a roughly constant mortality rate for the species through its entire life. This means that the individual's chance of dying is independent of their age. Which of the following best characterizes this type of animal?

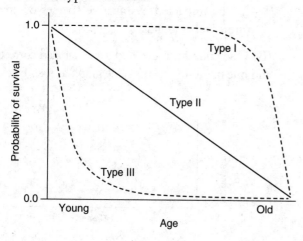

(A) Sparrows are k-selected species, displaying a Type III survivorship curve.
(B) Sparrows are r-selected species, displaying a Type I survivorship curve.
(C) Sparrows are k-selected species, displaying a Type II survivorship curve.
(D) Sparrows are r-selected species, displaying a Type III survivorship curve.

6. The idea that the carrying capacity for humans is fixed and the size of the human population will outgrow Earth's carrying capacity is best described by which of the following economic arguments?

(A) Malthusian Theory
(B) Keynesian Theory
(C) Hayek Theory
(D) Marshall Theory

7. A country had a population of 150,000 in 1980 and 210,000 in 2010. What is the percent change of the population in this country from 1980 to 2010?

(A) 4%
(B) 40%
(C) 1.33%
(D) 2,000%

› Free-Response Question

8. A population of elephants lives in sub-Saharan Africa. A female elephant will bear approximately 12 calves in her lifetime of almost 70 years and usually only one calf at a time. Elephants are herbivores who eat grasses, herbs, fruits, plants, and trees.

   (A) **Identify** the type of species the elephant would be, either r-selected or k-selected, and **explain** why you chose this as your answer.
   (B) **Draw** a survivorship curve that best describes an elephant.
   (C) In the early part of the twentieth century, there were as many as 5 million African elephants, but now there are approximately 415,000. **Calculate** the percent change in African elephants during this time span.

› Answers and Explanations

1. **A**—70/4 = 17.5 years

2. **B**—Countries in the transitional phase are the ones you will most likely be asked about on the exam because these are countries where birth rates stay high but death rates begin to drop due to improvements in health, food availability, and medicine. Infants begin to survive into childhood but because there are still so many births, the country's population begins to explode. The least developed countries today are in the transitional stage of the demographic transition.

3. **A**—Characteristics of r-selected species? They are small, mature early, and have short life spans. They have many offspring but don't take care of their offspring (or very little care). They can live almost anywhere and eat almost anything. They're not as impacted by invasive species or environmental changes.

4. **D**—Rapid growth countries: These are countries with a lot of infants, babies, and children. They grow very quickly because these children will grow up and have even more children because they are close to reproductive age. Some examples of countries with an age structure like this are Kenya, Nigeria, and Saudi Arabia.

5. **C**—Songbirds are an example of a Type II. In other words, the death rate for this species is constant during their entire lifetime. Some die young, others in middle age, and some live a long time. These are often k-selected species.

6. **A**—The Malthusian Theory of Population Growth proposed that if left unchecked populations (specifically the human population) will outgrow their resources, particularly food. In other words, humans will grow beyond the Earth's carrying capacity.

7. **B** $\dfrac{210,000 - 150,000}{150,000} \times 100\% = 40\%$

8. (A) One point for identifying that it would be a k-selected species and one point for explaining why from the list of characteristics below.

   K-selected species because the characteristics of k-selected species are:

   - Large size
   - Few offspring per year
   - Live in stable environments in certain places
   - Specialized diets
   - Spend a lot of time and energy caring for their offspring
   - Long life spans
   - Reproduce more than once in their lifetime
   - Can be impacted by invasive species or environmental changes

   (B) One point for the x- and y-axes labeled correctly and one point for a correct line graph as seen below.

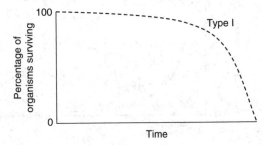

   (C) Two points possible: one point for correct setup and one point for correct answer.

   $$\dfrac{415,000 - 5,000,000}{5,000,000} \times 100 = -91.7\%$$

〉 Rapid Review

- Generalist—A species that can eat almost anything and live almost anywhere, like a cockroach.

- Specialist—A species that only eats a specific item or live in only one place/habitat, like a koala.

- K-selected species, like a kangaroo
  - Large size
  - Few offspring per year
  - Live in stable environments in certain places
  - Specialized diets
  - Spend a lot of time and energy caring for their offspring
  - Long life spans
  - Reproduce more than once in their lifetime
  - Can be impacted by invasive species or environmental changes

- R-selected species, like a roach
  - Small
  - Many offspring
  - Don't take care of their offspring (or very little care)
  - Mature early
  - Short life spans
  - Live almost anywhere
  - Eat almost anything
  - Not as impacted by invasive species or environmental changes

- Biotic potential—Maximum reproductive rate of a population if conditions were ideal. In other words, if there was plenty of room, plenty of food, no predators, and so on, then how many of a particular species could live in the area.

- Type of Survivorship Curves
  - Type I survivorship curve—Long life, not many die young. Example: humans.
  - Type II survivorship curve—Die at all stages of lifetime. Example: birds.
  - Type III survivorship curve—Almost all die young and only few live to adults. Example: fish.

- Carrying capacity—The number of organisms an ecosystem can support over time. This is often shown in a graph.

- Population overshoot—When a population exceeds its carrying capacity and there is a dieback.

- Age-structure diagrams—Pyramid-shaped graphs showing the number of female and males in each age group. See pictures of different shaped pyramids in the chapter.

- Total fertility rate—The total number of children born, or likely to be born, to a woman in her lifetime if she were subject to the prevailing rate of age-specific fertility in the population.

- Infant mortality rate—The number of infants that die before their first birthday out of 1,000 births.

- Density-dependent factors—Things that become worse as the density of the population is larger. Infectious disease is an example of this since the more humans there are, the faster the disease can spread.

- Density-independent factors—Things such as severe storms, droughts, heat waves, and fires that can influence populations regardless of their density. For example, a tornado doesn't hit a city more than a rural area; where people live doesn't matter to a tornado.

- Rule of 70—This is a calculation to solve for how many years it will take for a population to double. 70/growth rate = doubling time. If you are given the doubling time, then rearrange the formula to solve for the growth rate.

- Demographic transition—The demographic transition model is another way to look at populations. Similar to age-structure diagrams, these are broken up into four stages: pre-industrial, transitional, industrial, and postindustrial. It demonstrates how countries change as they develop.

CHAPTER 8

Earth Systems and Resources

IN THIS CHAPTER

Summary: This chapter is all about the nonliving part of our planet that supports our living systems. We will focus on how energy is transferred from the sun to different parts of Earth and how different parts of our planet interact with one another. We will cover geological concepts like plate tectonics, soil formation and composition, the atmosphere and wind, watersheds, and climate topics.

Key Ideas

✪ Earth's systems interact, resulting in a state of balance over time.
✪ Most of the Earth's atmospheric processes are driven by input of energy from the sun.

Key Terms

- Convergent boundaries
- Coriolis effect
- Divergent boundaries
- Earthquakes
- El Niño
- Erosion
- Exosphere
- Hot spot volcanism
- Island arcs
- La Niña
- Mesosphere

- Permeability
- Porosity
- Rain shadow effect
- Soil horizons
- Soil texture triangle
- Stratosphere
- Thermosphere
- Transform boundaries
- Troposphere
- Volcanoes
- Watershed

> These topics will cover about 10 to 12 percent of your AP Environmental Science exam, or about 8 to 10 questions out of the 80 multiple-choice questions. Unless you have taken an Earth Science class, some of topics may be new to you and you might need to review this chapter several times.

Plate Tectonics

Once again, this will be a topic that will be tested using a visual representation. In other words, you will be given a diagram and will need to answer questions based on the picture. Let's look at some of the diagrams they will ask you about.

The Earth's lithosphere, which includes the crust and upper mantle, is made up of a series of pieces, or tectonic plates, that move slowly over time (Figure 8.1).

The first way plates move is away from each other at **divergent plate boundaries**. When plates move apart we get seafloor spreading, rift valleys, volcanoes, and earthquakes. Along these boundaries, earthquakes are common and magma (molten rock) rises from the Earth's mantle to the surface (Figure 8.2). Once this magma solidifies we get new oceanic crust. The most common example of a divergent plate boundary is the Mid-Atlantic Ridge found in the middle of the Atlantic Ocean on the bottom of the seafloor.

The second way plates move is together at **convergent plate boundaries**. When two land (continental) plates come together, the land buckles and mountain ranges are formed. The Himalayan Mountains are an example of this. When a land plate and a sea (oceanic) plate collide, we get deep seafloor trenches with lines of volcanoes and earthquakes near them. The reason you will get a lot of volcanoes is seen in Figure 8.3.

As the ocean plate subducts, or is forced below the continental plate, the ocean plate melts and rises. Have you ever watched a lava lamp work? The wax (lava) is down on the bottom of the lamp where the heat source (light bulb) is found. As the heat melts the wax, the wax begins to rise up through the liquid to the top; this is like what is happening on our planet. As the ocean plate melts because of the heat in our Earth, it begins to rise forming a volcano.

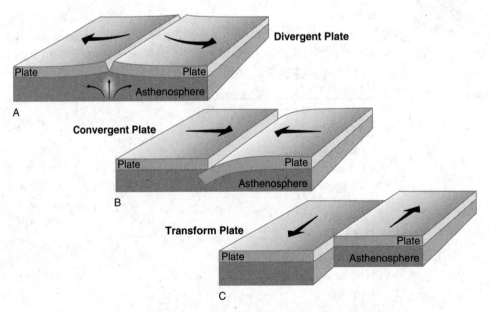

Figure 8.1   Plate tectonics.

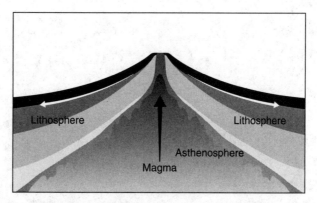

Figure 8.2   Divergent plate boundary.

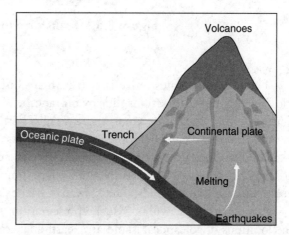

Figure 8.3   Convergent plate boundary.

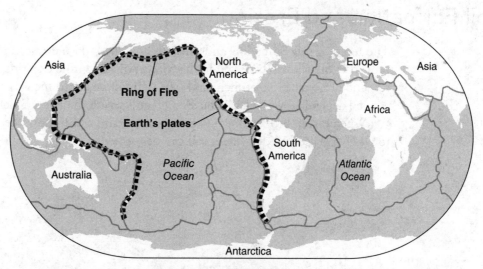

Figure 8.4   The Ring of Fire.

The **Ring of Fire** (see Figure 8.4) is an area around the Pacific Plate where a "ring" of volcanoes and earthquakes can be found because of convergent plate boundaries.

Island arcs are a chain of volcanic islands found on subduction zones and there are often earthquakes associated with these. Examples of island arcs are the Japanese islands, Kuril Islands, and the Aleutian Islands of Alaska.

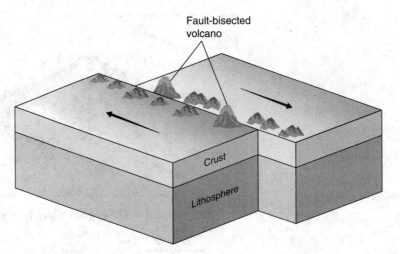

Fault-bisected
volcano

Crust

Lithosphere

Figure 8.5   Transform plate boundary.

The final way plates move is at **transform boundaries** (Figure 8.5) where two plates moving in opposite directions slide by one another. The most common example you may be familiar with is California's San Andreas fault. Earthquakes are common along these faults as the plates move past each other and stored energy becomes released as energy of motion.

Hot spots are areas where the magma from the mantle rises through the lithosphere creating a volcano (Figure 8.6). If the lithosphere is moving over a stationary hot spot, you can get a line of volcanic islands. The Hawaiian Islands are an example of a hot spot volcanism.

Remember, these will be visual representations so make sure you can identify on a map the locations of volcanoes, island arcs, earthquakes, and so on.

Soil Formation and Erosion

The topic of soil formation and erosion, as well as the next section on composition and properties of soil, will be tested in the context of a scientific experiment. You will be given a scenario of a science experiment and asked a question about the variables. Review independent and dependent variables if you aren't familiar with these topics before you take the exam.

When rock is broken down (weathered) by rain, wind, snow, ice, and so on, and carried to another place and deposited, soil can be formed.

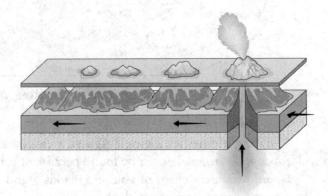

Figure 8.6   Hot spot volcanism.

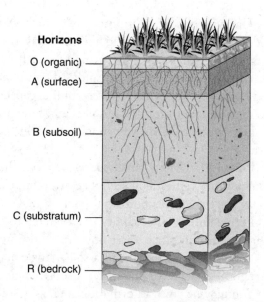

Figure 8.7   Soil profile.

Soil is broken down by many horizons as shown in Figure 8.7. The top layer is the "O" horizon, or organic layer, where freshly dead leaves and other organic matter are found. Lots of decomposition is happening here.

The second layer, the "A" horizon or surface layer, is often called topsoil and is rich in organic matter. The "B" horizon, or subsoil, often has a lot of clay from above layers. The "C" horizon, or substratum, is mostly weathered rock from the bedrock below.

Soil erosion can be caused from water and wind taking soil away. It is very important to stop soil erosion because of the importance of soil for plants, the ability soil has to clean and filter water, and the concern that when soil erodes it can damage the local waterways.

Soil Composition and Properties

Different types of soil allow water through at different rates, or not at all. For example, water goes easily through sand since the water is smaller than the particles of sand. Water can go through silt slower, because silt particles are smaller. Water can't go through clay at all because the particles of clay are so small that water can't squeeze between them (Figure 8.8).

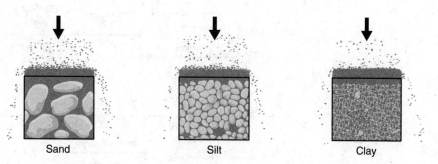

Figure 8.8   Infiltration by soil texture.

The type of soil determines how much water the soil can hold, or the soil's water-holding capacity. Think of it like this: clay is used to make things like pots and bowls. Why? Well, because clay has a high water-holding capacity. It can hold water for days. Would you make a cup out of sand? Of course not—the water would go right through the sand because sand has a low water-holding capacity. How much water the soil can hold can also determine how fertile the soil is and how productive the land might be.

Here are some terms you should know, including knowing how these affect the fertility of the soil:

Porosity—Having small spaces between the particles. The finer the particle size, the more porosity. This might seem backward but clay has tiny holes and very fine particle sizes so clay has the highest porosity.

Permeability—The ability of a material to allow liquid to flow through it. Sand has a high permeability since water flows easily through it.

You may be asked to read a soil triangle and determine the type of soil based on the percentage of sand, silt, and clay. A soil triangle looks like Figure 8.9.

You may be given information such as: a soil has 40 percent sand, 40 percent silt, and 20 percent clay. You would be asked to determine the type of soil texture using the soil pyramid.

To do this, you start with the sand and find the percentage along the bottom of the triangle, in this case 40 percent, and follow the line that goes up and to the left for sand. Then, you move to the right side of the triangle and find the line for silt, in this case also 40 percent. Follow this line down and to the left until it hits the line you had drawn for sand. They should cross. Then, where they cross, if you draw a straight line to the left, where you find clay, you should be at the 20 percent line, which is your percentage of clay. Where these three lines intersected is the type of soil you have; in this case, loam. You might want to use a ruler or a straight edge when drawing the three lines to make sure you are accurate.

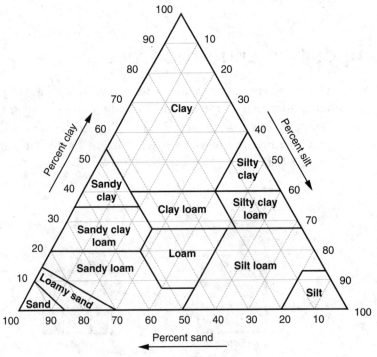

Figure 8.9   Soil triangle.

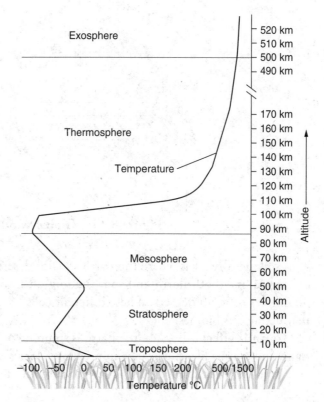

Figure 8.10   Layers of the earth's atmosphere.

Earth's Atmosphere

The Earth's atmosphere is mostly made of nitrogen gas. In fact, 78 percent of the atmosphere is nitrogen. The next highest is oxygen, making up 21 percent, followed by argon, which is 0.9 percent. The rest of the atmosphere is made up of what are known as trace gases, including carbon dioxide, methane, nitrous oxides, and ozone.

The Earth's atmosphere has layers as you move away from the land; the layers are seen in Figure 8.10. The layer we live in is called the troposphere, where all weather occurs. The layer that is farthest away is the exosphere. You can see the temperature line going up through each layer. As you move up through the troposphere, the temperature gets colder. Once you hit the stratosphere, the temperatures begin to go in the other direction, heating up. This back-and-forth continues as you move up through each layer. The thermosphere (*thermo* means "heat") has temperatures that reach hundreds to thousands of degrees! But, the air is so thin it would feel freezing cold to us if we went there. Don't be surprised if you see a picture just like this one on the exam since this section will be tested with a visual representation.

Global Wind Patterns

Another visual representation you will be tested on shows the global wind patterns.

Look at Figure 8.11. The Earth is tilted at a 30-degree angle. Because of this, the sun's radiation hits the Earth with different intensities. It hits the equator most directly since it is directly overhead most of the year. Remember that warm air rises and cooler air sinks because warm air is less dense than cold air. So, if you look at the 0-degree equator, you see rising, moist air that goes off in both directions and sinks at 30 degrees north and south.

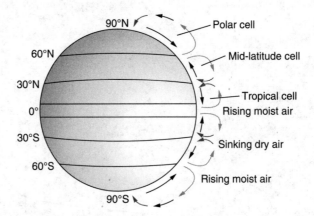

Figure 8.11 Global wind patterns.

This sinking, dry air is where the Earth's major deserts are found. Air is also rising at the 60-degree line (both north and south) going off in both directions and sinking again at 30 degrees or at 90 degrees. These different cells are responsible for the climate patterns that define our biomes.

Coriolis effect—Because the Earth is spinning on its axis, winds and water veer to the right, and storms like hurricanes spin counterclockwise in the Northern Hemisphere and veer to the left and spin clockwise in the Southern Hemisphere (Figure 8.12).

Watersheds

A watershed is a land area that directs water or snow to a river, creek, or stream and eventually to the ocean. Some watersheds are very large, like the Mississippi River watershed that covers about 40 percent of the United States. Watershed characteristics such as size, slope, shape, drainage density, land use/land cover, geology, soils, and vegetation are important factors of watersheds. Things that can affect a watershed would be a dam and housing developments.

Solar Radiation and Earth's Seasons

Our Earth is tilted 23.5 degrees and solar radiation hits the planet at different intensities depending on the season and latitude. So, let's look at the visual representation shown in Figure 8.13.

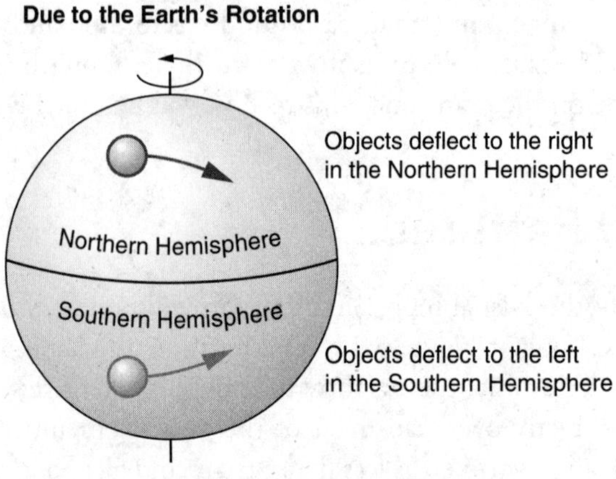

Due to the Earth's Rotation

Objects deflect to the right in the Northern Hemisphere

Northern Hemisphere

Southern Hemisphere

Objects deflect to the left in the Southern Hemisphere

Figure 8.12 The coriolis effect.

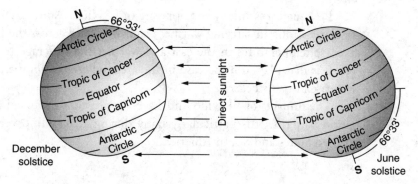

Figure 8.13   Solar radiation.

The diagram on the left is the Earth in December. Do you see how the Tropic of Capricorn is receiving the most direct (straight) sunlight in December? Now, look at the diagram on the right; this is the Earth in June. Where is the most direct sunlight now? Is it the Tropic of Capricorn? No, it is the Tropic of Cancer. The amount of sunlight varies seasonally. In addition, the equator gets direct sun year-round and as you move up or down to the poles the sunlight becomes less and less direct. The fact that the Earth is tilted and rotates around the sun accounts for the Earth's seasons.

Earth's Geography and Climate

Figure 8.14 shows the rain shadow effect. Our planet's weather and climate are impacted by other things in addition to the tilt of the Earth and the amount of sunlight. Weather and climate can be impacted by things like tall mountains. In the picture, the ocean is on the left, which provides a lot of moisture to the area. As the moisture evaporates and clouds are formed, there is a lot of rain on the windward side of the mountain. However, because the mountain is so tall, the rain clouds don't go over the mountain and it is very dry on the other side.

El Niño and La Niña

Every three to seven years on average, the Pacific Ocean has climate shifts with warmer surface waters known as the El Niño–Southern Oscillation (ENSO). Upwellings from the seabed occur in normal years that bring nutrients up for the plankton to feed on. Plankton are food for the marine life up the food chain. In an El Niño year, that upwelling does not occur so the plankton decrease and, in turn, so do the fish stocks.

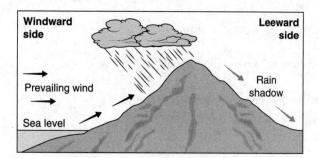

Figure 8.14   The rain shadow effect.

La Niña is essentially the opposite of El Niño. With La Niña, the trade winds are particularly strong in carrying warmer water westward across the Pacific leading to colder than average temperatures in the east and warmer than average temperatures in the west. The result is that plankton increase in the areas where the temperature is cooler, leading to an increase in fish stocks.

The impacts of El Niño and La Niña are changes to rainfall, wind, and ocean circulation patterns. It is particularly rainy during an El Niño year on the West Coast of the United States and South America.

› Review Questions

Multiple-Choice Questions

1. The graph below shows the difference in temperature in each layer of the atmosphere.

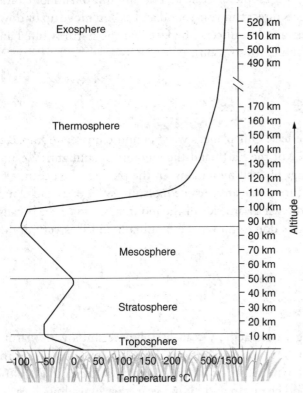

Which of the following correctly describes the Earth's atmosphere?

(A) The mesosphere is where temperatures get warmer.
(B) The troposphere is where the ozone layer is found.
(C) The troposphere is where all weather is found.
(D) The stratosphere contains most of the oxygen in our atmosphere.

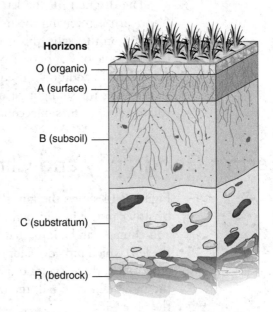

2. According to the diagram above, which layer would have the most organic material?

(A) O
(B) A
(C) B
(D) C

3. Which of the following would be found at the plate boundary seen below?

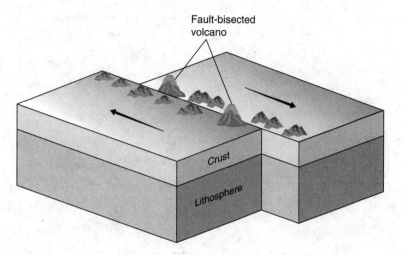

Fault-bisected volcano

Crust

Lithosphere

(A) Mountain formation, due to plates colliding together
(B) Deep ocean trenches
(C) Earthquakes, due to stored energy being released
(D) New crust being formed as magma rises

4. An experiment is done where water is poured through a soil sample as shown below.

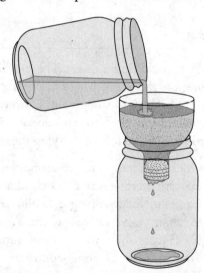

100 ml of water is added and after one hour, 2 ml is found in the bottom of the jar. Which type of soil is likely in the funnel?

(A) Sand
(B) Silt
(C) Loam
(D) Clay

5. Around December, fisherman off the coast of South America would discover that the normal numbers of fish they would catch would diminish every three to seven years. Which of the following is the best explanation of why this was happening?

(A) Warmer waters were causing the fish to move to colder waters.
(B) Overfishing was occurring in the region.
(C) Large predators such as sharks were frequenting the region.
(D) Fallout from local coal-burning power plants was generating acid rain.

6. What type of biome would you expect to find on the leeward side of the mountain?

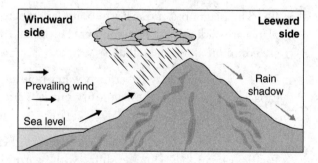

Windward side

Leeward side

Rain shadow

Prevailing wind

Sea level

(A) Tropical rainforest
(B) Desert
(C) Temperate forest
(D) Grassland

❯ Free-Response Question

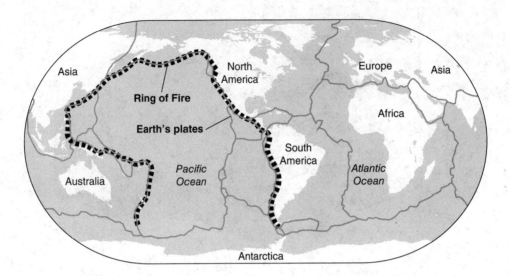

7. The Ring of Fire is a ring of volcanoes around the Pacific Ocean that result from subduction of oceanic plates beneath lighter continental plates. Most of the Earth's volcanoes are located around the Pacific Ring of Fire because that is the location of most of the Earth's subduction zones.

(A) **Explain** what happens when two plates collide along a subduction zone.

(B) Another common phenomenon around the equatorial Pacific Ocean is known as El Niño. **Describe** what an El Niño is and what impact it would have on the environment.

❯ Answers and Explanations

1. **C**—The troposphere is where we live and where all weather is found.

2. **A**—The top layer is the organic layer where dead and decaying leaves are found.

3. **C**—The diagram is a transform boundary where plates are sliding past one another. Earthquakes are common along these faults.

4. **D**—Clay, because clay has a high water-holding capacity. It has the highest porosity but it is not very permeable.

5. **A**—Every three to seven years on average, the Pacific Ocean has climate shifts with warmer surface waters known as the El Niño–Southern Oscillation (ENSO). Upwellings from the seabed occur in normal years that bring nutrients up to the plankton to feed on. The plankton are food for the marine life up the food chain. In an El Niño year, that upwelling does not occur so the plankton are reduced and, in turn, so are the fish stocks.

6. **B**—You would find a desert. The prevailing wind coming off the ocean brings a lot of rain to the windward side of the mountain. However, because the mountain is so tall, the rain clouds don't go over the mountain and it is very dry on the other side.

7. **(A)** One point for explaining that one plate is pushed beneath another and a trench may form.

(B) One point for describing an El Niño. Every three to seven years on average, the Pacific Ocean has climate shifts with warmer surface waters known as the El Niño–Southern Oscillation (ENSO). Upwellings from the seabed occur in normal years that bring nutrients up to the plankton to feed on. The plankton are food for the marine life up the food chain. In an El Niño year, that upwelling does not occur so the plankton decrease, and in turn, so do the fish stocks. One point for describing the impact of El Niño. The impact on the environment from El Niño is fewer fish on the West Coast of South America and increased rainfall on the western coasts of both North and South America.

❯ Rapid Review

- Convergent boundaries—Where two tectonic plates are colliding together.

- Divergent boundaries—Where two tectonic plates are moving apart.

- Transform boundaries—Where two tectonic plates moving in opposite directions are sliding by one another.

- Hot spot volcanism—A volcano created by the magma from the mantle rises through the lithosphere. If the lithosphere is moving over a stationary hot spot, you can get a line of volcanic islands.

- Island arcs—A chain of volcanic islands found on subduction zones. There are usually earthquakes associated with these.

- Erosion—Soil moving from one area to another caused by wind or water.

- Soil horizons—Layers of soil that include O, A, B, C, and bedrock. The top layer is the "O," or organic layer, where freshly dead leaves and other organic matter is found. Lots of decomposition is happening here. The second horizon, "A," or surface layer, is often called topsoil and is rich in organic matter. The "B" layer, or subsoil, often has a lot of clay from above layers. The "C" horizon is mostly weathered rock from the bedrock below.

- Porosity—Having small spaces between the particles. The finer the particle size, the more porosity. This might seem backward but clay has tiny holes and very fine particle sizes so clay has the highest porosity.

- Permeability—The ability of a material to allow liquid to flow through it. Sand has a high permeability, since water flows easily through it.

- Soil texture triangle—A way to determine the type of soil based on the percentage of clay, silt, and sand.

- The layers of the atmosphere—Troposphere, stratosphere, mesosphere, thermosphere, and exosphere. The temperature changes with each layer.

- Coriolis effect—Because the Earth is spinning on its axis, winds and water veer to the right, and storms like hurricanes spin counterclockwise in the Northern Hemisphere and clockwise in the Southern Hemisphere.

- Watershed—A watershed is a land area that directs precipitation to a particular creek, stream, or river and eventually to the ocean.

- Rain shadow effect—Where it rains on the side of the mountain with the ocean and is very dry on the other side of the mountain.

- El Niño and La Niña—Are opposite phases of what is known as the *El Niño–Southern Oscillation* (ENSO) cycle. The ENSO are the fluctuations in temperature in the ocean and atmosphere in the east-central Equatorial Pacific.

CHAPTER 9

Land and Water Use

IN THIS CHAPTER

Summary: This chapter explains that humans are doing things to the environment that are both positive and negative and gives examples of ways we can reduce the negative impacts humans are causing.

Key Ideas

✪ When humans use natural resources, they alter natural systems.

✪ Humans can mitigate their impact on land and water resources through sustainable use.

Key Terms

- Aquaculture
- Aquifers
- Biocontrol
- Clear-cutting
- Concentrated animal feeding operations (CAFOs)
- Contour plowing
- Crop rotation
- Desertification
- Drip irrigation
- Ecological footprint
- Flood irrigation
- Free-range grazing
- Fungicides

- Furrow irrigation
- Genetically modified organisms (GMOs)
- Green Revolution
- Herbicides
- Impervious surfaces
- Infiltration
- Insecticides
- Integrated pest management
- Intercropping
- No-till agriculture
- Overburden
- Overfishing
- Overgrazing

- Permeable surfaces
- Perennial crops
- Pesticides
- Prescribed burns
- Reforestation
- Rodenticides
- Rotational grazing
- Salinization
- Saltwater intrusion
- Slag and tailings
- Slash-and-burn farming
- Spray irrigation
- Strip cropping

- Strip mining
- Subsurface mining
- Surface mining
- Sustainability
- Terracing
- Tilling
- Tragedy of the commons
- Urban runoff
- Urban sprawl
- Urbanization
- Waterlogging
- Windbreaks

This chapter about land and water use will cover about 10 to 15 percent of your AP Environmental Science exam, or about 8 to 12 out of the 80 multiple-choice questions. The topics of irrigation, pest control, mining, urbanization, integrated pest management, sustainable agriculture, aquaculture, and sustainable forestry are all going to be tested on your ability to come up with the best environmental solution. So, make sure when you read the question you are thinking pro-environment and choose the best solution from the answer choices.

The Tragedy of the Commons

The **tragedy of the commons** holds that individuals tend to overexploit shared resources until the resource becomes unavailable to all. Garrett Hardin originally explained this concept using an analogy of ranchers taking their animals to a common field. Hardin said that when there are just a few animals feeding off the common area there is no problem. However, when many ranchers come and add more and more animals, and there are no rules as to how many or how long the animals can graze, with the rancher caring only about their own profits, soon the area will be decimated and unusable to anyone. This concept can be extended to many areas of environmental science (for example, polluting the air or water and overfishing our oceans).

Clear-Cutting

Forests are an important resource, both for the environment and for human use. The trees in forests are huge carbon sinks, meaning they are able to absorb large amounts of carbon dioxide from our atmosphere (carbon dioxide is a leading contributor to climate change that we will discuss in a future chapter). When we cut and burn the trees to make room for housing or agriculture, we release the carbon stored in the trees into the environment, leading to increased carbon dioxide levels and climate change. Forests also remove pollutants both from the atmosphere and from the water and soil.

Clear-cutting is a method of harvesting trees in the forest for human use. These uses can be for building materials, fuel for fires, paper, and so on. A cheap and easy method of harvesting these trees is to cut them all down at one time in large areas. This method is called clear-cutting (Figure 9.1).

Figure 9.1   Clear-cutting.

Clear-cutting has many environmental consequences even though from an economic standpoint it is a benefit since it is cheaper than other methods. Since trees have roots that hold the soil, when we clear cut large areas of land we expose this soil, leaving it vulnerable to erosion and/or flooding. This soil may end up in a river, lake, or stream leading to problems there. Trees also provide shade, so when we cut them down, the temperature in these areas is increased because the sun hits the ground directly.

The Green Revolution

In Mexico and India in the 1940s and beyond, the **Green Revolution** brought new disease-resistance varieties of plants like wheat and rice, new technologies for mechanized harvesting, and new chemical fertilizers, irrigation practices, and pesticides. The Green Revolution has allowed us to feed more people, to make larger profits, to create tastier and more nutritious food, and to use less pesticide and water, but there are some consequences to these practices. Increased mechanization has led to a greater use of fossil fuels, leading to climate change.

Genetically modified organisms (GMOs) are organisms (plants, animals, and micro-organisms) that have had their DNA modified in some way through genetic engineering. GMOs are often developed to increase food's flavor or to make the plant resistant to disease and drought. Some people are concerned that GMOs have increased allergic reactions in some individuals.

This topic will be tested using text analysis. This means that you will be given a short passage to read and will be asked questions based on that passage.

Impact of Agricultural Practices

Providing food for a growing human population is important and we are doing this in better and better ways. However, there are environmental impacts of many of the practices we use. For example, **tilling** the soil is how farmers dig, stir, and turn the soil over so they can plant new crops. This helps to aerate the soil and allows for the seedlings to get established.

However, when we till the soil it leaves the soil vulnerable to erosion, which we discussed as an environmental concern in a prior chapter. Also, many farmers use a technique called **slash-and-burn farming**, where they take wild or forested land and convert this to farmland. This devastates habitats and species, causes deforestation, and can lead to climate change. Fertilizers and pesticides also have large environmental problems. Fertilizers can run off the land and end up in the water causing a problem called eutrophication that we will discuss in a future chapter. Pesticides can contaminate the soil and water and be toxic to organisms that they were not intended to harm such as birds, fish, "good" insects, and plants.

Irrigation Methods

Seventy percent of all water used by humans is to irrigate crops. One reason for the large use is the wasteful way we water those crops. You will need to know the pros and cons of the different methods.

Drip irrigation—This method saves water because only about 5 percent of the water is lost to evaporation, but it is pretty expensive. You might have seen this at your house or in businesses. This method uses hoses with small holes where water seeps out slowly, getting the water down to the roots (Figure 9.2). Using this on a large scale for mass food production is costly, but it helps prevent erosion and nutrient runoff and discourages weeds since the water is targeted.

Flood irrigation—In flood irrigation the farmer floods an entire field with water (Figure 9.3). The benefits of this include the ability to produce more food (therefore increasing profits for the farmer) and incur less loss of crops from drought. However, the cons of this are that a lot of water is lost to evaporation and it can increase salinization of the soil. **Soil salinization** results when salt in the water is left on crops after the water evaporates. While water can evaporate, salt will not. After time, so much salt can be left on the soil that plants can't grow.

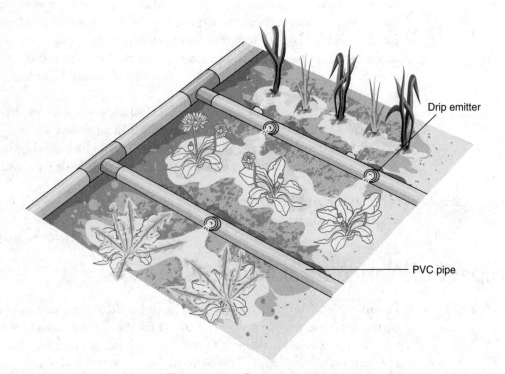

Figure 9.2 Drip irrigation.

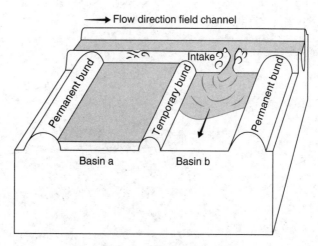

Figure 9.3 Flood irrigation.

Figure 9.4 Furrow irrigation.

Furrow irrigation—This method is similar to flood irrigation except that trenches are dug between rows of crops and that area is flooded with water. This allows the farmer to flow water down these trenches and the water is absorbed by the roots of the plants (Figure 9.4). The advantages and disadvantages are similar to flood irrigation with about 35 percent being lost to evaporation.

Spray irrigation—This method is the one you are probably most familiar with. You see this on lawns all the time with sprinklers, but on a large scale this is done on crops (Figure 9.5). This method loses less water than either flood or furrow but is more expensive.

There are several more terms relating to irrigation that you need to know for the exam. **Waterlogging** happens when so much water is left on the soil it is saturated. The water affects plants by lowering the levels of oxygen to the roots and impacting the germination of seeds and young plants. **Aquifers** are underground layers of water that can be tapped for irrigation and other uses. However, if too many wells are drilled, the water can be severely depleted depending on the type of aquifer and the demand for the water. In fact, the Ogallala Aquifer in the middle of the United States, where much of our food is grown, is being severely depleted due to massive overuse in the past century.

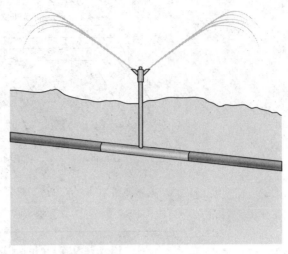

Figure 9.5   Spray irrigation.

Pest Control Methods

Pests such as insects, fungus, rodents and weeds are a common problem for our land use. To combat these pests, farmers, homeowners, and ranchers have used many different types of pest control methods. Make sure you are familiar with the different terms when it comes to pest control. **Pesticide** is a generic term that includes the others. The other terms are: **herbicides** that get rid of unwanted plants such as weeds; **fungicides** that get rid of fungal organisms; **rodenticides** that kill rodents including mice and rats; and **insecticides** that are designed to kill insects. There are many different types and they all kill in different ways.

One problem with many of these pesticides is that the organism that the pesticide is designed to kill builds up resistance over time. Pesticides are designed to prevent crop damage and increase crop profits, but if pesticide resistance becomes a problem, the pesticide will no longer work (or will not work as well). The farmer/homeowner will have to either use more pesticide or stronger doses, or switch to a new type, and this can impact both the profits and the environment. The **pesticide treadmill** is a term used for when a farmer continues to add more and more pesticides or switches from one to another as they become ineffective.

One method to help stop this is by genetically engineering crops so the pests don't or can't harm them. This has pros and cons. A pro is that there is less need for pesticides, which is good for the environment since pesticides can often harm other organisms that they weren't designed to harm. Other pros are increased profits for farmers and helping keep the cost of food affordable. However, on the negative side is the loss of diversity in the crop.

Meat Production Methods

You will be asked to look at various types of data and answer questions when it comes to meat production. Remember, this could be in the form of a graph or data table.

Concentrated animal feeding operations (CAFOs), also known as feedlots, are defined as a feeding operation involving more than 1,000 animal units (defined as 1,000 pounds of animal weight) held for more than 45 days, or any size feeding operation that discharges manure or wastewater into a natural or man-made ditch, stream, or other waterway. The pros of CAFOs are profits because you can get a lot of animals ready for slaughter very quickly and cheaply, which means increased profits for ranchers and lower priced food for consumers. The cons of CAFOs are many. Animals are usually packed into small enclosures with thousands of animals crowded into one CAFO, they are often fed a man-made feed rather than grass, and many times the animals are given large doses of antibiotics to prevent disease. Because of the number of animals crowded together, large amounts of waste are generated, which can pollute local rivers, streams, lakes, and land areas.

Free-range grazing is what it sounds like—animals are allowed to roam free and graze as needed on open land. The pros of this method are animals are free to roam, fewer or no antibiotics are given, and because there are fewer animals, the manure is less concentrated, leading to the waste being a beneficial fertilizer and not a problem. However, this is a more expensive choice for ranchers and large amounts of land are needed.

Farmers must be careful to not overgraze the land. **Overgrazing** happens when farmers/ranchers put too many animals on an area and the area begins to lose all plants. Any area that has low rainfall in general and then loses all plants is said to have undergone **desertification**. Overgrazing can also lead to soil erosion; the plants' roots hold the soil in place and when the plants are gone the soil can easily be eroded by wind or water.

Eating less meat has some big environmental advantages. First, it takes almost 20 times less land to get the same number of calories from growing plants. Animals also produce a lot of methane and carbon dioxide, two things we will discuss in detail in the chapter relating to climate change. Finally, if we don't eat as much meat, we lower the use of antibiotics and growth hormone, use less water, and prevent erosion of soil caused by overgrazing.

Impact of Overfishing

Overfishing is commercial fishing in which large quantities of fish are caught faster than the species can breed and replace itself. Since many people depend on fish for their food supply, overfishing can be very dangerous and can impact aquatic ecosystems by disrupting the food chain. When too many fish are taken out of the ocean, it can destroy food webs, lead to a loss of marine life, and can have a large socioeconomic impact on humans who rely on fishing for their livelihood and food needs.

Impact of Mining

There are many minerals found on Earth's surface and underground that we need for human purposes, for example, coal. When the mineral resource is found on the surface of the Earth and we extract this mineral resource, it is called **surface mining** (Figure 9.6). When the resource is found deep underground, it is called **subsurface mining**, which is more expensive (Figure 9.7).

There are many methods of surface mining, such as strip mining, open-pit mining, and mountaintop removal. Each of these has its own set of environmental impacts. In order to get to these resources, miners must first remove the soil, plants, and rock known as **overburden**. After mining, the wastes from mining, called **slag and tailings**, are left behind to be dealt with. Mining removes plant life, opens the soil up to erosion and runoff, harms habitats, can contaminate aquifers, releases methane from the soil, and causes fine particles of dust to be released.

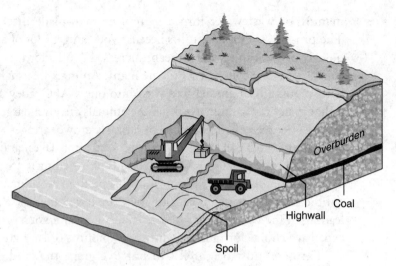

Figure 9.6 Surface mining.

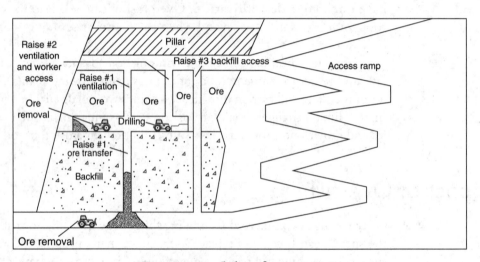

Figure 9.7 Subsurface mining.

Impact of Urbanization

Urbanization occurs as people move from rural areas and into cities, usually in search of job opportunities. Urbanization has many benefits such as increased job opportunities and access to basic needs like clean water and electricity. However, as more people live together there are some costs to the environment. For example, as we pave land to build roads, houses, and parking lots, water can't seep into the soil and refill aquifers. This can also cause increased runoff and flooding since the water runs off the pavement and doesn't **infiltrate** into the soil. In addition, as more people move to cities and gain access to electricity, we mine and burn more coal, oil, or natural gas. This can lead to an increase of carbon dioxide or land damaged from mining.

There are a couple more terms relating to irrigation that you need to be familiar with for the exam:

Saltwater intrusion—If there are too many people putting a demand on fresh water, and the city is located near the ocean, we can overdraw the aquifer allowing the saltwater to move into the freshwater aquifer. This can destroy aquifers.

Urban sprawl—The expansion of urban areas into rural areas. It can cause water and air pollution and destroy habitats.

Ecological Footprints

Each person or society has an ecological footprint, and it is measured by the amount of land (in hectares) needed by the person or society to support their way of life. To calculate the ecological footprint, you would take the person's or society's demands such as timber, electricity, food, gas, and so on, and assign a number to that need. For example, a person in the United States, who lives in a home that is heated by oil, drives a car using gas, has clothing and food needs, and produces carbon emissions would have a much greater ecological footprint than a person living in a poor country possibly living in a hut with no electricity, no car, and growing their own food or living off the land.

Introduction to Sustainability

Everyone needs access to a healthy environment, clean air and water, and natural resources. Sustainability is the access to each of these for human use without depleting them. There are many things we can do as humans to help, such as limiting our use of resources, reduce/reuse/recycle, green building, and employing sustainable agriculture. As long as we stick to a sustainable yield, or not taking more than can be regrown, replenished, or reused, we can live on this planet for many years to come.

Methods to Reduce Urban Runoff

As we discussed earlier in this chapter, as we pave surfaces, build buildings, and put in roads, we stop allowing water to infiltrate into the soil and we increase the amount of water that runs off. There are many ways to reduce this runoff. For example, if a company wanted to build a parking lot, they could add areas throughout the parking lot with plants and trees and soil. This way, although there are less actual parking spaces, when it rains the water can soak into the natural areas and the runoff will not be that bad. You can also plant trees around the parking lot that will absorb water and reduce runoff.

Impervious surfaces like concrete or asphalt don't allow for water to infiltrate into the ground. Using pavers instead of asphalt or concrete in a parking lot will allow water to seep into the ground between the pavers and not run off. These types of **permeable surfaces,** shown in Figure 9.8, allow water to seep into the ground and replenish aquifers or water plants. This topic will be given to you as a scientific experiment that you will need to read and come up with the best answer.

Integrated Pest Management

Pests are a huge problem for humans for many reasons. They eat our crops, make us sick, destroy our building structures, and can be nuisances in our lives. We often try to kill these pests using pesticides, herbicides, and fungicides. But, as mentioned earlier in this chapter, these can have devastating effects on the environment. Humans can mitigate this problem a little by implementing **integrated pest management (IPM)**, which is a method of killing

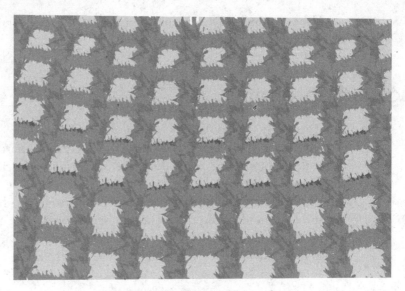

Figure 9.8   Permeable surfaces.

or preventing the bugs without using as much pesticide. So, we might step on the cockroach rather than grabbing the can of insecticide.

But, on a larger scale for crops, we need other methods. These can include biological methods like predator bugs that a farmer buys to eat the pests (**biocontrol**), or rotating crops to plant ones that naturally are resistant to the pest. We can also use intercropping, a method of planting rows of crops that are different; one row is a crop that repels the insect while another row is the crop the farmer wants to harvest. These methods are all better for the environment than the chemical pesticides that have historically been used. The problem with IPM for farmers is the expense it incurs.

Sustainable Agriculture

Our agricultural practices have environmental impacts. For instance, if we overgraze, we cause soil to erode, and we reduce soil fertility and its ability to sustain plant life. However, many farmers and ranchers are looking at ways to reduce this and still produce food for humans. The methods to make agriculture more sustainable are many. For example, ranchers can make sure to not overgraze by rotating their animals to different pastures, allowing the grass to regrow and recover. This is called **rotational grazing**. We can prevent soil from losing valuable nutrients by rotating the places we plant these crops or by adding manure to increase nutrient values and limestone to balance acidity to protect soil health.

We can prevent soil from eroding by each of the following techniques:

Contour plowing—Planting crops along the contours of the land as shown in Figure 9.9.

Windbreaks—Planting trees or shrubs to limit erosion as shown in Figure 9.10.

Perennial crops—Planting crops that don't need to be replanted each year and can be harvested multiple times during the year. After harvest, they automatically grow back. By eliminating replanting each year, perennial cropping can reduce soil erosion.

Terracing—Similar to contour plowing but when an area is very hilly or mountainous. The farmer will make step-like rows and plant the crops on these rows. This helps to reduce soil erosion. Figure 9.11 shows how the steep mountain was made into steps and crops were planted on the top of each step.

Figure 9.9   Contour plowing.

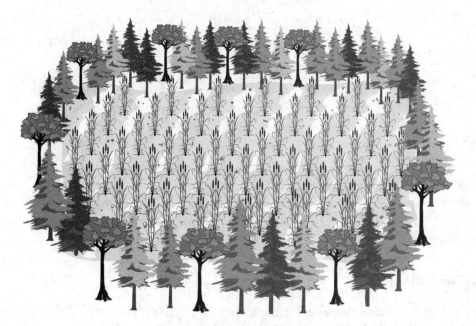

Figure 9.10   Windbreaks.

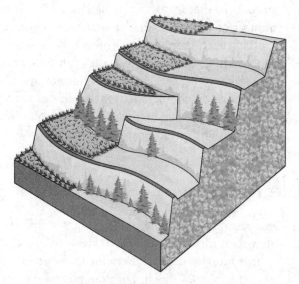

Figure 9.11   Terracing.

No-till agriculture—This method is what it sounds like, planting crops but without tilling the soil before planting. This reduces soil erosion because when we turn the soil over (tilling), it is vulnerable to wind and water erosion.

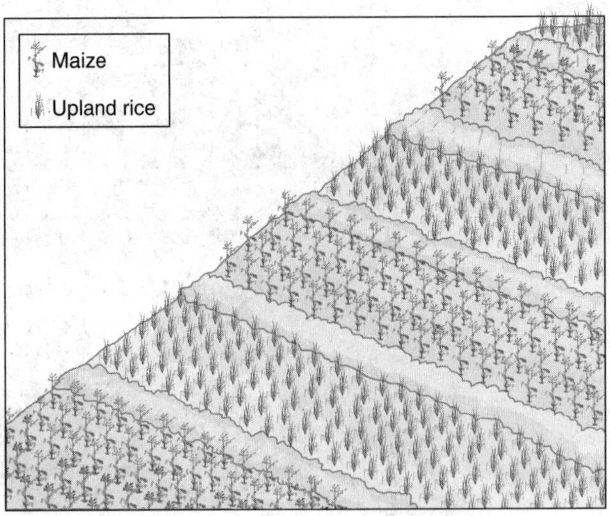

Figure 9.12   Strip cropping.

Strip cropping—Planting a strip of one crop, then a strip of another, alternating throughout the field. This prevents soil erosion because one row might have crops with deep roots, while the next one doesn't. The deep roots will hold in the soil for the plants that don't have deep roots. You can see an example of this in Figure 9.12.

Aquaculture

Aquaculture is a method of farm raising fish, shellfish, or aquatic plants. A farmer can build large ponds and stock these ponds with large numbers of animals or plants, or use a natural river, lake, or ocean to do this with nets and holding pens. The benefits of aquaculture are that it doesn't deplete our natural supplies of these organisms, it feeds a large number of people, it uses less water, it increases profits, and it uses very little fuel.

However, there are environmental problems; large numbers of fish, for example, can produce huge quantities of waste (fish poop, excess fish food, etc.), which can pollute the river, lake, or ocean. These fish might escape their enclosures and if they are not a natural species can outcompete natural species or breed with wild species. In addition, when we put large numbers of animals together in one area, disease can spread very quickly and these diseases might spread to wild populations.

Sustainable Forestry

Humans have a large need for resources made from forests. These include building materials, paper, medicine, and food. However, there are more sustainable ways to harvest forests so that humans can use them for many years and we don't harm the environment and the animal habitat as much. For example, we can replant trees after cutting them down (**reforestation**), we can do **prescribed burns** to clear out the brush, which can prevent larger "crown" fires. We can make sure to purchase wood that is grown on a tree farm rather than a natural forest. We can also reduce, reuse, and recycle wood products for future use. Using IPM to prevent trees from getting pests like fungus or bugs can also help sustain a forest for many years.

› Review Questions

Multiple-Choice Questions

1. A family of four realized their water bill was high and that a lot of water was being wasted in the shower. They replaced their 5-gallon-per-minute showerheads with ones that only use 3 gallons per minute. If each family member showers for 5 minutes per day and a typical month is 30 days long, how much water will the family save per month with the new showerheads?

   (A) 3,000 gallons
   (B) 1,800 gallons
   (C) 1,200 gallons
   (D) 9,000 gallons

2. A farmer is growing a crop that has historically been eaten by a particular insect. However, she has noticed that each year she puts the same amount of pesticide on and not as many insects are killed. She has begun to add more and more amounts of the pesticide to kill the same number of insects. What is the best explanation of why this is happening?

   (A) The company that sells the pesticide has begun lowering the percentage of chemical in the bottles to save money.
   (B) The insects are becoming resistant to the pesticide.
   (C) The insects are flying away during the times the farmer is spaying her crops and then returning afterward.
   (D) The farmer doesn't realize that this is a different species of insect than she had in previous years.

3. A sustainable society would choose which of the following things to impress upon its people?

   (A) Use fossil fuels for their energy use.
   (B) Produce meat by using concentrated animal feeding operations (CAFOs).
   (C) Use commercial fishing methods that can capture thousands of fish at one time.
   (D) Use integrated pest management to mitigate their impact on the land.

4. Which of the following best describes an environmental problem associated with urbanization near coastal areas?

   (A) Saltwater intrusion from overdrawing of water can harm aquifers.
   (B) Cities generally have a lower transportation carbon footprint.
   (C) It is more expensive to live in cities than in rural areas.
   (D) People in cities use less electricity than people in rural areas.

5. Which of the following best describes an environmental solution using aquaculture?

   (A) Aquaculture can produce large amounts of fish that humans can purchase or sell.
   (B) Aquaculture prevents diseases in wild fish populations because of the antibiotics used.
   (C) Aquaculture uses a small amount of water and very little fuel.
   (D) Aquaculture prevents wastewater contamination because of the environmental methods that are employed.

6. Which of the following is the best example of an environmental problem from clear-cutting forests?

   (A) Soil erosion increases.
   (B) Stream temperatures fall.
   (C) Carbon dioxide levels fall.
   (D) Flooding decreases.

› Free-Response Questions

7. **Identify** ONE method of mining that extracts natural resources from the earth and for the type you identified **describe** ONE environmental problem of this method.

8. **Describe** ONE ecological benefit that forests provide to the Earth.

› Answers and Explanations

1. **C**—1,200 gallons. Before: family of 4 × 5 gallons per minute × 5 minutes per day × 30 days per month = 3,000 gallons per month. Now: family of 4 × 3 gallons per minute × 5 minutes per day × 30 days per month = 1,800 gallons per month. 3,000 gallons per month − 1,800 gallons per month = 1,200 gallons per month.

2. **B**—One consequence of using common pesticides is the pests can develop a resistance to the pesticide.

3. **D**—Integrated pest management is a way to use less pesticides to minimize the harm done to the environment. A sustainable society would want to do this.

4. **A**—As more people put a demand for water in cities, those in coastal areas can have their aquifers impacted by saltwater intrusion, when saltwater from the oceans moves into freshwater aquifers.

5. **C**—Aquaculture uses little water and fuel.

6. **A**—The roots of trees help hold in the soil, so when a forest is clearcut, erosion of the soil will increase.

7. One point for the method and one point for the environmental problem of the method. The method must be linked to the correct problem.

METHOD	ENVIRONMENTAL PROBLEM OF THE METHOD
Surface mining (strip mining, open-pit mining, and mountaintop removal)	In order to get to these resources, miners must first remove the soil, plants, and rock known as overburden. After mining the wastes from mining, called slag and tailings, are left behind to be dealt with. Mining removes plant life, opens the soil up to erosion and runoff, harms habitats, can contaminate aquifers, releases methane from the soil, and causes fine particles of dust to be released.
Subsurface mining	Subsurface mining is more expensive and can be dangerous.

8. One point for describing that forests provide many benefits to Earth. They absorb pollutants, store carbon dioxide, prevent soil erosion, reduce flooding, and lower temperatures on the land and water around the forest.

⟩ Rapid Review

- Tragedy of the commons—A shared resource that no one owns and everyone can use is overexploited and eventually unavailable to all.

- Clear-cutting—An economically viable way of cutting down all the trees in an area of a forest for human use. This leads to erosion, flooding, and increased soil and water temperatures, and it removes the carbon sink that forests provide.

- Mechanization—Using mechanical means like tractors and farm equipment to harvest crops.

- Fertilization—Using man-made, chemical fertilizers on crops to help them grow better.

- Tilling—Turning the land over so you can plant crops, but this can lead to erosion of the soil from both water and wind.

- Slash-and-burn farming—This is an agricultural method for taking wild land such as a forest, and clearing it to grow crops. Usually this method involves slashing (cutting down) and burning the plants that were found there and planting a crop.

- Drip irrigation—Using hoses that slowly drip water onto the roots of plants. Pro: conserves water. Con: expensive.

- Flood irrigation—Flooding an entire crop with water. Pros: cheap and quick. Cons: uses large quantities of water and water is lost to evaporation.

- Furrow irrigation—Building rows between crops and flooding those rows with water. Pros: cheap and quick. Cons: uses large quantities of water and water is lost to evaporation.

- Spray irrigation—Using sprinkler-type devices to water crops. Pro: less water lost to evaporation. Con: expensive.

- Waterlogging—When soil gets so flooded with water, and the water then evaporates but the salt is left behind. After many years of this, the land is so salty that most plants can't grow.

- Salinization—Salt in the soil that limits plant growth.

- Aquifers—A layer of rock that is filled with water.

- Pesticides—A generic term to describe any herbicide, fungicide, rodenticide, or insecticide.

- Herbicides—A chemical that kills unwanted plants.

- Fungicides—A chemical that kills unwanted fungi.

- Rodenticides—A chemical that kills unwanted rodents such as mice and rats.

- Insecticides—A chemical that kills unwanted insects.

- Concentrated animal feeding operations (CAFOs)—Large feeding operations with many animals in a small area. Pro: increased profits. Cons: disease can spread so large amounts of antibiotics are used and manure and urine can run off into local waterways.

- Free-range grazing—Allowing animals to roam free and eat on grassy pastures.

- Overgrazing—When too many animals are allowed to eat in an area and the grass/plants can't recover. This often leads to desertification.

- Desertification—When an area is so overgrazed it can't recover and the area can become a desert.

- Overfishing—Taking too many fish at one time by commercial fishing and not allowing the breeding stock to reproduce and replenish.

- Surface mining—A type of mining where minerals are found near to the surface with only soil and small amounts of rock above it so it is inexpensive and relatively easy to obtain.

- Overburden—The rock and soil found above a mine that must be removed to get to the mineral resource.

- Slag and tailings—The waste from mining that must be dealt with and can be an environmental problem if it is not.

- Subsurface mining—Digging deep into the Earth to get to the mineral resource. Pro: can get to a resource that is abundant deep within the Earth. Con: expensive and sometimes dangerous.

- Urbanization—People moving from rural areas and into cities looking for jobs or other opportunities.

- Saltwater intrusion—Occurs when too many people living in cities close to the coastline draw on an aquifer for fresh water. The freshwater is removed and the salt water can move into the aquifer, destroying the aquifer.

- Impervious surfaces—Surfaces like concrete or asphalt that don't allow for water to infiltrate into the ground.

- Permeable surfaces—Surfaces that do allow water to seep into the ground and replenish aquifers or water plants.

- Urban sprawl—Term used to describe cities as they expand more and more into the surrounding ecosystems/habitats.

- Ecological footprint—The area of land (measured in hectares) that a person or society uses due to the pressures it puts on the environment. In other words, the amount of natural resources that it takes to support one person or one society. People living in developed nations have a greater ecological footprint than people living in developing nations.

- Urban runoff—Occurs when cities are so covered with concrete, asphalt, buildings, and so on, that water can't infiltrate into the land and runs off instead.

- Infiltration—The ability of water to move through the soil and perhaps into an aquifer.

- Integrated pest management—The method of killing pests without using as much pesticide; for example, using predator bugs and rotating crops.

- Biocontrol—A method of integrated pest management that uses predator bugs to control pest species.

- Intercropping—A method of integrated pest management where rows of crops that repel pests are planted next to the row of crops the farmer wants to sell.

- Crop rotation—A method of rotating crops to different fields so the soil has a chance to recover and minerals are not depleted.

- Contour plowing—Planting crops with the contour of the land to prevent erosion.

- Windbreaks—Planting trees or shrubs next to crops to prevent wind erosion.

- Perennial crops—Planting crops that don't need to be replanted each year but can be harvested multiple times throughout the year.

- Terracing—Creating flat terraces on mountainsides to plant crops and prevent erosion.

- No-till agriculture—Planting crops without tilling, or churning the soil, before you plant.

- Strip cropping—Planting crops in strips with one strip having a crop with deep, extensive roots and one that doesn't. The crop with roots will hold in the soil and prevent erosion that the other crop doesn't do.

- Rotational grazing—Moving animals around to various pastures to allow the grass to recover from grazing.

- Aquaculture—Farm raising fish, shellfish, or aquatic plants to sell. Pros: inexpensive and uses less water and energy. Cons: can cause disease and, if the farmed animal or plant escapes its enclosure, it could reproduce or outcompete with native species.

- Reforestation—Planting new trees after harvesting the adult ones.

- Prescribed burns—Intentionally starting a fire in a forest to allow the brush and dead trees to be burned and the larger trees to not be destroyed. This prevents a forest from having a larger "crown" fire that can destroy the entire forest.

CHAPTER 10

Energy Resources and Consumption

IN THIS CHAPTER

Summary: Humans use both renewable and nonrenewable forms of energy and each has an impact on the environment. This chapter will examine each energy type, both renewable and nonrenewable, and provide benefits and costs of each.

Key Idea

✪ Humans use energy from a variety of sources, resulting in positive and negative consequences.

Key Terms

- Active solar systems
- Anthracite
- Biomass
- Bituminous
- Chernobyl
- Cogeneration
- Combustion
- Ethanol
- Fission
- Fossil fuels
- Fukushima
- Geothermal energy
- Half-life
- Hydroelectric power

- Hydrogen fuel cells
- Hydrologic fracturing (fracking)
- Kinetic energy
- Lignite
- Nonrenewable energy source
- Passive solar systems
- Peat
- Photovoltaic solar cell
- Radioactivity
- Renewable energy source
- Thermal pollution
- Three-Mile Island
- Turbine
- Uranium-235

This chapter is about both renewable and nonrenewable energy use and resources and will cover about 10 to 12 percent of your AP Environmental Science Exam, or about 8 to 10 out of the 80 multiple-choice questions. For the test you will have to know where energy sources are found and the environmental problems related to different types of energy. You will be asked to solve mathematical problems and propose environmental solutions to energy problems.

Renewable and Nonrenewable Resources

Renewable energy resources are resources that can be replaced over a relatively short time scale. These include things like solar, wind, hydroelectric, geothermal, and biomass resources. **Nonrenewable energy resources** are not replaced quickly or not at all. These include things like coal, oil, natural gas, and nuclear energy resources.

Global Energy Consumption

This topic will be given to you as a math problem that you will need to solve. Remember, you can use a calculator so make sure you don't forget it. You might need to calculate a family's energy use or the energy use from a particular country and year. It should be simple math like addition, subtraction, multiplication, or division, but you should read carefully so you use the correct numbers in the correct way.

Developed countries use a lot more energy resources than developing countries, but as a country goes through the demographic transition and becomes more industrialized, they will begin to demand more and more energy. Currently, the major source of energy in the world comes from **fossil fuels** such as coal, oil, and natural gas. However, this depends on regional availability of other sources like geothermal, solar, and water or any government regulations that might influence the type of energy source a population uses or has access to.

Fuel Types and Uses

We use many different types of fuel. This can be a family burning wood or charcoal to cook or heat their houses or using **peat**, partially decayed plant matter that is burned for cooking or heating in parts of Europe. Of course, fuel can also be coal, oil, and natural gas.

Let's talk first about coal. There are different types of coal such as lignite, bituminous, and anthracite (Figure 10.1). As we move from lignite to anthracite, the coal gets harder and burns hotter. **Anthracite** is the highest rank of coal. It has the highest amount of carbon

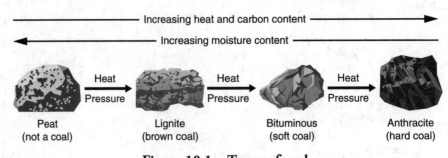

Figure 10.1   Types of coal.

and the lowest amount of volatile matter. **Lignite** is the lowest rank of coal with the least amount of carbon. **Bituminous** coal is the most abundant and extensively used.

Next, let's discuss oil. Oil or crude oil is made up of hydrogen and carbon with some other trace elements. It was formed millions of years ago as dead marine organisms sunk to the bottom of the ocean and under heat and pressure were changed to oil. We drill down to the oil reserves and pump it out. We can also find crude oil in tar sands, where a mixture of sand, clay, and water is saturated with petroleum known as bitumen. Oil is then burned for energy.

Natural gas is the fossil fuel that burns the cleanest and can be used for energy. It is made up mostly of methane but contains other things like carbon dioxide, nitrogen, and more. Natural gas can be used to create electricity, heat buildings, and fuel cars.

When an energy source is used to generate both heat and electricity, we say it is a combined heat and power (CHP) system or **cogeneration**.

Distribution of Natural Energy Resources

If we look at Figure 10.2, we can see where oil and gas energy sources are found. You will be given a diagram similar to this on the test and asked to draw some conclusions. First, the oil is found in a layer below the gas. This is because gas bubbles up from the oil and floats on top. The rock reservoir is the layer that has the rich organic matter from millions of years ago. This has then been subjected to heat and pressure. The oil has risen up through the next permeable layer but stopped at the layer that is impermeable. We then drill down through the impermeable layer and get the gas and oil.

Fossil Fuels

How do we actually get energy for electricity from a chunk of coal, or from a gallon of oil or natural gas? Well, since each of these energy items have stored energy, we can turn that stored energy into electrical energy. **Combustion** of these fossil fuels is burning the

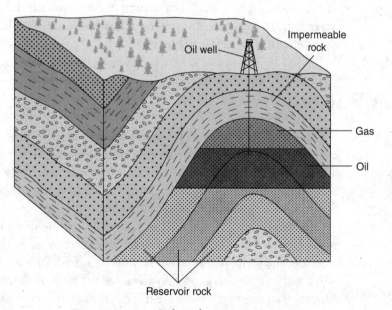

Figure 10.2   Oil and gas energy sources.

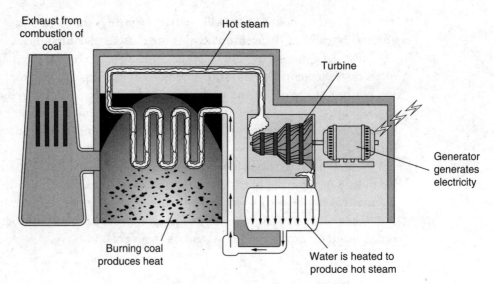

Figure 10.3   Coal power plant.

fossil fuel, which is a chemical reaction between fuel and oxygen, and turning it into carbon dioxide, water, and energy. Let's take coal as an example. First coal is pulverized into a very fine powder, which is then burned to make heat. This heat is used to boil water and produce steam. This steam is then pumped through a pipe at extremely high pressures and is focused on a giant **turbine**, causing the turbine to spin (similar to blowing on a pinwheel and causing it to spin). This turbine is connected to an electrical generator that generates electricity. The same is done when oil or natural gas is burned.

Figure 10.3 shows a typical coal energy generator.

When we burn fossil fuels we produce carbon dioxide and water. This carbon dioxide is a contributor to climate change that we will discuss in future chapters.

Another environmental problem of the use of fossil fuels for energy is caused when a method called **hydrologic fracturing,** commonly known as **fracking,** is used for extracting it. Fracking forces liquid at very high pressures down into the rock, which causes the oil or gas to be released. This can lead to groundwater contamination because the water that is used to release the oil or natural gas can contain contaminates that then run off into waterways. In addition, this process releases volatile organic compounds during the natural gas production process.

Nuclear Power

We can also split atoms of **Uranium-235**, in a process known as **fission**, to produce extremely high heat. Similar to how electricity is generated from coal, oil, or natural gas, the heat is used to boil water to make steam to turn a turbine to generate electrical energy. You will be asked to look at diagram of a nuclear power plant and answer some questions. Figure 10.4 is a picture of a typical nuclear power plant.

The uranium-235 is stored in fuel rods and the uranium atoms produce radioactivity as the isotopes lose energy. There are several cons of nuclear energy. First, when we use uranium, the waste that is left over must be stored for a very long time. This waste is radioactive and must be very carefully disposed of. In addition, uranium-235 is a nonrenewable resource that must be mined; we discussed the environmental problems with mining in the last chapter. Also, nuclear energy generation creates so much heat that it must be "dumped"

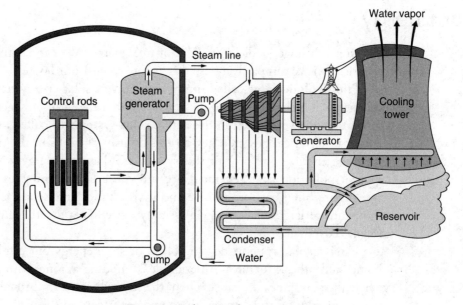

Figure 10.4 Nuclear power plant.

into a water source, which causes thermal pollution that we will discuss in a future chapter. However, the pro of nuclear energy is that because we aren't actually burning anything, no air pollution is produced and therefore this energy source does not cause climate change.

There have been three times in our history when a nuclear accident happened and radiation was released. The first was at **Three-Mile Island** in Pennsylvania, the second in **Chernobyl** in Ukraine, and the final one at **Fukushima**, Japan. In each of these cases radiation was released from the fuel rods and the environment was impacted, sometimes devastatingly.

Half-life is a term used to describe the amount of time it takes for a radioactive isotope to be half of its original value. We use this to calculate how long we must store the radioactive waste, and how radioactive the object is and for how long. For example, uranium-235 has a half-life of 700 million years! That's a long time to store radioactive waste and a lot of time for this waste to harm the environment.

Energy from Biomass

People in developing nations may not have access to good, reliable energy to cook and heat their homes. In this case, many will burn different types of **biomass** because it is cheap and usually easy to get. This might be as simple as burning wood from trees. However, this practice while inexpensive and abundant can cause some human health and environmental problems. For example, openly burning wood in a closed home or hut produces carbon dioxide, carbon monoxide, nitrogen oxides, particulates, and volatile organic compounds. None of these is good to be breathing for long periods of time and many lead to climate change. In addition, if a country is doing this on a large scale there are problems of deforestation and habitat destruction.

Another type of biomass fuel comes from ethanol. **Ethanol** is made by fermenting things like corn, wheat, potatoes, and so on. Because it can be grown over and over, it is a renewable resource and is used as an alternative to gasoline. It has a 34 percent average reduction in greenhouse gases that lead to climate change over gasoline. However, ethanol doesn't have a very large return of energy on investment and if we are converting natural areas of forest and grassland into large farms to produce corn to make ethanol, we are contributing to a problem of habitat loss and greater pollution due to agriculture.

Solar Energy

The sun is a huge, endless provider of free energy. We can capture this energy to create electricity or we can passively use this energy to heat our homes.

Photovoltaic solar cells capture and convert solar energy from the sun into electrical energy. The limitations of these cells are that they can only generate energy when the sun is out. However, we can use **active solar systems** to collect, store, and convert solar energy to electrical power. They do this by using heat from the sun to heat a liquid and store the energy. The pros of this system are that the energy is free and unlimited and that air pollution isn't generated because you aren't burning anything. However, these systems are often cost-prohibitive and if you build large solar "farms" with hundreds or thousands of large solar panels in a sunny place like a desert, you could be harming that fragile ecosystem.

Passive solar systems do not collect or store energy but can be used to heat or cool homes and other structures. An example is building a home with large windows that face where the sun shines the most. Then, the sun will come in through the windows and heat the home. During the summer the homeowner could put thick curtains on the windows to prevent the heat from coming in as well. Another option is planting shade trees to help keep a house cooler in summer.

Hydroelectric Power

Another form of renewable energy is using the power of running water to create electricity. This can be done by building a dam across a river; the dam has a turbine that the water passes over as it goes downstream. This turbine turns and is connected to a generator that converts energy of motion into electrical energy. Another way to generate electricity is to use the movement of the tides to turn a turbine. The ocean tides come in and out every day; in some places this large movement of water is greater than in others. If the movement is large enough a turbine can be built and again it can be connected to a generator to generate electricity.

The pro of hydroelectric power is that it doesn't produce any air pollution since nothing is burned. The cons are that building dams is expensive, and when you build a dam you change the river ecosystem. You flood an area above the dam, which was once a land habitat. If some of the water is diverted to irrigation, you reduce the flow of water downstream, reducing the amount of nutrients available and changing the ecosystems. In some cases the flow is so reduced that the water never reaches the sea. This can damage habitats and cause loss of biodiversity.

Geothermal Energy

Our planet has a huge amount of heat down in the subsurface of the Earth. If we can access this heat we can create steam and, again, turn a turbine to create electrical energy with a generator. We can also use geothermal heat pumps to take that heat to the surface and heat buildings with it. The pros of **geothermal energy** are it is renewable and very efficient. The cons are it is expensive, can release hydrogen sulfide, requires a lot of water, and isn't readily available everywhere in the world.

Hydrogen Fuel Cell

A **hydrogen fuel cell** is a device that converts potential energy into electrical energy. Fuel cells can be used in transportation and power. The cell uses hydrogen gas (H_2) and oxygen gas (O_2) and the products are water, heat, and electricity. Hydrogen is oxidized at the anode and flows to the cathode where oxygen reacts with hydrogen to make water.

The advantage of hydrogen fuel cells is they produce no carbon dioxide as they make electricity. The problems are they are still very expensive and, in order to create the hydrogen gas, a process called electrolysis is used, which requires energy possibly produced from nonrenewable sources such as coal.

Wind Energy

Another way to generate free, renewable energy is to capture the energy from the wind to turn a turbine. Kinetic energy is energy of motion; if we allow the wind to turn a turbine and turn it into electrical energy, we can use that kinetic energy. This method is especially good off the coasts of continents where the wind blows stronger and more often than on land. The pros of this type of power is it is clean, is free, and can be used in areas where you are doing other things such as ranching or growing crops. A con is that migrating birds, butterflies, and bats have been known to get caught in the turbines and killed. This problem can be mitigated by slowing the turbines down or shutting them off during migration times but then an alternate energy source will be needed at those times.

Energy Conservation

This is another topic where you will be asked to do some math to solve a problem. The calculation will involve ways to save energy. It might be in your home by lowering or raising the temperature on the thermostat, replacing an old appliance with a more energy efficient one, or conserving water. The question might also be about vehicles like hybrids, battery electric ones, or ones powered by hydrogen fuel cells. Regardless, read the question, do the math, and find the answer that best conserves energy or money.

› Review Questions

Multiple-Choice Questions

1. A family home uses five 80-watt lightbulbs every day for 10 hours a day. Approximately how many hours of electrical energy will the family consume in one year using these bulbs?

   (A) 1,460 kwh
   (B) 1,460,000 kwh
   (C) 120 kwh
   (D) 120,000 kwh

2. One way to decrease our dependence on fossil fuels is to use renewable energy resources. However, there are still environmental concerns from renewable energy. Which of the following correctly describes an environmental concern of getting energy from biomass?

   (A) Burning biomass is too expensive for people in developing countries.
   (B) Burning biomass reduces the emission of volatile organic compounds.
   (C) Burning biomass leads to deforestation.
   (D) Burning biomass releases large amounts of hydrogen sulfide.

3. The diagram below shows a typical nuclear power plant.

Nuclear Power Plant

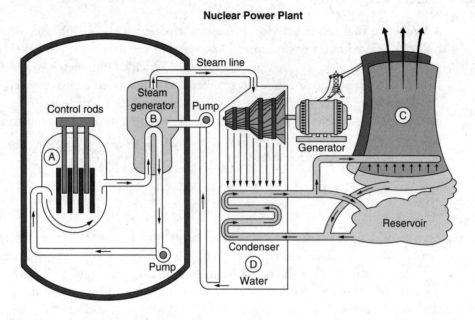

At which of the following labels is water heated, causing thermal pollution, which can be an environmental problem?

(A) A
(B) B
(C) C
(D) D

4. Which of the following would be the best way to reduce the risk of wind farms to the environment?

(A) Slow down or stop the speed of the turbines during times of bird or bat migration.
(B) Don't build windfarms on ranches where cattle graze.
(C) Add orange flashing lights to alert animals.
(D) Plant trees around the windfarm to absorb the carbon emissions that are produced.

5. Which of the following is an example of an environmental disadvantage of geothermal energy?

(A) Geothermal energy is expensive.
(B) Geothermal energy generates carbon dioxide emissions that lead to climate change.
(C) Geothermal energy is dangerous to harvest.
(D) Geothermal energy releases hydrogen sulfide.

6. People that live in the northern part of the United States can reduce their energy cost by lowering their thermostat by 2 degrees in the winter. This reduces their energy costs by about 8 percent in many homes. If the family was paying $120 per month, how much will their bill be if they lower the thermostat by the 2 degrees?

(A) $110.40
(B) $9.6
(C) $100.80
(D) $24

› Free-Response Questions

7. Identify ONE environmental benefit of wind energy.

8. Dams are built to provide electricity to towns with no air pollution or waste. However, there are environmental concerns of dams.

(A) **Identify** ONE environmental cost of a dam.
(B) **Explain** how electrical energy is made at a hydroelectric dam.

› Answers and Explanations

1. **A**—5 × .080 kw × 10 hours × 365 days a year = 1,460 kwh

2. **C**—Biomass can come from cutting down trees, which leads to deforestation if done at an unsustainable rate.

3. **D**—Thermal pollution is the heat produced that is then dumped into a local river or lake.

4. **A**—Wind farms can kill migrating birds and bats.

5. **D**—Geothermal energy can release hydrogen sulfide gas.

6. **A**—$120 × .08 = $9.60 less, so $120 − $9.60 = $110.40

7. One point for describing one environmental benefit of wind energy. The benefits: it's renewable and it's a clean energy source with no air pollution.

8. **(A)** One point for identifying one environmental cost of a dam. The environmental costs are change of habitats by flooding areas above the dam and, if water is extracted from the reservoir for irrigation or other purposes, lowering the water flow below the dam. Sometimes, if enough water is taken from the reservoir, the water flow below the dam is so decreased that no water reaches the sea; this destroys estuary habitats.
(B) One point for explaining how energy is generated at a dam. A turbine is placed in the water running through the dam; the rushing water turns the turbine. This generator then turns the energy of movement into electrical energy.

› Rapid Review

- Nonrenewable energy source—Coal, oil, natural gas, and nuclear energy resources that can't be renewed or regrown for thousands or millions of years.

- Renewable energy source—Wind, biomass, hydrogen, water, and solar energy resources that can be renewed or regrown rather quickly.

- Fossil fuels—Energy sources that come from organisms that lived millions of years ago. After being buried with heat and pressure, they have become coal, oil, or natural gas.

- Peat—Partially decayed plant matter that is used for cooking or heating in parts of Europe.

- Lignite—The least efficient type of coal that generates the least amount of heat and isn't very common.

- Bituminous—The type of coal used the most because it is very abundant and generates a lot of heat.

- Anthracite—The most efficient type of coal that generates the maximum amount of heat but isn't very common and is more expensive.

- Cogeneration—Creating electricity and heat from one energy source.

- Turbine—A giant fan-type structure that is turned by steam or water (hydroelectric power) and connected to a generator to make electrical energy.

- Hydrologic fracturing (fracking)—Forcing liquid at very high pressures down into the rock to cause the oil or gas to be released.

- Combustion—The burning of fuel to produce energy.

- Fission—The splitting atoms for energy.

- Uranium-235—The radioactive isotope used to create nuclear power.

- Radioactivity—The radiation emitted from a nuclear isotope.

- Thermal pollution—The heat that is produced by nuclear power generation that can be a pollutant to aquatic organisms.

- Three Mile Island—A nuclear power plant in Pennsylvania where a small nuclear accident occurred, releasing some radiation.

- Chernobyl—A nuclear power plant in the Ukraine where a large nuclear meltdown occurred, releasing a lot of radiation.

- Fukushima—A nuclear power plant in Japan where a tsunami and earthquake caused a release of radiation.

- Half-life—The time it takes for nuclear isotope to lose half of its radioactivity.

- Biomass—Organic matter that can be used for heating or cooking or fuel. Example: wood from trees or ethanol from decaying plant matter.

- Ethanol—A substitute for gasoline that is made from decaying plant matter.

- Photovoltaic solar cell—A cell that captures light from the sun and converts it into electricity.

- Active solar energy—Turning solar energy into electricity or heat and can be stored.

- Passive solar energy—Using the sun to heat or blocking the sun to cool a house or building.

- Hydroelectric power—Using the power of a river or tides to turn a turbine to generate electricity.

- Geothermal energy—Using the heat below the surface of the Earth to make steam to turn a turbine to generate electricity.

- Hydrogen fuel cells—Taking H_2 and O_2 and producing water, heat, and electricity.

- Kinetic energy—The energy of motion as in the turning of a turbine.

CHAPTER 11

Atmospheric Pollution

IN THIS CHAPTER

Summary: Air pollution is a problem both inside and outdoors. This chapter will cover the sources and effects of both indoor and outdoor air pollution and the human activities that have caused these issues. Included will be topics such as photochemical smog, thermal inversions, atmospheric CO_2 and particulates, indoor air pollutants, how to reduce air pollution, acid rain, and noise pollution.

Key Idea

✪ Human activities have physical, chemical, and biological consequences for the atmosphere.

Key Terms

- Acid deposition
- Acid rain
- Anthropogenic
- Carbon dioxide
- Carbon monoxide
- Catalytic converter
- Clean Air Act
- Electrostatic precipitators
- Formaldehyde
- Hydrocarbons

- Lead
- Nitric acid
- Nitrogen oxides
- Noise pollution
- Ozone
- Particulates
- Photochemical smog
- Primary air pollutants
- Radon-222
- Secondary air pollutants

- Sulfur dioxide
- Thermal inversion
- Toxic metals

- Vapor recovery nozzle
- Volatile organic hydrocarbons
- Wet and dry scrubbers

Atmospheric pollution will account for about 7 to 10 percent of your AP Environmental Science exam, or about 5 to 7 questions out of the 80 multiple-choice questions. This chapter is all about air pollution. You will need to be able to predict trends and data as well as draw conclusions from the data and/or graphs. You may also be asked to propose solutions to environmental problems and describe a research method to understand the problem.

Introduction to Air Pollution

When coal combusts, or burns, carbon dioxide, sulfur dioxide, nitrogen oxides, toxic metals, and particulates are released. These go into the air and can result in both environmental and human health concerns. Let's go through each of these air pollutants, discuss what they do that is harmful, and consider how we can prevent this and still get the needed energy from these resources.

Carbon dioxide (CO_2) traps heat, leading to climate change, melting ice caps, rising sea levels, and coastal flooding. Carbon dioxide can be removed from the atmosphere through a few processes, but the main one is **carbon sequestration**. This is the process of capturing and storing atmospheric carbon dioxide in either rock formations or through terrestrial and aquatic ecosystems.

Sulfur dioxide (SO_2) can harm trees and plants by damaging leaves and decreasing growth when the SO_2 leads to acid rain. Human health is impacted by sulfur dioxide by making it difficult to breathe, particularly for people with asthma, or other respiratory health concerns. Sulfur dioxide can be removed by gas scrubbing or by using fluidized bed combustion from coal-fired power plants.

Nitrogen oxides come from a mixture of NO_x and NO_2. They are colorless, acidic when combined with water, and highly corrosive. They contribute to the formation of photochemical smog (to be covered in the next section) and to the formation of tropospheric ozone, another component of photochemical smog. They can form a secondary pollutant, nitric acid, which contributes to acid deposition. Nitrogen oxides can be removed during burning of fossil fuels by catalytic converters in vehicles. In manufacturing plants, they can be removed by H_2O_2 or sodium hydroxide scrubbers. Catalytic converters remove pollutants using redox reactions that convert about 98 percent of the fumes from a car into less harmful gases and scrubbers remove it by spraying the gas through a liquid substance. Make sure you are familiar with pollution remediation strategies, as they can show up in many different question types.

There are many **toxic metals** that can be released from burning coal. These include things like lead, mercury, nickel, tin, cadmium, and arsenic. The type of toxic metal will determine the environmental and human health effects. We can limit the amount of toxic metals by using catalytic reduction, electrostatic precipitators, and other technologies to address these pollutants.

Particulates are simply small solid or liquid particles that are suspended in the air. These include things like dust, dirt, soot, and smoke. The size of the particle can determine the harm they can do to humans. They can get into the lungs and some are even small enough to get in the bloodstream. They can cause haze and, depending on what the particle is, can acidify lakes and streams, deplete the soil of nutrients, and damage materials. Particulates can be prevented by using baghouse filters or electrostatic precipitators.

In the United States, a law was passed called the **Clean Air Act** that has helped control air pollution. The Environmental Protection Agency, the enforcer of the Clean Air Act, has eliminated **lead** from gasoline, protecting us from lead poisoning. Lead poisoning leads to permanent nerve damage, anemia, or mental retardation, and is particularly dangerous for children since their nervous system is still developing.

Primary air pollutants come directly from a source, say your car. Primary pollutants include sulfur dioxide, carbon monoxide, nitrogen oxides, and particulate matter. **Secondary air pollutants** form when two or more primary air pollutants react in the atmosphere. Examples of secondary pollutants are photochemical smog, ozone, and secondary particulate matter.

Photochemical Smog

Photochemical smog occurs in sunny places that have a lot of people, cars, factories, and power plants. It is formed when volatile organic hydrocarbons and nitrogen oxides, along with heat and sunlight, mix and pollution occurs. The major contributors are coal-burning power plants and cars. This is worse in the summer because of the long hours of sunlight. It usually forms in the morning as people are driving to work and can be affected by rainfall, wind, daily temperatures, and topography.

Photochemical smog can cause eye irritation and respiratory illness. In the morning, nitrogen oxide is high because of so many cars on the road; we discussed the problems with this in the prior section. In the afternoon when it gets hot and the sunlight is the most intense, ozone is produced. Ozone can cause a variety of health effects such as chest pain, throat irritation, coughing, and congestion. It is particularly dangerous to people with asthma, bronchitis, and emphysema.

Volatile organic compounds (VOCs) come from many things. They are up to 10 times higher inside than outside and can come from paints, fuels, formaldehyde, gasoline, varnishes, and wax. Trees can also be a natural source of these. They can cause eye, nose, and throat irritation as well as headaches and nausea. Symptoms depends on the exposure level and the health of the person. We can reduce photochemical smog by reducing VOCs and nitrogen oxide.

Thermal Inversion

If you look at Figure 11.1, you can see what happens during a **thermal inversion**. This is a weather condition when warm, less dense air moves over dense, cold air. Because of

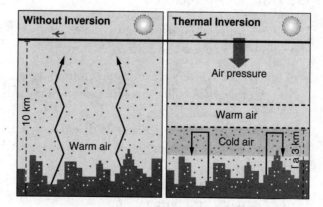

Figure 11.1   Thermal inversion.

the thermal inversion and the dense air, pollution, particularly smog and particulates, gets trapped near the ground and can't "escape" to space. Normally, the temperature would get colder as you go away from the Earth.

Look at the first illustration; warm air rises and pollutants move upward and are dispersed into space. Look at the second illustration; cold air is dense and sinks, trapping the pollutants with it. Warm air above the polluted cold air traps the particles and creates poor air quality. This often occurs in regions surrounded by mountains.

Atmospheric CO_2 and Particulates

There are many natural forms of CO_2 and particulates found on Earth. For example, every time you exhale, you exhale CO_2 and add it to the atmosphere. CO_2 is also formed as things decompose and when volcanoes erupt. CO_2 is measured in parts per million (ppm). Natural sources of particulates are things like dust, sea salt, pollen, and also things from volcanic eruptions. For the test, they will give you a scientific experiment and you will have to answer questions about atmospheric CO_2 and particulates from that experiment.

Indoor Air Pollutants

This section will be tested by giving you questions on data in the form of a chart or graph. The indoor air pollutants that you might be asked about are carbon monoxide, particulates, asbestos, dust, smoke, radon, mold, dust, nitrogen oxides, sulfur dioxide, particulates, and tobacco smoke.

Indoor air pollutants come from natural sources; from man-made things like furniture, carpet, and paneling; or from burning things like wood or cigarettes.

Another natural source is **radon-222**, which comes from the decay of uranium that is found in the ground. This is a particularly dangerous indoor air pollutant because radon decays quickly and when it does tiny radioactive particles are released. When these are inhaled they can damage the lining of the lungs. Long-term exposure can lead to lung cancer. When we build homes, and particularly homes with basements where we dig down into the rock or soil, radon gas can work its way into the home via cracks. It can also enter homes through the groundwater from a local well.

Reduction of Air Pollutants

We have already discussed most of the methods for reducing air pollutants in the topics above. But let's review and learn a few more:

Catalytic converters are used on automobiles, electrical generators, locomotives, and so on and they take pollutants like carbon monoxide, NO_x, and hydrocarbons and make them less harmful.

Scrubbers remove particulates so they don't get into the atmosphere.

Vapor recovery nozzles are put on gasoline pumps to capture the fumes that are produced.

Electrostatic precipitators remove fine particles like dust, smoke, soot, and ash before they leave the coal-burning smokestack.

Acid Rain (Acid Deposition)

Coal-burning power plants, vehicles, manufacturing, and even volcanoes release nitrogen oxides (NO_x) and sulfur oxides (SO_2) into the atmosphere. When these chemicals go into the atmosphere and mix with atmospheric water like rain, snow, fog, hail, or dust, they can become **acid rain** and fall to Earth. This can be in wet or dry forms. Winds can then blow this far away from the source, so usually places downwind from the pollution have the biggest problems. Because acid rain comes from things that humans are doing such as burning coal and driving vehicles, acid rain is considered an anthropogenic pollutant. **Anthropogenic** means "caused by human activity."

When soil or water becomes acidified because of acid deposition there can be some environmental effects. For example, often you will see dead or dying trees in areas affected by acid rain. The soil may have higher levels of aluminum in it since acid rain can leach aluminum from the soil; this is toxic to plants and animals. In aquatic biomes acid rain can be harmful to fish and other wildlife. The aluminum that was leached from the soil on the land may run off into the water and lead to a loss of biodiversity.

The impact on the environment from acid rain depends on the type of soil and rock that is found in the area. For example, limestone and dolomite have a natural ability to neutralize acid because of the high amounts of calcium carbonate. Calcium carbonate helps to maintain a constant pH as the minerals react with the acid rain. One way to remediate the problem is to add limestone (lime) to the soil; lime is a base that counters the effects of the acidic soils.

Noise Pollution

This topic will be tested by giving you a short text about noise pollution; you will be asked to answer questions about the text. Make sure you read the text carefully and answer with evidence from the text.

The definition of noise pollution is "harmful or annoying levels of noise, as from airplanes, industry, etc." Noise pollution can be high enough to cause damage to people's hearing and can cause anxiety, poor concentration, loss of productivity, difficulty communicating, lack of sleep, and stress. It can also cause problems to animals by altering their behavior, making them relocate to quieter places, and impacting migration routes. It can also impair their ability to navigate, communicate, and reproduce. In marine ecosystems, animals can be impacted because of boats, sonar, and oil and gas drilling.

› Review Questions

Multiple-Choice Questions

1. A coal-burning power plant is located on a lake. The citizens of the town are concerned that the power plant might be doing harm to the organisms living in the lake by increasing acid levels in the lake. Which of the following would be the best way to test and see if the citizen's concerns are valid?

   (A) Take the temperature of the water in the morning, mid day, and evening and see if the temperature changes over time.
   (B) Test the water for radon-222 to see the levels of this in the lake.
   (C) Take blood samples from fish in the lake to see if they have elevated levels of mercury and lead in their bloodstream.
   (D) Test the pH levels in the lake to see if it is elevated.

2. An electricity company wants to lower the amount of fine particles like dust, smoke, soot, and ash before the particles leave the smokestack. Which of the following would be the best addition to the power plant to accomplish this?

   (A) Install electrostatic precipitators.
   (B) Install catalytic converters.
   (C) Install vapor recovery nozzles.
   (D) Install fluidized-bed combustion devices.

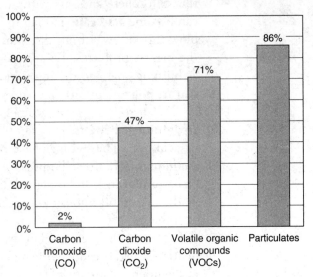

AirAdvice 2004 IAQ Findings: Problem Type and Occurrence

3. The percentages of homes that tested positive for certain pollutants is shown above according to a study in 2004. Which of the following would most likely help solve the problems with indoor air pollutants as seen in the graph?

   (A) Vent all combustion appliances outdoors and install and use exhaust fans vented to the outside when cooking.
   (B) Use fireplaces with wood to heat homes rather than electrical heat.
   (C) Open windows to allow fresh air to enter the home.
   (D) Install asbestos siding in homes to prevent fires.

4. "When we start to add artificial, unfamiliar noises to natural soundscapes, it can alter the acoustic environment of these marine and terrestrial habitats. This can cause a range of problems. It can affect an animal's ability to hear or make it difficult for it to find food, locate mates and avoid predators. It can also impair its ability to navigate, communicate, reproduce and participate in normal behaviors. Interest in the way sound affects wildlife has intensified over the last decade as more and more studies begin to explore how these changes in behavior could have flow-on effects for not only individual animals and their populations, but for whole ecosystems."

—Reprinted with permission from the Australian Academy of Science, "Noise Pollution and the Environment." (https://www.science.org.au/curious/earth -environment/noise-pollution-and-environment)

Which of the following best describes the author's claim about noise pollution?

(A) Noise pollution can cause physiological stress and hearing loss in humans.
(B) Switching from burning fossil fuels to wind energy would lower the concern about noise pollution.
(C) Noise pollution has affected wildlife in many ways and is now being studied more.
(D) Noise pollution is worse in industrialized countries than in developing countries.

5. Based on the diagram below, which of the following best describes why pollution tends to be trapped near the ground during a thermal inversion?

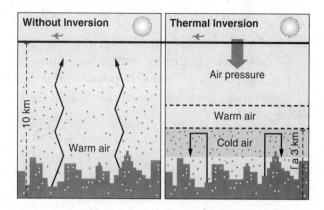

(A) A cold front has moved into the area and caused heavy rainfall.
(B) Warm, less dense air moves over dense, cold air over a city and traps the pollution near the ground.
(C) Warm air rises pushing the denser pollutants toward the ground.
(D) Cold air pushes its way through the warm air, which has a greater pollutant load than cold air has.

› Free-Response Question

6. Air pollution, both indoors and outside, can have large environmental and human health effects.

(A) **Identify** ONE way that particulates are commonly introduced into the atmosphere.
(B) **Describe** ONE way to reduce the number of particulates in the atmosphere.

› Answers and Explanations

1. **D**—pH is a measure of hydrogen ion concentration that determines the amount of acid in a solution.

2. **A**—Electrostatic precipitators remove fine particles like dust, smoke, soot, and ash before they leave the smokestack.

3. **A**—Indoor particulate matter can be generated through cooking, combustion activities (including burning of candles, use of fireplaces, use of unvented space heaters or kerosene heaters, or cigarette smoking).

4. **C**—Only choice C correctly states the author's claim.

5. **B**—A thermal inversion occurs when warm, less dense air moves over dense, cold air over a city and pollutants are unable to escape to space.

6. **(A)** One point for identifying one way particulates are commonly introduced into the atmosphere. Some answers include: fossil fuel combustion, dust, tobacco smoke, pollen, burning wood.

(B) One point for describing one way to reduce the amount of particulates in the atmosphere. Some answers include scrubbers, electrostatic precipitators, not burning wood inside, closing windows to stop dust and pollen from getting in.

› Rapid Review

POLLUTANT	HUMAN HEALTH EFFECT	ENVIRONMENTAL EFFECT	WAYS TO PREVENT
Carbon dioxide	Not applicable except in high quantities	Traps heat leading to melting ice caps, rising sea levels, and coastal flooding; causes climate change	Carbon sequestration
Sulfur dioxide	Makes it difficult to breathe, particularly for people with asthma	Harms trees and plants by damaging leaves and decreasing growth; leads to acid rain	Gas scrubbing or by using fluidized bed combustion
Nitrogen oxides	Photochemical smog because of the formation of ozone molecules; cause acid rain	Chronic lung disease and damage to the respiratory system	Catalytic converters in vehicles; H_2O_2 or sodium hydroxide scrubbers in manufacturing plants
Toxic metals	The type of toxic metal will determine the environmental and human health effects	The type of toxic metal will determine the environmental and human health effects	Catalytic reduction, electrostatic precipitators, and other technologies
Particulates	Can get into the lungs; some are even small enough to get into the bloodstream	Cause haze and, depending on what the particle is, can acidify lakes and streams, deplete the soil of nutrients, and damage materials	Baghouse filters or electrostatic precipitators

- Ozone—Photochemical smog can cause ground-level ozone to occur particularly in the afternoon when it gets hot. Ozone can cause a variety of health effects such as chest pain, throat irritation, coughing, and congestion. It is particularly dangerous to people with asthma, bronchitis, and emphysema.

- Photochemical smog—This type of smog occurs in warm places that have a lot of people, cars, factories, power plants, etc. It is formed when volatile organic hydrocarbons, nitrogen oxides, heat, and sunlight mix. Photochemical smog can cause eye irritation and respiratory illness; ground-level ozone is produced.

- Acid rain (acid deposition)—When nitrogen oxides (NO_x) and sulfur oxides (SO_2) in the atmosphere mix with the rain, snow, fog, hail, or dust, they can become acid rain and fall to the Earth. This can be in wet or dry forms.

- Clean Air Act—American law that regulated the use of lead in fuels and the atmosphere.

- Lead—Leads to permanent nerve damage, anemia, or mental retardation.

- Volatile organic hydrocarbons—When they mix with nitrogen oxides and heat they can form photochemical smog.

- Thermal inversion—Occurs when pollution gets trapped near the Earth's surface because of warm air trapping cooler, denser air near the Earth.

- Radon-222—A gas that comes from uranium decay and is the second leading cause of cancer in America.

- Catalytic converter—A device that converts pollutants into less dangerous things.

- Vapor recovery nozzle—A device added to gasoline fuel pumps that traps the vapors before they can be released to the atmosphere.

- Wet and dry scrubbers—Air pollution devices that remove particulates so they don't get into the atmosphere.

- Electrostatic precipitators—Remove fine particles like dust, smoke, soot, and ash before they leave the smokestack.

- Anthropogenic—Caused by humans.

- Noise pollution—Sound that is loud and long enough to cause harm to humans and animals.

CHAPTER 12

Aquatic and Terrestrial Pollution

IN THIS CHAPTER

Summary: Pollution is a major problem that has been caused by humans and impacts ecosystems as well as human health. While we have laws that have helped in the United States, there are global concerns for the animals and plants on our planet from the pollution that we have created.

Key Ideas

○ Human activities, including the use of resources, have physical, chemical, and biological consequences for ecosystems.

○ Pollutants can have both direct and indirect impacts on the health of organisms, including humans.

Key Terms

- Bioaccumulation
- Biomagnification
- Cholera
- Composting
- Dead zones
- Dose-response curve
- Dysentery
- E-waste
- Endocrine disruptors
- Eutrophication
- Hypoxic

- Lethal Dose 50% (LD_{50})
- Malaria
- Middle East respiratory syndrome (MERS)
- Nonpoint source
- Oligotrophic
- Oxygen sag curve
- Pathogens
- Persistent organic pollutants (POPs)
- Plague

- Point source
- Primary sewage treatment
- Recycling
- Sanitary municipal landfill
- Secondary sewage treatment
- Severe acute respiratory syndrome (SARS)

- Tertiary sewage treatment
- Tuberculosis
- West Nile virus
- Wetland
- Zika

Aquatic and terrestrial pollution will cover about 7 to 10 percent of your AP Environmental Science Exam, or about 5 to 8 questions out of the 80 multiple-choice questions. This chapter all about pollution is usually not familiar to students since a lot of the concepts are not covered in prior science courses. You will be asked to propose solutions to environmental problems and do some calculations around environmental problems.

Sources of Pollution

I always teach my students that **point source** is pollution you can point to and say, "There it is." For example, a pipe that is dumping waste into a river. A smokestack that is spewing out soot and smoke. You can literally point to it. On the flip side is **nonpoint source** pollution. You can't point to any particular thing, like cars on the road. You can't point with your finger to all the cars on the road, or farmers spraying pesticide on all the crops in an area. As you read the question think about it like this: is that a single thing or a bunch of things? If it is a single thing, it is most likely point source. Many things are most likely nonpoint source pollution.

Human Impacts on Ecosystems

This topic is broad, covering many ways that humans impact aquatic ecosystems. It will be tested using mathematical routines, so you need to know the information on how humans impact ecosystems but also be able to take a word problem and do some math. Let's look at the topics you could be asked about.

Organisms have specific ranges of tolerance that they can live within, known as a species range of tolerance. Think of yourself. If you go outside without any protection in below-freezing weather, you could survive for a while but pretty quickly you would begin to shiver, get frostbite, and if you couldn't protect yourself, you might even die from the cold. Other organisms have similar ranges of tolerance and humans are putting stresses, particularly pollutant stresses, on them. That can have many different impacts, depending on the organism and the pollutant. For example, many aquatic organisms would die if the salinity were to exceed the species range of tolerance.

One example is coral reefs. Corals are very delicate animals that live in shallow, warm waters where they can get lots of sunlight and food. When corals die they turn white because their exoskeletons are white and the coral animal, which can be many beautiful colors, is no longer alive. Humans are doing harm to corals through global climate change, which has caused water temperatures to rise past the range of tolerance for coral animals to live. We are also causing erosion on the land, which runs off into the water and clouds the water so the coral animals can't get sunlight. There are also fishing techniques that are harming the corals when fisherman drag nets across them or drop anchors down on top of the coral reefs.

Oil spills are another way humans are harming the oceans. Oil that spills from drilling platforms, pipes, and ships can cause damage to animals that live on the surface of the water such as birds and mammals, where the oil gets in their feathers or fur and they lose their ability to fly or stay warm. Some oil components sink to the ocean floor where they can do damage to organisms like oysters and clams that live on the ocean floor. In addition, some of the oil might end up on the beach or in the estuaries and cause damage to organisms that live there.

Dead zones are being formed in the ocean where there is low oxygen (hypoxic) caused by too many nutrients coming from the land. For example, the Gulf of Mexico has a huge "dead zone" that varies in size but can be 6,000 to 8,000 square miles large. This is because of the fertilizers that are coming from the Mississippi River watershed. The map in Figure 12.1 shows the Mississippi River watershed.

Since a lot of the area in the watershed is farmland and very dense urban populations that use a lot of fertilizer, this amount adds up to millions of tons of nitrogen and phosphorus fertilizers in the Gulf. The Gulf of Mexico is just one example; there are ocean dead zones all over the world.

An **oxygen sag curve** is a graph of discharged pollutant and the distance from the discharge. It is usually sewage pollution but can be other things.

Figure 12.2 shows a graphical view of a river. The point of discharge is where the sewage is being dumped into the river. The dissolved oxygen begins to drop because sewage contains millions of organisms, like fungi and bacteria, that need oxygen. This increases the **biological oxygen demand (BOD)** on the oxygen in the river and lowers the amount of dissolved oxygen. Usually there are very few organisms that can live in the area where the dissolved oxygen is at the lowest. However, since this is a river and the pollutant will eventually get diluted, the dissolved oxygen goes up again as you get farther downstream

Mississippi watershed

Figure 12.1 Mississippi watershed.

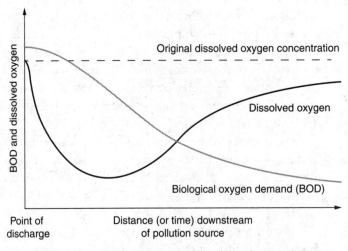

Figure 12.2 Biological oxygen demand.

from the pollutant. One great way to remember this is "dilution is the solution to pollution." This helps you remember that time and space disperse pollutants!

Other things that can harm aquatic ecosystems are litter, heavy metals from industry, and mercury that is released into the air from coal-burning power plant smokestacks, among other sources. The bacteria in the water can take the mercury and convert it to an extremely toxic form called methylmercury. Another concern with mercury is Minamata disease, which is a neurological syndrome caused by severe mercury poisoning.

Endocrine Disruptors

Endocrine disruptors are chemicals that can mimic hormones in organisms; they can come from a variety of things, like pesticides, food, and pharmaceuticals. These can cause birth defects and have been linked to developmental, reproductive, neural, immune, and other problems in animals. The endocrine disruptor can block the receptor protein so that the cell can't receive a hormone signal. This can also lead to fertility problems.

Human Impacts on Wetlands and Mangroves

Swamps, marshes, and bogs are the three main types of **wetlands** that have a huge ecological importance. They do things like clean the water naturally, protect from floods, and provide habitats to many plants and animals. This ecosystem service helps humans and has ecological importance as well for animals. Mangroves are trees and shrubs found near the coastal zone that protect the coast from erosion and flooding and provide habitat to many organisms. These are being harmed by humans when we drain and build on the areas and pollute with trash and chemical waste.

Eutrophication

Eutrophication occurs when a body of water has so many nutrients (fertilizers like nitrogen and phosphorus) that have run off from the land that the nutrients "fertilize" the algae that live in the water. This comes from agriculture runoff, mainly from fertilizers and waste water runoff from concentrated animal feeding operations (CAFOs). This can cause the water to become so thick and green with algae that no light can penetrate it. The water can literally look like pea soup. Then, when the algae die, microbes like bacteria and fungi that live in the water eat the algae and in doing so take up a lot of oxygen. As with an oxygen sag curve, when there isn't enough oxygen, it results in large die-offs of fish and other aquatic organisms that need to oxygen to survive. When a body of water has little to no oxygen it is known as **hypoxic**.

On the flip side, we have waters that have very few nutrients in them. These are known as **oligotrophic** (*oligo* meaning "few") and they have normal-to-low algae levels, high amounts of oxygen, and very few nutrients. The water is usually very clear and often very deep.

Thermal Pollution

Thermal pollution is often from a nuclear power plant where large amounts of heated water are being dumped into a body of water. The heated water doesn't have to have any pollutants in it, but just being warm can cause problems. This is because warm water can't hold as much oxygen as cold water. The oxygen diffuses out of the water and into the air. If an organism such as fish that need dissolved oxygen in the water can't get it, they might die. In addition, the higher temperatures may exceed an organism's range of temperature tolerance.

Persistent Organic Pollutants (POPs)

There are 12 key **persistent organic pollutants (POPs)** that were targeted in the 2001 Stockholm Convention to be reduced or eliminated. You are probably most familiar with DDT (dichlorodiphenyltrichloroethane), a synthetic organic chemical used as an insecticide, and PCBs (polychlorinated biphenyls), used as dielectric and coolant fluids in electrical equipment. POPs do not break down in the environment very quickly and can build up in the tissues and the fat of animals. This accumulation of POPs in an organism's tissues can be toxic. In addition, because they are persistent (they don't break down quickly), because animals migrate long distances, and because these chemicals can travel in wind and water very far distances, we have POPs in almost all parts of our planet.

Bioaccumulation and Biomagnification

As mentioned above, chemicals like the pesticide DDT can build up in the fatty tissues of animals because they don't break down but accumulate there. This is referred to as **bioaccumulation**. In addition, because animals eat other animals, these chemicals can magnify up the food chain; this is referred to as **biomagnification.** It occurs because top predators eat many different prey; each prey may have eaten many different organisms as well. Figure 12.3 is an illustration of how things magnify up the food chain.

As you can see in the illustration, the water has only a small amount of DDT, but as the zooplankton pick this up it gets a little more, then because the small fish eat many zooplankton, it gets even more. Then, when large fish eat many small fish, the amount of DDT greatly increases and finally when we get to the birds, it is at the highest. This amount of DDT is now high enough to cause major problems to the birds that might not have happened to the organisms down the food chain.

Figure 12.3   Biomagnification.

Persistent chemicals like DDT, PCBs, and mercury can have environmental and human health effects. For example, when DDT made its way up to predatory birds like bald eagles, the chemical interfered with the ability of the bird to make strong eggshells. The shells were so soft that they often broke during incubation and the baby birds died. It went on for many generations with the bald eagle population, and we had entire species on the brink of extinction due to this problem. In humans, persistent chemicals can damage the reproductive, nervous, and circulatory systems.

Solid Waste Disposal

Humans generate large amounts of solid waste. This can be normal household trash; e-waste from electronics like computers, televisions, and cell phones; or waste from industrial and agricultural processes.

Most waste in the United States is sent to a landfill. A landfill must be carefully maintained and monitored or the waste can leach out and contaminate groundwater. As the waste decomposes it can produce methane and carbon dioxide, which can lead to climate change.

Sanitary municipal landfills have been designed to control the disposal of solid waste so that our water and air is protected. Look at Figure 12.4. There is a clay and plastic lining to prevent leaks, a leachate pump to collect the liquid that passed through the trash, and, in addition, there are pipes to collect the methane gases produced as a result of decomposition. The methane is either used to create electricity or burned off safely. There are also ways to collect large amounts of storm water so it doesn't end up in the landfill.

How quickly the trash decomposes depends on many things. For example, what is the trash consisting of? Where is the landfill located? What is the temperature? How much rainfall is there? All of these factors can determine how fast items decompose.

In addition to putting trash into a landfill, we can also burn the trash at high temperatures. It is important that this is done carefully as air pollutants can be released. But, as a result of burning, the volume of the trash is greatly reduced and the concern of water pollution goes way down.

Other concerns about solid waste are people illegally dumping it into our oceans and people putting things into landfills that are not allowed.

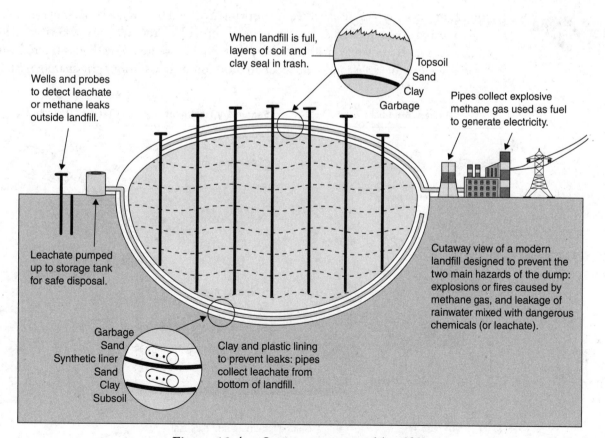

Figure 12.4   Sanitary municipal landfills.

Waste Reduction Methods

We know that solid waste is going to be a problem because of the numbers of people on Earth. However, there are other ways to reduce the amount of waste or to recycle the waste. **Recycling** is taking something like plastic and turning it into something new. This does a few things: first, it means that new oil doesn't have to be pumped to make more plastic, and it also means that the plastic doesn't end up in the landfill or the ocean. However, recycling can be expensive and require a lot of energy.

Another way to reduce the waste that is generated is to compost it. **Composting** works well for food waste, paper waste, and yard trimmings. Rather than throwing these products into the landfill, we can put them in composting piles, and after they decompose, we can use it for fertilizer. Some people don't like composting because it can attract rodents and can have a pungent odor. However, it produces some of the best fertilizer and is chemical free.

Computers, TVs, cell phones, and other **e-waste** can also be recycled for their parts and turned into new items. Like the example above, this avoids having to mine new metals and prevents the items from ending up in a landfill.

Another way to lessen the impact of landfills can be done after they are full. If we cap them and plant trees and other plants to restore habitats or use as city parks, we can help lower the impact they have on the environment.

Finally, the methane and CO_2 gas from a landfill can be captured. Then it can be burned to heat water, produce steam, and turn a turbine to generate electrical energy.

Sewage Treatment

Figure 12.5 shows a typical sewage treatment plant. You will be given a visual representation like this one and asked questions about it. Let's go through all the steps of sewage treatment.

The first step is known as **primary treatment**. This is where the sewage is filtered with grates and screens for large solid items that are not liquid. In addition, grit chambers allow

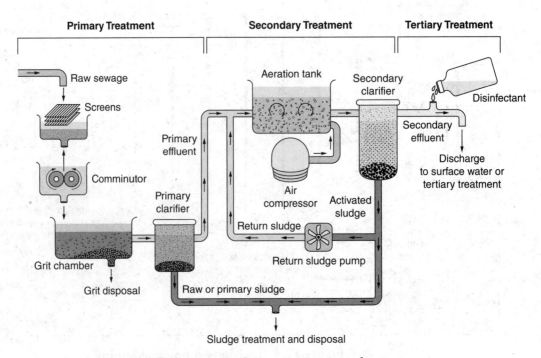

Figure 12.5   Sewage treatment plant.

the sewage to slow down so things like ground-up eggshells and coffee grounds that also are not liquid can sink to the floor and be disposed of in a landfill.

Now, only liquid waste is going to move into the next stage, **secondary treatment**. The bacteria found in the sewage is given lots of air so it can begin to consume the waste and break it down into carbon dioxide and inorganic sludge. The sludge sinks to the bottom of the tank and is disposed of as well.

Finally, we move to the last stage known as **tertiary treatment**, where either chemicals like chlorine and ozone gas or water disinfectants like UV light kill any bacteria that remain. Then the water is released to a river or lake.

Lethal Dose 50% (LD$_{50}$)

Lethal Dose 50% is a term used in toxicology to say the amount of a toxin that kills 50 percent of the organisms that are being tested. This can be any animal but usually refers to test rats and mice in a laboratory. This concept is useful for toxicology because it can help us determine the relative short-term toxicity of a substance. For example, the LD$_{50}$ of nicotine is 50 milligrams per kilogram for a rat; for table salt it is 3,000 milligrams per kilogram for a rat. This is commonly used to measure the toxicity of a chemical's active ingredient and is a way to measure the short-term poisoning potential of a substance.

Dose-Response Curve

The **dose-response curve** (or dose-response relationship) is a curve plotting the relationship between the dose of a drug administered and its pharmacological effect. This is usually graphed with the dose on the *x*-axis and the effect on the *y*-axis. You will be given a graph or chart to read and you will need to explain what the graph says about an environmental issue.

A dose-response is curve is usually shaped like the letter "S." This is because usually small doses are not toxic and as you increase the dose, the individuals show a response to that dose. Look at the example of a dose-response curve in Figure 12.6; the sharp increase in the graph of the line shows that there are increasingly higher risks of toxic response as the dose amount increases until almost 100 percent of the organisms are experiencing toxicity.

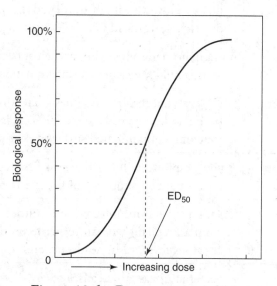

Figure 12.6   Dose-response curve.

Pollution and Human Health

Humans are exposed to many different chemicals every day. This can be in what we eat, what we breathe, where we live, and so on. Therefore, it is hard to directly say if a particular chemical causes a particular human health issue. However, there are a few that can be significantly linked to particular things.

For example, **dysentery** is an infection of the intestines resulting in severe diarrhea with blood and mucus in the feces. This comes from untreated sewage in streams and rivers that become drinking water or food contaminates. Another is asbestos, a building material that was used because it was flame resistant. That seemed like a good idea—build homes that couldn't catch on fire! What we didn't know at the time was that when these panels, floor boards, or ceiling tiles began to break down, tiny fibers would be released into the air that people breathed in. This led to various serious lung conditions such as lung cancer. Also, as tropospheric ozone from the chemical reaction between NO_x and VOCs is formed and we breathe it in we can get respiratory problems like asthma, emphysema, and COPD.

Pathogens and Infectious Disease

A **pathogen** is a bacterium, virus, or other microorganism that can cause disease. This disease can be transmitted from human to human or animal to human. You could be asked about a number of pathogens and how they are transferred. Let's look at Table 12.1 with the pathogens you need to know:

Table 12.1

PATHOGEN	INFORMATION ABOUT
Plague	A bacterial infection transmitted by fleas, famous for killing millions in Europe in the Middle Ages. Modern antibiotics are effective in treating this.
Tuberculosis (TB)	A bacterial infection that usually attacks the lungs and is spread from one person to another. TB can be treated by taking several drugs for six to nine months.
Malaria	A parasitic disease transmitted by mosquitos. People get fever, chills, and flu-like illness. However, if left untreated it can be deadly. Nearly half a million people die each year, mostly in the African region.
West Nile virus	A mosquito-transmitted virus and most people show no signs or symptoms. However, fever, a mild headache, and inflammation of the spinal cord or brain can occur.
Severe acute respiratory syndrome (SARS)	SARS is a viral respiratory illness that was first reported in 2003 but there haven't been any known cases since 2004. It is spread easily by coughing and sneezing, touching contaminated surfaces, skin-to-skin contact, or kissing.
Middle East respiratory syndrome (MERS)	A viral respiratory illness that was first reported in 2012. This causes fever, coughing, and shortness of breath. It is transferred from animal to human.
Zika	Zika is a virus from infected mosquitoes, sexual contact, blood transfusions, or from a pregnant woman to her fetus. There is no vaccine or medicine for Zika. It causes fever, rash, headache, and joint/muscle pain.
Cholera	A bacterial disease that causes severe diarrhea and dehydration and is spread in water. Rehydration and antibiotics are the treatment for this disease.

As our climate is changing and the Earth is getting warmer, diseases from insects like West Nile and malaria are spreading to areas that they were not in before. In addition, many of these diseases are spread in areas that are poor and lack sanitation or clean water.

》 Review Questions

Multiple-Choice Questions

1. The graph below shows the dose-response curves for three common pesticides.

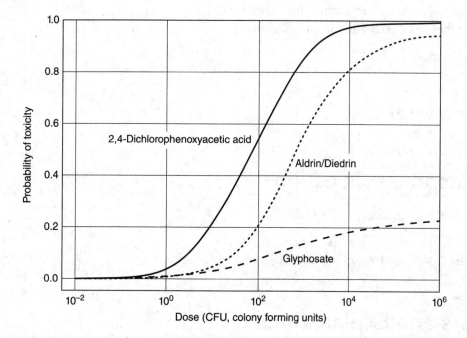

All three of these pesticides are used to kill pests such as rodents, insects, or plants. Which of the three would have the greatest dose response according to the graph?

(A) 2,4-Dichlorophenoxyacetic Acid
(B) Aldrin/Dieldrin
(C) Glyphosate
(D) DDT

2. A scientist is trying to discover why large amounts of lake trout are dying in a particular area. He discovers that the temperature in the water is much warmer than it would be naturally. He explores the area and discovers what he thinks is causing the problem. Which of the following would most likely be what is killing the lake trout?

(A) Pesticides are raising the temperature in the lake, killing the lake trout.
(B) Electricity from a local power plant is shocking the lake trout.
(C) Persistent organic pollutants (POPs) are being dumped into the lake from a local pesticide plant.
(D) Heated water from a nuclear power plant is being dumped into the lake.

3. The LD_{50} for caffeine in humans is approximately 180 mg/kg. If a person weighs 150 lbs and 1 kg = 2.2 lbs, how many grams of caffeine would it take to reach the LD_{50} for a human?

(A) 12.27 grams
(B) 12,272 grams
(C) 2.64 grams
(D) 2,640 grams

4. Which of the following is true about persistent organic pollutants (POPs)?

   (A) POPs are only a concern in areas where they were used, particularly developed nations.
   (B) The Montreal Protocol was written to stop the problem of POPs.
   (C) POPs pose the biggest problem to producers.
   (D) POPs are soluble in fat and they can accumulate in organisms' fatty tissues.

5. Dioxins, PCBs, pesticides, and perfluorinated chemicals are all types of endocrine disruptors. What would they most likely affect in an organism?

   (A) Nervous system
   (B) Hormones
   (C) Skin
   (D) Circulatory system

6. Which of the following is a point source pollutant that might affect the oysters and clams living at the bottom of the ocean floor?

   (A) CO_2 from the cars in a large city near the ocean
   (B) Fertilizer runoff from local farms and feedlots
   (C) Oil spilling from a tanker with a leak
   (D) Pesticides sprayed on the estuary system to prevent disease from mosquitoes

› Free-Response Question

7. Eutrophication is a problem in many lakes.

   (A) **Identify** ONE cause of eutrophication.
   (B) **Describe** ONE way to stop the problem of eutrophication.

› Answers and Explanations

1. **A**—2,4-Dichlorophenoxyacetic acid has the highest probability of toxicity.

2. **D**—Thermal pollution is what is lowering the dissolved oxygen and this is most likely coming from a nuclear power plant, which generates a lot of heat.

3. **A**—$\dfrac{150 \text{ lb} \times 1 \text{ kg} \times 180 \text{ mg} \times 1 \text{ g}}{2.2 \text{ lb} \times 1 \text{ kg} \times 1{,}000 \text{ mg}} = 12.27$ grams

4. **D**—POPs do not break down in the environment very quickly and can build up in the tissues and fat of animals. This bioaccumulation of POPs in organisms, tissues can be toxic.

5. **B**—Endocrine disruptors are chemicals that can mimic hormones in organisms and can come from a variety of things, like pesticides, food, pharmaceuticals, etc. These can cause birth defects and have been linked to developmental, reproductive, neural, immune, and other problems in animals.

6. **C**—Point source pollution is pollution you can point to and say, "There it is." In this example, the oil tanker with the leak.

7. **(A)** One point for stating one cause of eutrophication. Eutrophication is the term used to describe a body of water that has so many nutrients (fertilizers like nitrogen and phosphorus) that have run off from the land and these nutrients have "fertilized" the algae that live in the water.
   (B) One point for describing one way to stop eutrophication. Possible answers include plant vegetation around farms or streambeds to slow erosion and absorb fertilizer; construct barriers; control the application, amount, and timing of fertilizers; use no-phosphorus fertilizer on lawns and gardens; use better drainage systems; remove pet waste.

〉 Rapid Review

- Point source—A pollutant that you can see and point to. Usually a single source.

- Nonpoint source—A pollutant that comes from many sources such as pollution from cars in a city. You can't point to one particular place or thing.

- Dead zones—Formed in the ocean where there is low oxygen (hypoxic) caused by too many nutrients coming from the land.

- Oxygen sag curve—A graph of discharged pollutant and the distance from the discharge. It is usually sewage pollution but can be other things.

- Endocrine disruptors—Chemicals that can mimic hormones in organisms and can cause birth defects and have been linked to developmental, reproductive, neural, immune, and other problems in animals.

- Wetland—Land consisting of marshes, swamps, or bogs; saturated land.

- Eutrophication—A body of water that has so many nutrients (fertilizers like nitrogen and phosphorus) that have run off from the land that the nutrients have "fertilized" the algae that live in the water.

- Hypoxic—A body of water with little to no oxygen in the water.

- Oligotrophic—A body of water with normal to low algae levels, high amounts of oxygen, and very few nutrients.

- Thermal pollution—Occurs when warm water is pumped into a lake or river, lowering the oxygen levels and harming biodiversity.

- Persistent organic pollutants (POPs)—POPs do not break down in the environment very quickly and can build up in the tissues and fat of animals.

- Bioaccumulation—POPs, like the pesticide DDT, can accumulate in the fatty tissues of animals; this is referred to as bioaccumulation.

- Biomagnification—When animals eat other animals and the prey have POPs that have bioaccumulated in their tissues, the POPs can magnify up the food chain. This biomagnification occurs because top predators eat many different prey.

- E-waste—Electronic waste like TVs, computers, phones, etc.

- Sanitary municipal landfill—Where solid waste from homes, businesses, and more is stored. It has a clay or plastic liner, leachate detection systems, a way for the gas to be collected or burned, and a way to make sure storm water doesn't enter the landfill.

- Recycling—Taking solid waste and turning it into something new rather than throwing it away.

- Composting—Taking food, yard, or other organic waste and letting it decompose to form good soil.

- Primary sewage treatment—The first stage of sewage treatment in which the sewage is filtered in grates and screens for items that are not liquid. In addition, the sewage is slowed down so things like eggshells and coffee grounds that also are not liquid can sink to the bottom and be disposed of in a landfill.

- Secondary sewage treatment—The second stage of sewage treatment where lots of air is added so the bacteria found in the sewage can begin to consume the waste and break it down into carbon dioxide and inorganic sludge. The sludge sinks to the bottom of the tank and is disposed of as well.

- Tertiary sewage treatment—The stage of sewage treatment where either chemicals like chlorine and ozone gas or UV light kills any remaining bacteria. Then the water is released to a river or lake.

- Lethal Dose 50% (LD_{50})—A term used in toxicology to indicate the amount of a toxin that kills 50 percent of the organisms that are being tested.

- Dose-response curve—A curve plotting the relationship between the dose of a drug administered and its pharmacological effect. This is usually graphed with the dose on the x-axis and the effect on the y-axis.

CHAPTER 13

Global Change

IN THIS CHAPTER

Summary: Global climate change, ozone depletion, ocean warming, and endangered species are just a few of the ways humans have impacted the Earth. This chapter focuses on environmental solutions to environmental problems that are caused by man. You will need to look at global changes and be able to explain the causes and consequences of these. Make sure you can look at data and use this data to propose solutions or legislation to global problems. One of the most important aspects that students confuse is the difference between global climate change and ozone depletion. You need to be experts on these two concepts and make sure you can differentiate between them before you take the AP Environmental Science Exam.

Key Ideas

○ Local and regional human activities can have impacts at the global level.
○ The health of a species is closely tied to its ecosystem, and minor environmental changes can have a large impact.

Key Terms

- Chlorofluorocarbons (CFCs)
- Coral bleaching
- Endangered species
- Habitat fragmentation
- Hydrofluorocarbons (HFCs)

- Invasive species
- Ocean acidification
- Ozone depletion
- Positive feedback loop
- Stratospheric ozone layer

Global change will account for 15 to 20 percent of your AP Environmental Science exam, or about 12 to 16 questions out of the 80 multiple-choice questions. That means that you *must* know this chapter to be successful on this exam. This chapter contains by far the most covered topics on the exam and therefore the most important. This chapter is all about global changes that man has made on the environment. You will learn all about global climate change and ozone depletion. You will be asked multiple questions about these two concepts and must be sure you know the difference! In addition, other important topics you need to know are ocean acidification and ocean warming, as well as invasive and endangered species.

Stratospheric Ozone Depletion

The **stratospheric ozone layer** is a shield around the Earth that absorbs most of the sun's ultraviolet radiation (UV). This layer of our atmosphere contains ozone (O_3). It is the ozone (O_3) and oxygen molecules (O_2) in this layer that absorb the UV light. The stratosphere is above the troposphere, which is the layer closest to the Earth's surface; it extends from 10 km (6 miles) to about 50 km (31 miles) into space.

Because of the stratosphere's ability to absorb the sun's UV light, this dangerous radiation is prevented from passing to the Earth's surface. Without this stratospheric ozone layer life on Earth as we know it would not be possible.

Ozone is produced naturally in the stratosphere when the sun's UV rays split O_2 molecules into single oxygen atoms. These oxygen atoms then combine with O_2 to form O_3 molecules, which are very good at absorbing UV light.

However, human-produced chemicals, such as **chlorofluorocarbons (CFCs)**, although they are heavier than air, have been carried into the stratosphere by the air currents and mixing processes of the atmosphere. These CFC molecules are hit by the sun's UV energy and break up, releasing chlorine atoms. The chlorine atoms then react with the O_3 molecules, breaking up the O_3 by taking one oxygen atom to form chlorine monoxide and O_2. The chemical equation, which you need to know and memorize, looks like this:

$$Cl + O_3 \rightarrow ClO + O_2$$

Next, if the ClO molecule finds a free oxygen atom, the oxygen atom will steal the O from the ClO to become O_2, which releases the Cl atom back into the stratosphere to destroy more ozone. The second equation looks like this:

$$ClO + O \rightarrow Cl + O_2$$

Now the Cl can repeat the process again, taking another ozone molecule and breaking it down as in the first equation. A single CFC molecule can destroy 100,000 ozone molecules and it is thought that chlorine can remain in the stratosphere for 50 years or so.

UV light naturally breaks O_3 down, and O_3 is still formed naturally, but chlorine accelerates this process and puts the cycle out of balance.

One example of **ozone depletion** is the "hole" over Antarctica. This isn't really a "hole" but rather very low levels of ozone over this area during the Antarctic spring. However, the South Pole isn't the only place with very low levels of ozone.

The result of all this chemistry is more UV light is able to get through the stratosphere and to the surface of the Earth. UV light is dangerous because it damages the DNA in skin cells and leads to skin cancer, eye damage such as cataracts, and premature aging. It can also suppress the immune system. In plants it can affect their growth and has been shown to cause problems for marine phytoplankton, the foundation of the marine food web.

Reducing Ozone Depletion

The main way we have tried to stop the problem of ozone depletion is to stop using ozone-depleting substances. The Montreal Protocol (1987) and the Vienna Convention (1985) were treaties to control the release of these substances. The main ozone-depleting substances are chlorofluorocarbons (CFCs), hydrochlorofluorocarbons, and halons. Using things like hydrofluorocarbons can be a helpful replacement, but some are very potent greenhouse gases. CFCs may also be reduced by inspecting and maintaining air conditioners and refrigeration appliances to prevent leaks.

The Greenhouse Effect

The greenhouse effect is shown in Figure 13.1. As you can see, solar radiation (infrared) from the sun is absorbed by Earth's surface, warming the surface, and some is reflected back to space. This is important because without the greenhouse effect, it would be too cold on Earth for life.

The main gases that are in our atmosphere that absorb the solar radiation are carbon dioxide, methane, water vapor, nitrous oxide, and chlorofluorocarbons. Each of these has a different amount of global warming potential (GWP). Let's look at each in Table 13.1.

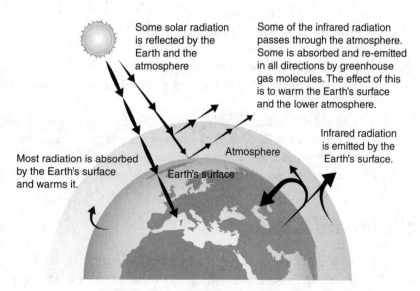

Figure 13.1   The greenhouse effect.

Table 13.1

GAS	SOURCES	GWP	ATMOSPHERIC LIFETIME
Carbon dioxide	Decomposition, respiration, burning fossil fuels, deforestation	1	50–200 years
Methane	Burning of fossil fuels, livestock, landfills, decomposition, burning biomass, natural wetlands	21	12 years
Nitrous oxide	Soils, livestock manure, biomass or fossil fuel combustion, wastewater management	310	120 years
Chlorofluorocarbons	Refrigerants, aerosols, aircraft halons, solvents	12,000–16,000	20–100 years

Water vapor's GWP is unknown but not of great concern since the water cycle cycles relatively quickly.

Increases in the Greenhouse Gases

There are many things that have increased the amount of greenhouse gases in the troposphere. For this topic, you will be given an image and asked questions about that image. You will need to know the things responsible for increasing the amount of greenhouse gases: transportation, electricity production, industry, businesses and homes, agriculture, and reduction of forested land.

Some results of increased greenhouse gases that have impacted either the environment or harmed humans are:

- Glaciers have shrunk.
- Ice sheets are melting.
- Plant and animal ranges have shifted.
- Sea levels are rising.
- Seas expand from thermal expansion.
- Insects are moving to places that used to be too cold for them, and these insects can carry disease.
- Droughts are threatening crops, wildlife, and freshwater supplies.
- Biodiversity is affected as many species depend on ice for food and for a place to live.
- Many organisms cannot move or adapt quickly enough to survive, so population numbers decrease, particularly specialist populations.

Global Climate Change

As you can see in Figure 13.2, Earth has had many different changes in temperature over its history. There are times when it has been much warmer and times when it has been much colder. Currently, we are in a warming trend, which as mentioned in the topic above,

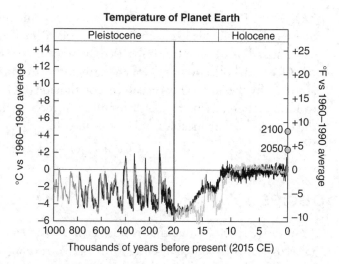

Figure 13.2   Historical data of temperatures on earth.

has led to many impacts on the environment and human health. Let's look at a few other impacts, both positive and negative, of a warmer Earth:

- Sea levels are rising, which can flood coastal communities, impact ocean organisms that are now too deep to photosynthesize, and may create new habitats for other organisms.
- Weather patterns are changing due to changes in the circulation of winds in the atmosphere.
- Ocean currents, which push tropical heat toward the poles, are changing and weakening the oceans' global conveyor belt as warm freshwater melts into the sea, which stops the sinking of cold, salty water. This is changing climates across the globe.
- Soil can be impacted if we have droughts and increased soil erosion from wind and water.
- There is a positive feedback loop in the polar regions, where normally the ice reflects the sun's rays back (albedo effect). With a warmer planet we have more melting of the ice and less sunlight being reflected back to space. This then increases the temperatures on Earth even more, causing more melting. A **positive feedback loop** is when one thing gets worse and worse, as in this example. In addition, as ice and permafrost areas melt, methane is released; this a global warming gas mentioned above. This is another example of a positive feedback loop.

Ocean Warming

As our oceans get warmer because of climate change from greenhouse gases, there is a negative impact to ocean biodiversity. For example, corals need zooxanthellae, an algae that lives in the tissues of coral and captures sunlight and converts this into energy for the coral animals. When the temperature of the ocean is too warm, the zooxanthellae become under stress and can die or leave their coral host, causing the coral to die and turn white, a process known as coral bleaching. A warmer ocean also can lead to loss of habitat to marine organisms.

Ocean Acidification

The ocean absorbs carbon dioxide from the atmosphere and the carbon dioxide reacts with the ocean water creating carbonic acid. The oceans absorb almost a quarter of global CO_2 emissions we create from burning fossil fuels and deforestation. As the

CO$_2$ enters the ocean it causes the ocean to become more acidic (lower pH). This acidity doesn't allow animals like clams and mussels to make protective shells, due to the loss of calcium carbonate, and can impact corals since they also make protective shells.

Ocean acidification is happening because excess CO$_2$ in the atmosphere is being absorbed by the ocean. This excess carbon dioxide (CO$_2$) reacts with water molecules (H$_2$O) to form carbonic acid (H$_2$CO$_3$), resulting in more hydrogen ions and lowering the pH of the ocean. The chemical formula looks like this:

$$CO_2 + H_2O \rightarrow H^+ + HCO_3^-$$

Invasive Species

An invasive species is one that is not native to an area. Invasive species can harm the natural ecosystems by outcompeting with native species, reducing biodiversity, and altering habitats, sometimes leading to extinctions of native plants and animals. Invasive species tend to be generalists and r-selected species, and they become invasive because of a lack of competition, no predators, and/or abundant resources.

The three main ways to control invasive species are:

- Biological—Using natural enemies to control the pest species. This can work but sometimes the biological control backfires and the new species becomes a problem.
- Mechanical—Mowing, hoeing, hand pulling, and more to control the pest species. This is expensive and time consuming.
- Chemical—Using pesticides (such as herbicides, insecticides, and rodenticides). This can lead to the problems discussed earlier in this book on pesticides.

Many species are introduced to environments by human transport, either with the global trade of species (for example, exotic pets) or with humans traveling and intentionally or unintentionally bringing the species back with them.

Endangered Species

An endangered species is any animal or plant that is considered at risk of extinction. A species can be listed as endangered at the international, national, or state level. The Endangered Species Act has the endangered species listed on it and it is managed federally and allows the United States to enforce the international treaty known as CITES.

A species may become endangered for many reasons. Habitat loss, invasive species, poaching, climate change, taking too many of a species in hunting and fishing, pollution, if the animal is highly specialized (lives in a certain place, eats a certain thing), competition within or with other species, and selective pressures on the species are all reasons animals and plants might become endangered. If the species can't adapt or move it might be in danger.

Humans can help prevent and can combat species becoming endangered by protecting the habitats where they live and protecting the species itself.

Human Impacts on Biodiversity

 A way to remember how we harm biodiversity is the mnemonic device HIPPCO. Let's look at each letter:

H—Habitat loss
I—Invasive species

P—Population growth

P—Pollution (but always name a chemical if you want to use this one—just "pollution" is too general)

C—Climate change, which leads to droughts, floods, sea level rising, and so on

O—Overharvesting (overfishing, overhunting)

So, if asked to give a solution to a problem, you can think of each of these reasons and come up with a way to stop this loss to biodiversity.

Of all these reasons for loss of biodiversity, the greatest one is habitat loss. We harm habitats by cutting down forests, by building roads, by building human habitation in areas where there used to be large areas of land (habitat fragmentation), and so on.

We can prevent this loss of habitat by protecting large tracts of land so it can't be developed, creating and enforcing legislation to protect biodiversity, preventing importation of nonnative species, creating habitat corridors so animals can move between native areas, preventing deforestation, using sustainable farming and ranching practices, and helping to restore areas that have been harmed by human or natural disasters.

› Review Questions

Multiple-Choice Questions

1. Which of the following correctly describes the problem of coral bleaching?

   (A) Factories are dumping chemicals into the ocean water that cause corals to fade in color.
   (B) Sewage that is dumped into the ocean smothers the coral causing it to turn white.
   (C) Parrot fish, a main predator on the reefs, are voraciously eating coral animals.
   (D) The algae that lives in the tissues of the coral die and, as a result, the coral animals die and turn white.

2. Use the graph below to answer the question.

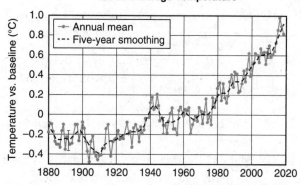

Which of the following can you conclude from the data above?

   (A) The Earth was warmer in 1920 than in 1980.
   (B) The temperature lines go up and down each year because people drive cars more in the winter than in the summer.
   (C) The average global temperature fluctuates, but the average for the last five years was hotter than at any time previously.
   (D) Temperature data on the graph is correlated with soil erosion rates.

3. The graph below shows the total number of species that are listed under the Endangered Species Act.

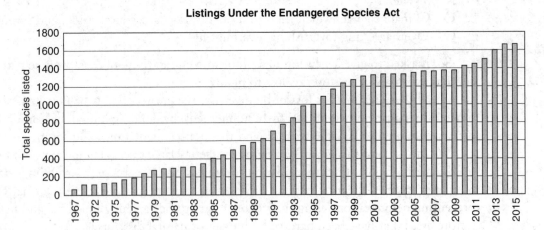

Listings Under the Endangered Species Act

Which of the following conclusions is the correct solution to the problem shown above in the graph?

(A) Protecting the habitat of the species would help to lower the number of species listed each year.

(B) Removing fishing regulations would help lower the number of species listed each year.

(C) Invasive species have little effect on the total number of species listed each year.

(D) Decriminalizing poaching would help lower the number of species listed each year.

4. Which of the following best describes the environmental disadvantage of habitat fragmentation?

(A) Profits decrease when you build homes in forested areas.

(B) Habitat fragmentation has negative impacts on many species in the ecosystem.

(C) Building habitat corridors prevents animals from migrating from one area to another.

(D) Habitat fragmentation lessens the impact from invasive species.

5. Which of the following best describes why the stratospheric ozone layer is so important to life on Earth?

(A) The stratospheric ozone layer absorbs most of the UV rays that come from the sun.

(B) The stratospheric ozone layer traps the infrared rays from the sun and keeps our Earth warm.

(C) The stratospheric ozone layer is replaced annually by an interaction between CFC molecules and O_3 molecules.

(D) Greenhouse gases are destroying the ability of the stratospheric ozone layer to reflect the sun's energy back to space.

6. Which of the following is correct about the ability of greenhouse gases to trap infrared heat from the sun?

(A) Carbon dioxide has the greatest global warming potential of any greenhouse gas.

(B) Because water vapor remains in the atmosphere for many years at a time, it has the greatest global warming potential of any greenhouse gas.

(C) Chlorofluorocarbons have the greatest global warming potential of any greenhouse gas.

(D) Ozone depletion in the stratosphere is increasing Earth's ability to absorb the sun's infrared heat.

7. Ocean acidification would be increased by which of the following activities?

(A) Switching to solar power for homes and businesses

(B) Stopping the deforestation of national forests

(C) Increasing fishing practices in coastal waters

(D) Burning coal, oil, and natural gas as energy sources

❭ Free-Response Question

8. (A) As cities expand habitat destruction can occur. **Identify** ONE activity that occurs as cities are built that can destroy habitats.

(B) For the activity you identified in Part (A), **describe** TWO ways to reduce this effect on biodiversity.

❭ Answers and Explanations

1. **D**—When the temperature of the ocean is too warm, the zooxanthellae become under stress and can die or leave their coral host, causing the coral to die and turn white, a process known as coral bleaching.

2. **C**—The last five years have been the hottest in history as shown on the graph.

3. **A**—Habitat protection is the best way to protect species.

4. **B**—When we take large natural areas and break them up into smaller areas with roads and buildings in the middle, we get loss of biodiversity.

5. **A**—Because of the stratosphere's ability to absorb the sun's UV light, the dangerous radiation is prevented from passing to the Earth's surface. Without this stratospheric ozone layer life on Earth as we know it would not be possible.

6. **C**—Chlorofluorocarbons have a GWP of 12,000–16,000.

7. **D**—Burning of fossil fuels increases CO_2 concentrations, which leads to a lower pH of oceans and ocean acidification.

8. (A) One point for correctly identifying an activity that occurs as cities are built that can destroy habitats. Possible answers include hunting, loss of habitat to homes, roads, businesses, pipelines, climate change, introduction of invasive species, etc.

(B) Two points, one for each correct description of a way to reduce the effect on biodiversity. Possible answers include building wildlife habitat corridors, promoting sustainable land use practices, remediating habitat that has been destroyed, switching to renewable energy resources, etc.

〉 Rapid Review

- Stratospheric ozone layer—The protected layer of our atmosphere that absorbs UV light.
- Chlorofluorocarbons (CFCs)—A man-made chemical that works its way through the troposphere and into the stratosphere where it can destroy ozone molecules.
- Ozone depletion—$Cl + O_3 \rightarrow ClO + O_2$ and $ClO + O \rightarrow Cl + O_2$ are the chemical formulas for ozone depletion. This is caused by chemicals like CFCs breaking down ozone in the stratosphere. This means less natural ozone to absorb UV light coming to Earth.
- Greenhouse effect—The natural ability of Earth to absorb heat from the sun (infrared) and keep our planet warm enough to live on.
- Global climate change—As more and more greenhouse gases are emitted into the atmosphere, we are trapping more heat from the sun and the temperature of the Earth is getting warmer. Sea levels are rising, estuaries are getting deeper, storms get stronger, insects are moving farther away from the equator, ice caps are melting, and permafrost is melting.
- Positive feedback loop—When one thing causes something else to get progressively worse. An example is as the Earth warms, the ice caps melt, causing the water to be warmer, causing more ice to melt, causing the water to be warmer, and so on and so on.
- Coral bleaching—When the algae that lives in the coral animals dies or leaves the coral and causes the coral to die and turn white.
- Ocean warming—When the Earth is getting warmer the oceans are also getting warmer. This is causing ice to melt, sea levels to rise, etc.
- Ocean acidification—As more carbon dioxide is added to the atmosphere it gets into the ocean causing the ocean to have a lower pH and harming things like coral animals.
- Invasive species—Nonnative species that are introduced to an environment and might outcompete the native species.
- Endangered species—Any species that is threatened to go extinct. Usually from one of the reasons in HIPPCO (see previous explanation).
- Habitat fragmentation—When a habitat is split up into smaller areas with roads, homes, and more in the middle, it leads to loss of biodiversity.

Building Your Test-Taking Confidence

AP Environmental Science Practice Exam 1
AP Environmental Science Practice Exam 2

AP Environmental Science Practice Exam 1
Multiple-Choice Questions

ANSWER SHEET

1 Ⓐ Ⓑ Ⓒ Ⓓ	31 Ⓐ Ⓑ Ⓒ Ⓓ	61 Ⓐ Ⓑ Ⓒ Ⓓ
2 Ⓐ Ⓑ Ⓒ Ⓓ	32 Ⓐ Ⓑ Ⓒ Ⓓ	62 Ⓐ Ⓑ Ⓒ Ⓓ
3 Ⓐ Ⓑ Ⓒ Ⓓ	33 Ⓐ Ⓑ Ⓒ Ⓓ	63 Ⓐ Ⓑ Ⓒ Ⓓ
4 Ⓐ Ⓑ Ⓒ Ⓓ	34 Ⓐ Ⓑ Ⓒ Ⓓ	64 Ⓐ Ⓑ Ⓒ Ⓓ
5 Ⓐ Ⓑ Ⓒ Ⓓ	35 Ⓐ Ⓑ Ⓒ Ⓓ	65 Ⓐ Ⓑ Ⓒ Ⓓ
6 Ⓐ Ⓑ Ⓒ Ⓓ	36 Ⓐ Ⓑ Ⓒ Ⓓ	66 Ⓐ Ⓑ Ⓒ Ⓓ
7 Ⓐ Ⓑ Ⓒ Ⓓ	37 Ⓐ Ⓑ Ⓒ Ⓓ	67 Ⓐ Ⓑ Ⓒ Ⓓ
8 Ⓐ Ⓑ Ⓒ Ⓓ	38 Ⓐ Ⓑ Ⓒ Ⓓ	68 Ⓐ Ⓑ Ⓒ Ⓓ
9 Ⓐ Ⓑ Ⓒ Ⓓ	39 Ⓐ Ⓑ Ⓒ Ⓓ	69 Ⓐ Ⓑ Ⓒ Ⓓ
10 Ⓐ Ⓑ Ⓒ Ⓓ	40 Ⓐ Ⓑ Ⓒ Ⓓ	70 Ⓐ Ⓑ Ⓒ Ⓓ
11 Ⓐ Ⓑ Ⓒ Ⓓ	41 Ⓐ Ⓑ Ⓒ Ⓓ	71 Ⓐ Ⓑ Ⓒ Ⓓ
12 Ⓐ Ⓑ Ⓒ Ⓓ	42 Ⓐ Ⓑ Ⓒ Ⓓ	72 Ⓐ Ⓑ Ⓒ Ⓓ
13 Ⓐ Ⓑ Ⓒ Ⓓ	43 Ⓐ Ⓑ Ⓒ Ⓓ	73 Ⓐ Ⓑ Ⓒ Ⓓ
14 Ⓐ Ⓑ Ⓒ Ⓓ	44 Ⓐ Ⓑ Ⓒ Ⓓ	74 Ⓐ Ⓑ Ⓒ Ⓓ
15 Ⓐ Ⓑ Ⓒ Ⓓ	45 Ⓐ Ⓑ Ⓒ Ⓓ	75 Ⓐ Ⓑ Ⓒ Ⓓ
16 Ⓐ Ⓑ Ⓒ Ⓓ	46 Ⓐ Ⓑ Ⓒ Ⓓ	76 Ⓐ Ⓑ Ⓒ Ⓓ
17 Ⓐ Ⓑ Ⓒ Ⓓ	47 Ⓐ Ⓑ Ⓒ Ⓓ	77 Ⓐ Ⓑ Ⓒ Ⓓ
18 Ⓐ Ⓑ Ⓒ Ⓓ	48 Ⓐ Ⓑ Ⓒ Ⓓ	78 Ⓐ Ⓑ Ⓒ Ⓓ
19 Ⓐ Ⓑ Ⓒ Ⓓ	49 Ⓐ Ⓑ Ⓒ Ⓓ	79 Ⓐ Ⓑ Ⓒ Ⓓ
20 Ⓐ Ⓑ Ⓒ Ⓓ	50 Ⓐ Ⓑ Ⓒ Ⓓ	80 Ⓐ Ⓑ Ⓒ Ⓓ
21 Ⓐ Ⓑ Ⓒ Ⓓ	51 Ⓐ Ⓑ Ⓒ Ⓓ	
22 Ⓐ Ⓑ Ⓒ Ⓓ	52 Ⓐ Ⓑ Ⓒ Ⓓ	
23 Ⓐ Ⓑ Ⓒ Ⓓ	53 Ⓐ Ⓑ Ⓒ Ⓓ	
24 Ⓐ Ⓑ Ⓒ Ⓓ	54 Ⓐ Ⓑ Ⓒ Ⓓ	
25 Ⓐ Ⓑ Ⓒ Ⓓ	55 Ⓐ Ⓑ Ⓒ Ⓓ	
26 Ⓐ Ⓑ Ⓒ Ⓓ	56 Ⓐ Ⓑ Ⓒ Ⓓ	
27 Ⓐ Ⓑ Ⓒ Ⓓ	57 Ⓐ Ⓑ Ⓒ Ⓓ	
28 Ⓐ Ⓑ Ⓒ Ⓓ	58 Ⓐ Ⓑ Ⓒ Ⓓ	
29 Ⓐ Ⓑ Ⓒ Ⓓ	59 Ⓐ Ⓑ Ⓒ Ⓓ	
30 Ⓐ Ⓑ Ⓒ Ⓓ	60 Ⓐ Ⓑ Ⓒ Ⓓ	

AP Environmental Science Practice Exam 1
Section I: Multiple-Choice Questions

Time: 90 minutes

Directions: For the multiple-choice questions that follow, select the best answer and fill in the appropriate letter on the answer sheet.

Questions 1–3 refer to the information below.

For many years, subsistence farmers in Brazil, Peru, Colombia, Bolivia, Venezuela, Suriname, Guyana, and French Guiana have cut down trees to grow crops for their families and to sell in local markets. This changed during the 1970s to mid-2000s as more than ¾ of the clear-cutting in the Amazon was for cattle ranching. Cattle ranching takes approximately 20 times more land to get the same calories from meat as it does from crops.

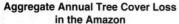

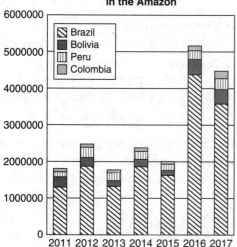

1. Based on the data in the graph, which country far exceeds the others in tree cover loss between 2011 and 2017?

   (A) Brazil
   (B) Bolivia
   (C) Colombia
   (D) Peru

2. Which is most likely the consequence of tree cover loss in the Amazon?

   (A) Lower levels of carbon dioxide
   (B) Decreased stream temperatures
   (C) Decreased need for pesticides
   (D) Soil erosion

3. Forest clearing began to decline in 2004 due to increased law enforcement, pressure from environmentalists, satellite monitoring, and protection of new areas. Changes in agricultural strategies and practices in order to increase food production including mechanization, genetically modifying organisms, fertilization, irrigation, and the use of pesticides can be attributed to what movement?

   (A) Agricultural Revolution
   (B) Green Revolution
   (C) Industrial Revolution
   (D) Cultural Revolution

4. Island biogeography is the theory and study of the species composition and species richness on islands. According to this theory, which island would have fewest number of species found on the island?

   (A) A large island far away from the mainland
   (B) A small island far away from the mainland
   (C) A small island close to the mainland
   (D) A large island close to the mainland

Use the image below to answer questions 5–6.

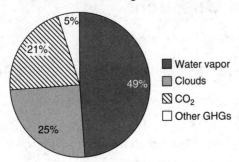

Greenhouse Gas Forcings on Earth's Climate

- Water vapor
- Clouds
- CO_2
- Other GHGs

5. As shown in the image above, water vapor and carbon dioxide are the two most abundant greenhouse gases on the planet. However, the greenhouse gas with the highest global warming potential (GWP) is which of the following?

   (A) Methane
   (B) Nitrous oxide
   (C) Chlorofluorocarbons
   (D) Water vapor

6. As more carbon dioxide is released into the atmosphere, a large part is also absorbed by the oceans. This increase in CO_2 causes a phenomenon known as ocean acidification. Which of the following is the greatest impact of ocean acidification?

   (A) Corals are damaged due to the loss of calcium carbonate making it difficult for them to form shells.
   (B) Ocean temperature drops causing salt to precipitate out and accumulate on the ocean floor.
   (C) Marine mammals are forced to move farther north in search of food supplies.
   (D) Beach erosion is accelerated due to stronger ocean currents.

7. The graph below shows many of the threats to wetlands worldwide. This loss has many impacts because of the ecosystem services that wetlands provide. Which of the following would be the best way to protect wetlands from further destruction?

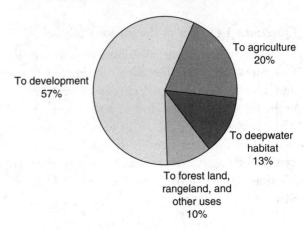

Wetland Converted to Other Uses

To agriculture 20%
To development 57%
To deepwater habitat 13%
To forest land, rangeland, and other uses 10%

   (A) Build dams to divert water from flowing downstream.
   (B) Encourage commercial development to the area to bring in revenue and increase tourism.
   (C) Strengthen legislation to regulate development and agriculture around wetlands areas.
   (D) Regulate pesticide and fertilizer use on agriculture and rangeland areas.

8. The demographic transition describes population change over time. According to the four-stage demographic transition model, during what stage will the population be growing the fastest?

   (A) Preindustrial
   (B) Transitional
   (C) Industrial
   (D) Postindustrial

9. During what stage do births and deaths begin to fall but the population continues to increase due to population momentum?

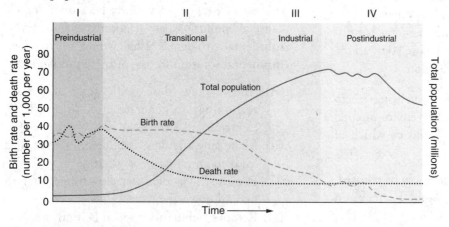

(A) Preindustrial
(B) Transitional
(C) Industrial
(D) Postindustrial

10. In which demographic stage seen in the graph above would the population growth be the highest?

(A) Preindustrial
(B) Transitional
(C) Industrial
(D) Postindustrial

11. A small lake in a deciduous forest has become covered in a thick bed of green algae. Large numbers of fish have died and the oxygen level in the water is extremely low. The diagram on the right shows an example of the lake over time.

What has most likely caused this problem?

(A) Ocean acidification
(B) An oil spill in the area
(C) Pesticide spraying on local crops
(D) Eutrophication caused by overuse of fertilizers on local crops

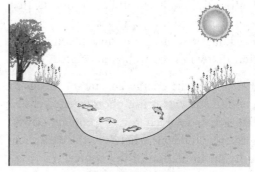

Oligotraphic stage
Deep and nutrient-poor system

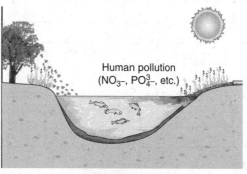

Mesotrophic stage
Nutrient enrichment

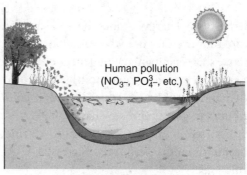

Eutrophic stage
Nutrients saturated—shallow algae and bacteria development

Questions 12–14 refer to the information below.

A local school district is looking to replace their current electricity source with a new, more reliable source that has less environmental consequences than the coal and oil they currently use. They hire an energy consultant to give them different options before going to the school board with their recommendation.

12. One option the energy consultant brings them is to use geothermal energy. The environmental consequences of this choice would be which of the following?

   (A) Hydrogen sulfide could possibly be released.
   (B) Excess carbon dioxide would be removed from the atmosphere.
   (C) Radioactive waste will be produced that must be stored for many years.
   (D) Fracking can cause groundwater contamination that will need to be remediated.

13. Another option the energy consultant brings to the school district is to use photovoltaic cells to generate active solar energy to produce power. Using the graph below, what does the data show would be the limitation of this source?

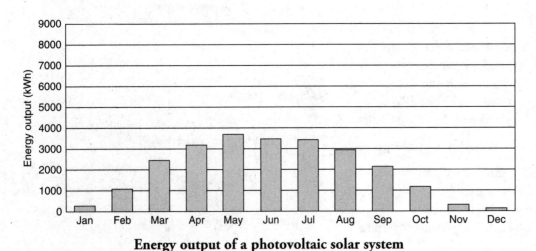

Energy output of a photovoltaic solar system

   (A) Active solar energy cannot be collected or stored for evening use without a battery.
   (B) Active solar energy may not generate enough energy during the winter months.
   (C) Methane is produced, which is a lead contributor to global climate change.
   (D) Excess solar energy production during summer months results in increased CO_2 emissions.

14. The final option given to the school district is to move to a cleaner renewable energy resource, hydroelectric power. Hydroelectric power is considered a cleaner energy source because it doesn't cause air pollution, but it does have some environmental problems. What would be an environmental solution to one of these problems?

   (A) Add a new dam with state-of-the-art technology to generate more kilowatts of electricity.
   (B) Make sure the dam is built on a river that leads to an estuary ecosystem.
   (C) Remove fish ladders that allow fish to migrate up and down the river.
   (D) Remove pollutants trapped behind the dam that can cause damage to wildlife.

15. Using the image below, explain what tectonic features you would find around the pacific plate and why these would be found here.

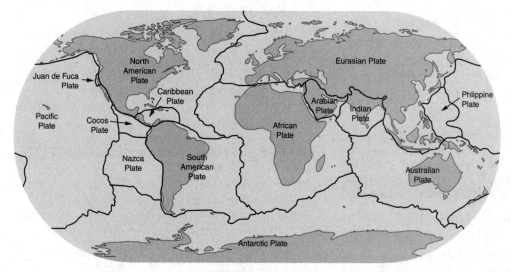

Earth's tectonic plates

(A) Divergent boundaries due to seafloor spreading
(B) Divergent boundaries due to excessive earthquakes and volcanoes
(C) Convergent boundaries, creating mountains, earthquakes, volcanoes, and island arcs
(D) Convergent boundaries, producing soil and sand due to erosion and sedimentation

16. In the Tropical Grasslands of Africa there is a relationship between a cheetah and a gazelle. Gazelles are herbivores who live in herds because there is really nowhere for the gazelle to hide. The cheetah can attack and try to outrun the gazelle. What type of relationship does this represent?

(A) Commensalism
(B) Mutualism
(C) Parasitism
(D) Predator-prey

17. Another example of this relationship is a lynx and hare. In 1865, the hare population was at an all-time high of 160,000. There was also a high of 80,000 lynx during that same year. Why would both organisms increase at the same time to reach such large populations?

(A) When the lynx was scarce, the hare numbers rose, which allowed for plenty of food for the lynx, who then increased in number due to so much food availability.
(B) When the lynx numbers were high, the hare numbers became even higher due to so much food availability.
(C) When the lynx numbers were at their lowest, the hare numbers were at their lowest due to increased environmental pressures.
(D) Lynx and hare numbers do not respond to one another because they are geographically isolated from each other.

18. The picture below is of a thermal inversion, when warm air traps the cooler air below. Why does this situation cause an atmospheric pollution problem?

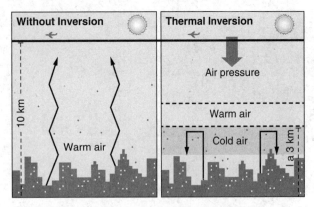

(A) Sinking air pressure causes pollutants from high in the atmosphere to settle onto a city.

(B) Thermal inversions cause pollution to be trapped close to the ground, especially smog and particulates.

(C) The warm air trapped above the cooler air can lead to an increase in global climate change.

(D) When there is not a thermal inversion, the warm air is released into space causing global cooling and an increase in energy demand to cool populated areas.

Questions 19–20 refer to the information below.

In the 1960s and 1970s the Texas horned toads and lizards were found all over Central and North Texas. However, in 1977 the Texas horned lizard was put on the threatened species list because of many reasons, one being the invasion of the invasive species, the fire ant. The fire ant pushed out the harvester ants (big red ant), which was the majority of the horny toad's/lizard's diet. In addition, farmers began to use pesticide to get rid of the fire ants, an action that also killed the red ants.

19. What is one solution that has helped bring the Texas horned toads and lizards back from endangerment?

(A) Texas Parks and Wildlife asked people to capture and breed these in their homes.

(B) A new invasive species was brought in to kill the fire ant.

(C) The Endangered Species Act was passed for protecting endangered and threatened animals and their habitat.

(D) Since the fire ant is a specialist species, Texas Parks and Wildlife just waited for the fire ant to die from lack of resources found in Texas.

20. In toxicology, many pesticides, like those used to control the fire ant, are tested according to the LD_{50} levels. LD_{50} levels are best described by which of the following?

(A) The level that kills 50 pests in 50 minutes

(B) The level that kills 50 pests out of 500

(C) The level that kills the pests but leaves 50 percent of the predators alive

(D) The level that kills 50 percent of the pest population of a particular species

Use the figure below to answer questions 21–22.

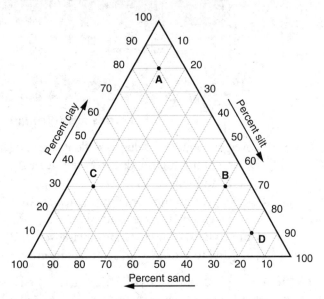

21. A scientist is trying to determine the best location for agriculture. After taking a sample of the soil and doing a texture analysis, he plots the texture on the pyramid at point A. What are the proportions of sand, silt, and clay he found for the soil at point A?

(A) 10 percent sand, 90 percent silt, 80 percent clay

(B) 10 percent sand, 10 percent silt, 80 percent clay

(C) 50 percent sand, 40 percent silt, 10 percent clay

(D) 0 percent sand, 90 percent silt, 10 percent clay

22. At which point would the scientist find the soil that is most porous and least permeable?

    (A) Point A
    (B) Point B
    (C) Point C
    (D) Point D

23. Which scenario best represents tragedy of the commons?

    (A) Farmers are allowing their cattle to graze on public land in the western United States, which results in overgrazing.
    (B) A tree farmer uses clear-cutting to bring in the highest profits on their own land.
    (C) A public municipality puts a tax on homes that use more than 10,000 liters of water per day.
    (D) Farmers in the Alps agree to keep cattle in barns in high altitude over the winter before allowing them to graze on the Alpine pastures in the summer.

24. Aquaculture has many benefits, both environmental and economical. What is one example of an economic benefit of aquaculture?

    (A) Aquaculture allows for competition and therefore lowers the number of fishing companies in the area.
    (B) Aquaculture uses large amounts of water and therefore brings revenue to the local economy.
    (C) Aquaculture promotes investment in large fishing boats.
    (D) Aquaculture requires small areas of water and little fuel.

Use the image of the Earth below to answer the following question.

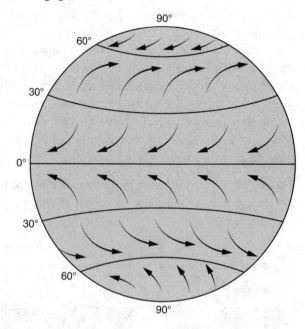

25. What is the cause of the global wind patterns seen in the image above?

    (A) The location of the land masses in relationship to the oceans
    (B) The amount of ice found on the planet, causing global climate change
    (C) The most intense solar radiation arrives at the equator and results in density differences and the Coriolis effect
    (D) Human-induced heat from energy production, causing global climate change

Use the following information to answer questions 26–27.

According to the Australian Department of Health, "Disease-causing germs can be spread from sewage if it is not disposed of properly or if people do not practice proper toilet hygiene (cleanliness). If a sewage disposal system is not properly maintained it will not be able to get rid of the sewage safely. For a sewage system to be properly maintained, all faulty (blocked, damaged, broken or worn-out) parts must be mended as soon as possible after they stop working correctly."

26. Which of the following properly names the order and processes of sewage treatment as seen in the image below?

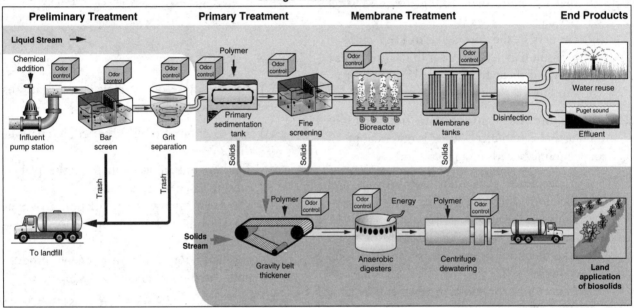

	PRIMARY	SECONDARY	TERTIARY
(A)	Physical removal of large objects with screens and grates	Bacteria break down organic matter	Ecological or chemical processes are used and the water is exposed to disinfectants
(B)	Bacteria break down organic matter	Physical removal of large objects with screens and grates	Ecological or chemical processes are used and the water is exposed to disinfectants
(C)	Bacteria break down organic matter	Ecological or chemical processes are used and the water is exposed to disinfectants	Physical removal of large objects with screens and grates
(D)	Ecological or chemical processes are used and the water is exposed to disinfectants	Physical removal of large objects with screens and grates	Bacteria break down organic matter

27. A scientist is looking for ways to bring down the disease problems in a developing country. Which of the following human health issues would be linked to installing and properly maintaining sewage treatment plants?

(A) Zika
(B) Malaria
(C) Tuberculosis
(D) Dysentery

Use the graph below to answer questions 28–30.

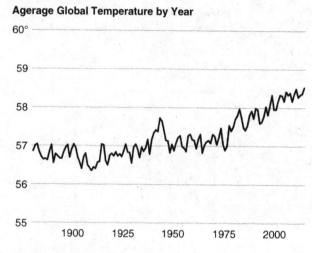

28. According to the graph above, the temperature has been going up from 1900 to 2000. What could we attribute this increase in temperature to?

(A) Increase in ocean levels
(B) Increased levels of carbon dioxide
(C) Increased numbers of specialists living in fragile ecosystems
(D) Difference in seasonal amounts of plants that photosynthesize

29. What is the change in temperature from 1900 to 2000?

(A) 1.5 degrees
(B) 3 degrees
(C) 57 degrees
(D) 100 degrees

30. This increase in average global temperatures are warming both the land and the oceans. Which of the following would be an environmental impact of the warming of the oceans?

(A) Generalist species would risk becoming endangered.
(B) R-strategists would risk becoming endangered.
(C) Sea levels would fall, leading to specialists becoming endangered.
(D) Coral bleaching would occur because of loss of algae in the corals.

31. The image below is of the nitrogen cycle. Which of the following steps takes the most amount of nitrogen and adds it to the atmosphere?

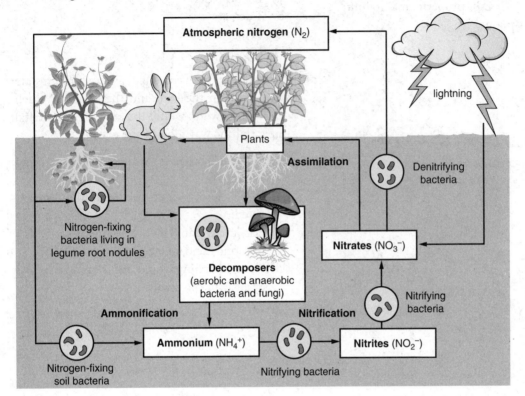

(A) Plants
(B) Lightning
(C) Denitrifying bacteria
(D) Decomposers

32. What might be a result of a population over-shooting its carrying capacity?

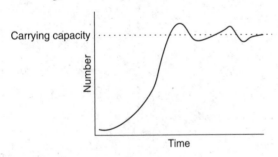

(A) Famine and disease
(B) Decreased competition
(C) Increase in available resources
(D) Nitrogen levels reaching record high levels

33. As energy transfers from one trophic level to the next, energy is lost. If 1,000 kilocalories of energy are available at the producer level, how much would be available at the herbivore level?

(A) 1 kilocalorie
(B) 100 kilocalories
(C) 10,000 kilocalories
(D) 1,000 kilocalories

34. A population is growing at a rate of 3 percent per year. The population will double in approximately how many years?

(A) 3 years
(B) 210 years
(C) 23 years
(D) 300 years

35. A fire has burned its way through an oak-hickory deciduous forest. Which of the following claims can be supported in the graph?"

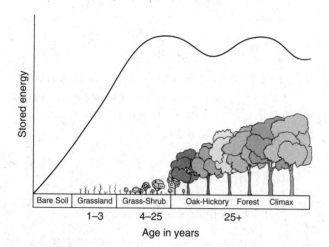

(A) The area will not begin to grow back for at least 25 years.
(B) The first plants move in in the first few years.
(C) The climax community takes a minimum of 100 years to establish.
(D) Soil must first be established from bare rock.

36. Which of the following would help reduce the problem of overfishing?

(A) Encourage the use of purse seines and long-line fishing to fisherman.
(B) Encourage bottom trawling near coral reefs.
(C) Pass legislation for catch limits per boat.
(D) Pass legislation to allow fishing in areas that are currently prohibited.

37. The fishermen off the coast of Chile have noticed that they are not catching near as many fish as in previous fishing seasons. The reason for this would most likely be which of the following?

(A) The melting of the sea ice has killed the fish due to warmer ocean temperatures.
(B) The fish have moved into the local rivers and streams to spawn.
(C) The fishermen have used new methods of fishing that are not sustainable.
(D) It is an El Niño event and the fish have moved to colder waters.

38. What causes the rain to fall on one side of the mountain and not on the other?

(A) As the air rises and cools it loses its moisture before it reaches the other side of the mountains.
(B) Dry air on the sea side rises and sinks on the other side of the mountain.
(C) The vegetation on the sea side of the mountain attracts all the moisture preventing it from reaching the other side.
(D) Cool air rises and sinks on the leeward side.

Use the figure below to answer questions 39–40.

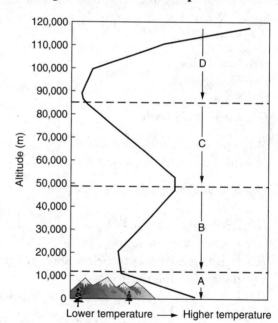

39. Which letter indicates where the protective ozone layer is found?

(A) A
(B) B
(C) C
(D) D

40. What gas would make up the majority of layer A?

(A) Oxygen
(B) Carbon dioxide
(C) Nitrogen
(D) Phosphorus

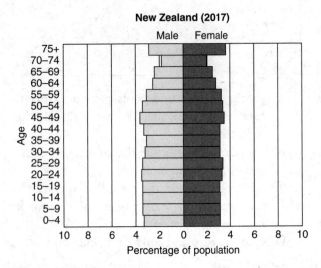

New Zealand (2017)

41. New Zealand's age-structure diagram is pictured above. What type of growth does the diagram demonstrate?

(A) Rapid growth
(B) Slow growth
(C) Stable growth
(D) Declining growth

42. Why would phytoplankton usually be found only in the first few meters of water?

(A) Red and blue light can only penetrate this deep.
(B) Zooplankton are their food source and this is where they are found.
(C) It becomes too salty below this level for phytoplankton to survive.
(D) Phytoplankton are unable to swim below 30 meters.

43. Which of the following would be considered a cultural ecosystem service of a river?

(A) Hiking, birdwatching, and photography
(B) Food sources
(C) Timber harvesting of hardwoods
(D) Water purification

44. The Montreal Protocol is a global agreement to phase out which of the following chemicals with the goal of reducing stratospheric ozone depletion?

(A) Carbon dioxide
(B) Organophosphates
(C) Volatile organic compounds
(D) Chlorofluorocarbons

45. A decrease in stratospheric ozone has led to which of the following?

(A) Melting of the polar ice caps
(B) Increased cases of lung cancer and COPD
(C) Skin cancer and cataracts
(D) An increase in atmospheric circulation

Use the figure below to answer questions 46–47.

Food Webs

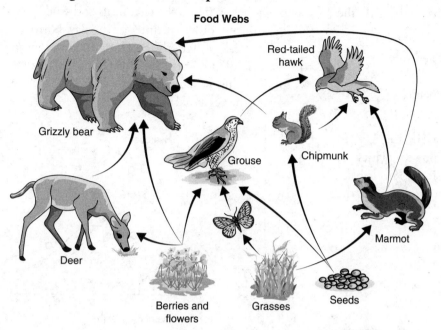

46. What organisms are missing in the above food web?

    (A) Herbivores
    (B) Decomposers
    (C) Carnivores
    (D) Producers

47. What would happen if you removed the marmot from the food web above?

    (A) Red-tailed hawks would increase in number.
    (B) The habitat for butterflies would be lost.
    (C) The deer population would decline.
    (D) The grasses would increase in number.

Use the graph below to answer questions 48–49.

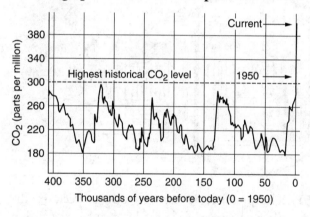

48. Based on the graph above, global climate change has caused a rise in carbon dioxide levels to the highest in history. Which of the following would be an impact on biodiversity because of this anthropogenic event?

    (A) Increased temperature will cause sea levels to rise.
    (B) Decreased temperature will harm fragile generalist species.
    (C) Ocean organisms would thrive because they now will live past the dangerous photic zone.
    (D) The dangerous UV-B rays will be blocked by the higher levels of CO_2.

49. Which of the following human activities has caused the increase in CO_2 that is seen in the graph?

 (A) Overuse of hairsprays and aerosols
 (B) Production of Styrofoam
 (C) Use of Freon and other coolants
 (D) Burning of fossil fuels

50. The Clean Air Act regulations in the United States require coal-burning power plants to remove sulfur from their emissions. This legislation has greatly reduced what problem in the United States?

 (A) Global climate change
 (B) Acid rain
 (C) Ozone depletion
 (D) Radon poisoning in homes

Use the diagram below to answer questions 51–52.

Nuclear Power Plant

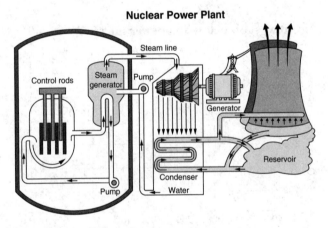

51. The presence of control rods, as seen in the diagram above, is required to regulate the fission reaction of which of the following?

 (A) Carbon-14
 (B) Uranium-235
 (C) Deuterium
 (D) Boron

52. What is an environmental problem with the generation of the energy above?

 (A) Air pollution
 (B) Noise pollution
 (C) Indoor air pollution
 (D) Thermal pollution

53. Photochemical smog is a problem in cities. The graph below shows the chemicals and when they peak during different times of the day. Nitrogen oxides peak early in the morning followed by an increase of ozone in the afternoon. This ozone peak is due to a reaction between oxygen and what other external input?

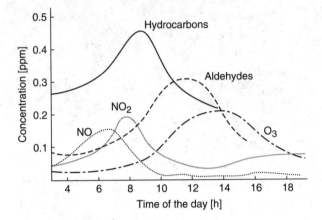

 (A) Sunlight
 (B) Carbon dioxide
 (C) Methane
 (D) Organophosphates

54. Indoor air pollutants are a problem in both developed and developing countries. According to the graph below, what is the biggest cause of death from indoor air pollutants?

Deaths Related to Indoor Air Pollution Breakdown by Disease

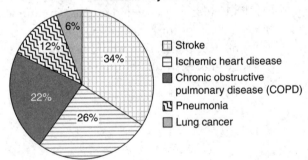

 (A) Ischemic heart disease
 (B) Lung cancer
 (C) Stroke
 (D) Pneumonia

55. A scientist is studying an area that has had an increase of acidification to its local soil and water. He sets up an experiment to see what is causing the acidification of the soil. What would his experiment most likely point to as the cause of this acidification?

(A) A farmer spraying pesticides on his corn crop

(B) Increased air traffic from a change in flight patterns

(C) A recently built hydroelectric dam above the area of concern

(D) A coal-burning power plant that is upwind from the area

56. Cockroaches can live in many different environments, can eat many different things, and can reproduce quickly. Which of the following best identifies a cockroach?

(A) An herbivore
(B) A carnivore
(C) A generalist
(D) A specialist

57. Using the data table below, which species would most likely be considered a r-strategist?

SPECIES	(A) MUSSEL	(B) RABBIT	(C) OPOSSUM	(D) BEAR
Number of off-spring produced per year	1,000,000	14	2	2

58. A farmer uses a method of irrigation where he cuts furrows between the crops and floods those with water. Which of the following would be a disadvantage of this method?

(A) Wildlife would be attracted to his crops.

(B) One-third of the water is lost to evaporation and runoff.

(C) It is extremely expensive.

(D) Eutrophication of local groundwater would be a result.

59. Which of the following would result as a country becomes more developed?

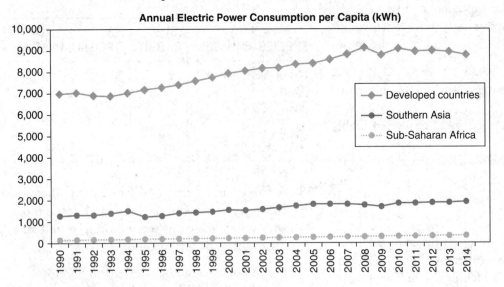

Annual Electric Power Consumption per Capita (kWh)

Legend:
- Developed countries
- Southern Asia
- Sub-Saharan Africa

(A) Annual electrical power is inversely proportional to the GDP of the country.

(B) Annual electrical power consumption remains the same.

(C) Annual electrical power consumption decreases.

(D) Annual electrical power consumption increases.

60. Which of the following fossil fuels burns the cleanest?

(A) Coal

(B) Oil

(C) Nuclear

(D) Natural gas

61. Which of the following best describes an environmental cost of hydrologic fracturing?

(A) Release of volatile organic compounds

(B) Long-term storage of radioactive waste

(C) Energy produced is expensive

(D) Disrupts migratory birds

62. According to the USGS website: "Zebra Mussels are a fingernail-sized mollusk that is native to fresh waters in Eurasia. Their name comes from the dark, zig-zagged stripes on each shell. Zebra Mussels probably arrived in the Great Lakes in the 1980s via ballast water that was discharged by large ships from Europe. They have spread rapidly throughout the Great Lakes region and into the large rivers of the eastern Mississippi drainage. They have also been found in Texas, Colorado, Utah, Nevada, and California being spread by boats traveling from lake to lake with Zebra Mussels attached to the sides and bottom. Zebra Mussels negatively impact ecosystems in many ways. They filter out algae that native species need for food and they attach to—and incapacitate—native mussels. Power plants must also spend millions of dollars removing zebra mussels from clogged water intakes."

Which of the following would best stop the spread of this environmental problem?

(A) Add pesticides that kill all mussel species to lakes with zebra mussels.

(B) Find an invasive species that preys on zebra mussels and introduce that species to the lakes that contain zebra mussels.

(C) Inspect boats for zebra mussels and remove before moving the boat to a new lake.

(D) Drain rivers and physically remove the zebra mussels from the river beds.

63. How does ocean acidification damage coral reefs?

   (A) Heat melts the tiny coral animals.
   (B) Loss of calcium carbonate doesn't allow shell formation.
   (C) Sea levels rise disrupting photosynthesis of the zooxanthellae.
   (D) Minerals precipitate out and cover the coral shells.

64. Climate change is increasing the greatest in the polar regions due to a positive feedback loop. The graph below shows the sea ice extent over the past 35 years.

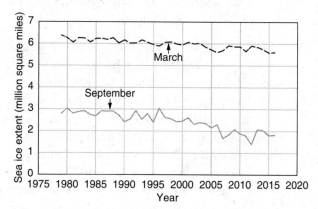

Which of the following best describes the phenomenon you see in the graph above?

   (A) We have lost about 1 million square miles of sea ice in March and September in 35 years.
   (B) We have gained about 1 million square miles of sea ice in March and September in 35 years.
   (C) Sea ice extent has remained fairly constant over the past 35 years.
   (D) Sea ice extent has dropped by over 4 million square miles in 35 years.

65. Which of the following would be the primary reason for ocean warming?

   (A) Ocean acidification
   (B) Thermal pollution from nuclear power plants
   (C) Global temperature increase due to climate change
   (D) Shifts in global wind patterns from El Niño

66. Which of the following is true of how an ecosystem can recover after a large fire breaks out in the area?

   (A) The area will remain plant and animal free for many years.
   (B) K-selected species will recover before r-selected species.
   (C) Salinization of the soil will happen disrupting plant recovery.
   (D) If the area had more species diversity it will generally recover more quickly than if it had lower species diversity.

Use the graph below to answer questions 67–68.

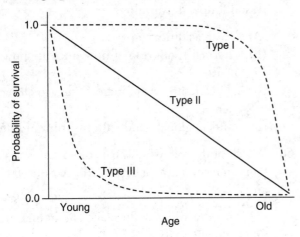

67. Kangaroos usually have one offspring per year. The joey will remain in the mother's pouch for nine months and will nurse until 17 months of age. Using this information and the graph above, which statement best characterizes a kangaroo?

    (A) Kangaroos are r-strategists and demonstrate a Type I survivorship curve.
    (B) Kangaroos are k-strategists and demonstrate a Type I survivorship curve.
    (C) Kangaroos are r-strategists and demonstrate a Type III survivorship curve.
    (D) Kangaroos are k-strategists and demonstrate a Type III survivorship curve.

68. Using the graph above, what can we expect from a species that demonstrates a Type III survivorship curve?

    (A) The species is a K strategist that has many offspring that live a long time.
    (B) The species is a K strategist that has many offspring that die young.
    (C) The species is a R strategist that has many offspring that survive a short time.
    (D) The species is a R strategist that has many offspring that survive a long time.

69. When rivers are dammed for recreation and hydroelectric power, there can be environmental problems that result. Which of the following would be a problem of this type of power?

    (A) The area downstream can flood and be disastrous to cities below the dam.
    (B) The area downstream can have huge amounts of soil and sediment build up below the dam.
    (C) Less water may flow to the area downstream causing a decrease in water and sediment from flowing below the dam.
    (D) The lake created above the dam may become a habitat for water fowl.

70. A farmer sprays an organophosphate pesticide on his crops. The first year he notices a 90 percent reduction in his crops being eaten by the pest. In year two he sprays again but this time notices a 50 percent reduction in his crops being eaten by the pest. In year three when he sprays the crops with the same pesticide he notices only a 10 percent reduction in his crops being eaten by the pest. What would be a solution the farmer could implement to stop this pesticide resistance?

    (A) Use genetically engineered crops that are resistant to the pest.
    (B) Continue adding the organophosphate because the resistance will stop in future years.
    (C) Move his crops to a neighboring field and use the organophosphate on the crop there.
    (D) Plant more of the same crops to get larger crop yields.

71. The graph below is from the United States Department of Agriculture website.

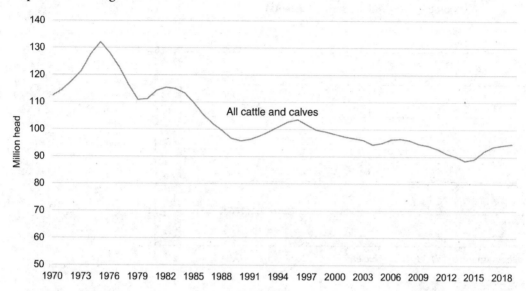

What could be a reason for the trend in the graph from 1996 to 2015?

(A) As demand for beef increased, ranchers bred more cattle.

(B) As drought conditions increased, ranchers slaughtered their cattle.

(C) The supply of domestic pork decreased.

(D) Ranchers began to use concentrated animal feeding operations (CAFOs) rather than free-range cattle farming.

72. Many resources are extracted from the Earth by both surface and subsurface mining. These methods can have a large environmental impact such as groundwater contamination, habitat destruction, and methane production. Which of the following would be the best environmental solution to this problem?

(A) Rely greater on subsurface mining than on surface mining.

(B) Switch to other methods such as hydraulic fracturing.

(C) Use the slag and tailings produced from the mining in manufacturing and building projects.

(D) Switch to a greater reliance on renewable energy resources.

73. Which of the following would be an environmental solution to the problem of urbanization?

(A) Provide private automobiles to allow easier commuting for citizens.

(B) Switch to fossil fuels to meet the greater energy demands from urbanization.

(C) Build homes that take up more land space rather than high-rise buildings.

(D) Use paving stones with grass in between for parking spaces rather than asphalt and concrete to allow water infiltration into aquifers.

74. Which of the following correctly describes renewable and nonrenewable energy resources?

(A) A nonrenewable example would be solar and a renewable would be coal.

(B) Nonrenewable energy can be replaced in a relatively short period of time.

(C) Nonrenewable energy has a fixed amount that can't be easily replenished.

(D) Nuclear energy is a renewable energy source.

75. Which of the following statements about geothermal energy is correct?

(A) Steam is generated from water that is heated from the Earth's interior and is used to drive an electric generator.

(B) Geothermal energy is inexpensive.

(C) Geothermal energy is extremely inefficient.

(D) Geothermal energy is a nonrenewable resource.

Use the graph below to answer questions 76–77.

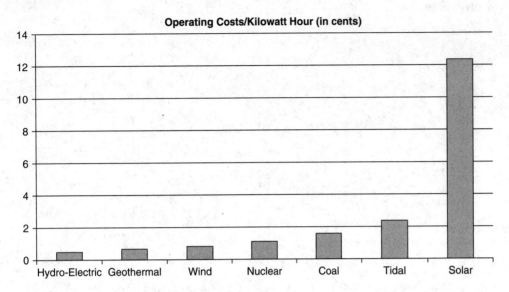

76. According to the graph above, solar energy has a much higher operating cost than any of the others. What is the percent increase in price of operating solar versus coal?

    (A) 5 times
    (B) 12 times
    (C) 100 percent
    (D) 550 percent

77. The costs above are associated with an active solar energy system. Which of the following would be an example of a passive solar energy system?

    (A) Photovoltaic cells that heat a liquid through mechanical and electric equipment
    (B) Solar energy farms that can be set up in desert ecosystems
    (C) Large windows to let heat from the sun into a building or home
    (D) Battery systems to collect solar power and store for evening use

78. Hydrogen fuel cells have many environmental benefits such as producing no carbon dioxide. However, they still have an environmental footprint. Which of the following best describes a negative environmental consequence of hydrogen fuel cells?

   (A) Water and energy are released as a product of these.
   (B) Hydrogen fuel cell technology is expensive.
   (C) Energy is needed to create the hydrogen gas which can cause climate change.
   (D) Combining hydrogen and oxygen in the air can form water.

79. A student enters a science fair competition with a project on demonstrating how CO_2 and particulates come from a variety of natural sources. Which of the following would her experiment most likely conclude?

   (A) CO_2 comes from decomposition and respiration and particulates from pollen and dust.
   (B) Volcanic eruptions do not produce CO_2 or particulates.
   (C) CO_2 is produced from nuclear energy power plants.
   (D) Particulate matter is completely anthropogenic.

80. According to the Australian Academy of Science: "We live in a noisy world, and much of that noise is made by humans. Traffic, machinery, electronics—it's a constant barrage of sound. How does our noise affect the animals around us? Unlike us, they can't put in some earplugs, close a window or turn off the stereo. Recent studies are showing that our increasingly loud world is having negative effects on a range of animals, across a variety of habitats."

   According to this passage, which of the following would most likely be a result of the environmental problem of noise pollution?

   (A) Loss of hearing to humans living in cities
   (B) Stress and changes to migratory routes for wildlife
   (C) Acidification on soil from the machinery that causes noise pollution
   (D) Groundwater pollution from machinery and electronic production

STOP. End of Section I.

AP Environmental Science Practice Exam 1
Section II: Free-Response Questions

Time: 70 minutes

Directions: Answer all three questions below. Where an explanation or discussion is needed, support your answers with relevant information and/or specific examples. If a calculation is required, clearly show all your work and how you arrived at your answer.

1. **Design an investigation.**

   A park ranger in Texas decides to begin a scientific experiment by monitoring the river in an area of the park. Each morning in August he goes out and takes water samples and goes back again in the afternoon once the park is full of visitors. He does this for three days and records the following data:

	DISSOLVED OXYGEN	CARBON DIOXIDE	TEMPERATURE	pH	NITRATES	PHOSPHATES
Day 1 AM	7.8%	14 ppm	30°C	7	2.0 ppm	0.1 ppm
Day 1 PM	7.2%	16 ppm	32°C	7	3.8 ppm	1.3 ppm
Day 2 AM	7.7%	14 ppm	30°C	7	2.0 ppm	0.1 ppm
Day 2 PM	7.2%	16 ppm	32°C	7	3.8 ppm	1.3 ppm
Day 3 AM	7.7%	14 ppm	30°C	7	2.0 ppm	0.1 ppm
Day 3 PM	7.1%	15 ppm	32°C	7	3.8 ppm	1.3 ppm

   (a) After completing his tests, the park ranger determines that the levels of nitrates and phosphates in the river are surprisingly high in the afternoon. He begins to look for reasons why this might be the case. **Identify** ONE possible reason for an increased level of nitrates and phosphates in the stream.

   (b) Design a laboratory experiment to determine why the river is testing high for nitrates and phosphates. For this experiment, be sure to:
   (i) State the hypothesis.
   (ii) Describe the method you would use to test your hypothesis.

   (c) **Describe** ONE step that could be taken to reduce the phosphates in the river from the activity you described in (a) and **explain** ONE environmental consequence of high levels of nitrates and phosphates in a body of water.

   (d) The park ranger is worried about the number of visitors he sees in the park because he knows human activities might result in a loss of biodiversity. **Identify** TWO specific human activities that could result in a loss of biodiversity in the park, and **explain** how each activity lowers biodiversity.

2. **Analyze an environmental problem and propose a solution.**

   According to the Everglades Cooperative Invasive Species Management Area, Tegu lizards are from South America and have escaped or been released into Southern Florida. The three species that have been found in Florida are the Argentine black-and-white Tegu, who can grow up to 4 feet long; the gold Tegu, who can grow up to 3 feet long; and the red Tegus, who can reach 4.5 feet long. The Tegus are generalists who eat many of the native wildlife, including small animals like lizards and rodents. They also dig in alligator and turtle nests and eat the eggs. They are becoming a threat to crocodiles, sea turtles, ground-nesting birds, and small mammals.

(a) Most invasive species are r-selected species. **Identify** ONE characteristic of an r-selected species and **explain** why they often can outcompete native species.

(b) **Identify** another invasive species other than the Tegu lizard and **describe** ONE negative impact it has had.

(c) Many times humans have introduced another nonnative species to an environment to control an invasive species. **Identify** ONE example of when this strategy was implemented and **discuss** ONE problem that resulted when this occurred.

(d) Florida scientists have recorded Tegus eating eggs from an alligator nest—a behavior that could be a problem for the threatened American crocodile population that lives nearby. **Describe** TWO important characteristics of an endangered species that would cause it to be slow to recover.

(e) Economic incentives have often helped solve environmental problems. **Identify** ONE example of an economic incentive the government of Florida could offer to stop Tegu lizards before they become a larger problem and **explain** how that incentive would work.

3. **Analyze an environmental problem and propose a solution using calculations.**

The graph below from the OurWorldinData annual report shows the historical estimates of the world population and the UN projections until 2100.

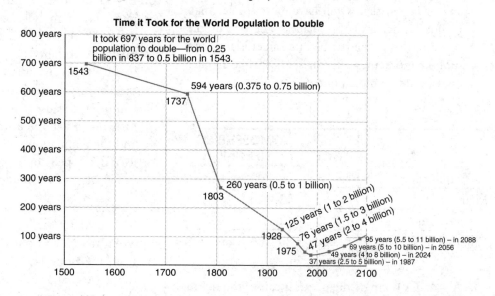

(a) **Calculate** the population growth rate between 1543 and 1803. **Calculate** the population growth rate between 1803 and 1928. **Explain** the general trend shown in the graph.

(b) **Describe** the difference between a density-independent and a density-dependent factor. **Identify** ONE density-independent factor and ONE density-dependent factor that could impact population growth.

(c) **Identify** ONE action a government could do that would affect the growth or decline of a population and **identify** whether or not that action would raise or lower a population.

(d) **Identify** ONE way an increased human population can impact biodiversity and **explain** a strategy that would combat that problem.

STOP. End of Section II.

Answers and Explanations for the Multiple-Choice Questions

1. **A**—Brazil makes up the majority of each of the bars in each year in the graph.

2. **D**—When deforestation occurs, the trees' roots no longer hold the soil in place and erosion becomes a huge problem.

3. **B**—The Green Revolution has allowed us to feed more people and has provided larger profits, tastier and more nutritious food, and less use of pesticides and water, but there are some consequences to these practices.

4. **B**—Island biogeography is the study of the species and distribution that would occur on islands. The theory states that islands closer to the mainland (where the animals/plants have moved from) and/or larger islands will have more species than islands farther away or smaller. The size of the island in theory matters because larger islands can support more and different species while smaller ones would be more limited.

5. **C**—

GAS	GWP	ATMOSPHERIC LIFETIME
Carbon dioxide	1	50–200 years
Methane	21	12 years
Nitrous oxide	310	120 years
Chlorofluorocarbons	12,000–16,000	20–100 years

6. **A**—As CO_2 enters the ocean it causes the ocean to become more acidic (lower pH). This acidity doesn't allow animals like clams and mussels to make protective shells, and can impact coral since they also make protective shells.

7. **C**—If laws regulating development and agriculture in wetland areas were strengthened, then wetlands would be protected and would recover.

8. **B**—Transitional countries are those where birth rates stay high but death rates begin to drop due to increases in health, food availability, and medicine. Infants begin to survive into childhood but because there are still so many births the country's population begins to explode. In addition, because education and birth control for women is limited, the TFR will remain high and the population will grow exponentially. The least developed countries today are in the transitional stage of the demographic transition.

9. **C**—Industrial, or stage 3, countries have birth rates that begin to drop due to access to reliable birth control, family planning, and women getting educations and jobs. This applies to most developing countries today. The population begins to slow, but not as quickly as you would think due to the concept of population momentum.

10. **B**—Transitional countries are those where birth rates stay high but death rates begin to drop due to increases in health, food availability, and medicine. Infants begin to survive into childhood but because there are still so many births the country's population begins to explode. In addition, because education and birth control for women is limited, the TFR will remain high and the population will grow exponentially. The least developed countries today are in the transitional stage of the demographic transition.

11. **D**—*Eutrophication* is the term used to describe a body of water that has many nutrients (fertilizers like nitrogen and phosphorus) that have run off from the land. These nutrients have "fertilized" the algae that live in the water. This can cause the water to become so thick and green with algae that no light can penetrate through the water.

12. **A**—Geothermal energy uses heat to create steam to turn a turbine that creates electrical energy with a generator. The cons are it is expensive, can release hydrogen sulfide, requires a lot of water, and isn't readily available everywhere in the world.

13. **B**—The graph is showing that the solar energy output is much less in the winter months.

14. **D**—Hydroelectric power cons are when you build a dam you change the river ecosystem.

You flood an area above the dam, which was once a land habitat. If water is taken from the reservoir for irrigation or other purposes, you reduce the flow of water and the amount of nutrients available downstream. In some cases, the flow is so reduced that the water never reaches the sea. This can damage habitats and cause loss of biodiversity.

15. **C**—The Ring of Fire is an area around the Pacific Plate where a "ring" of volcanoes and earthquakes is found because of convergent plate boundaries.

16. **D**—In predator-prey relationships, a predator, such as a cheetah, eats his prey, such as a gazelle. The cheetah and gazelle are a predator-prey relationship.

17. **A**—With many prey, there can be a lot of predators because of the ample prey availability.

18. **B**—A thermal inversion is a weather condition when warm, less dense air moves over dense, cold air over a city. Because of the thermal weather condition and the dense air, pollution, particularly smog and particulates, get trapped near the ground and can't "escape" to space.

19. **C**—The Endangered Species Act is a law for the conservation of threatened and endangered plants and animals and the habitats where they are found.

20. **D**—Lethal Dose 50% is a term used in toxicology to indicate the amount of a toxin that kills 50 percent of the organism that is being tested. This can be any animal but usually refers to test rats and mice in a laboratory.

21. **B**—To do this, you start with the sand and find the percentage along the bottom of the triangle, in this case 10 percent, and follow the line that goes up and to the left for sand. Then, you move to the right side of the triangle and find the line for silt, in this case also 10 percent. Follow this line down and to the left until it hits the line you had drawn for sand. They should cross. Then, where they cross, if you draw a straight line to the left, where you find clay, you should be at the 80 percent line, which is your percentage of clay.

22. **A**—Porosity is having small spaces between the particles. The finer the particle size, the more porosity. This might seem backwards but clay has tiny holes and very fine particle sizes so clay has the highest porosity. Permeability is the ability of a material to allow liquid to flow through it. Clay has the lowest permeability, since water can't flow easily through it.

23. **A**—This is the concept where individuals tend to over exploit shared resources until the resource becomes unavailable to all. So, if farmers are overgrazing on public lands, it is a tragedy of the commons.

24. **D**—Aquaculture is a method of farm raising fish, shellfish, aquatic plants, and so on. A farmer can build large ponds and stock these ponds with large numbers of animals or plants, or use a natural river, lake, or ocean to do this with nets and holding pens. The benefits of these are: no depletion of our natural supplies of these organisms, feeding a large number of people, less use of water, increased profits, and the use of very little fuel.

25. **C**—The sun's radiation hits the Earth with different intensities. It hits the equator most directly since it is nearly directly overhead most of the year.

26. **A**—The first step is known as primary treatment. In this step, the sewage is filtered with grates and screens for large items that are not liquid. In secondary treatment, we take the bacteria that is found in the sewage and give it lots of air so it can begin to consume the waste and break it down into carbon dioxide and inorganic sludge. In the last stage, known as tertiary treatment, chemicals like chlorine, ozone gas, or UV light kill any bacteria. Then the water is released to a river or lake.

27. **D**—Dysentery is an infection of the intestines resulting in severe diarrhea with blood and mucus in the feces. This comes from untreated sewage in streams and rivers that become drinking water or contaminates food.

28. **B**—Increases in carbon dioxide from burning fossil fuels have led to more heat being trapped and increased temperatures.

29. **A**—From 57 degrees to 58.5 degrees is a difference of 1.5 degrees.

30. **D**—Corals need zooxanthellae, an algae that lives in the tissues of coral and captures sunlight and converts it into energy for the coral animals. When the temperature of the ocean is too warm, the zooxanthellae become under stress and can die or leave their coral host, causing the coral to die and turn white, a process known as coral bleaching.

31. **C**—

D—Denitrification	N— Nitrogen gas	Bacteria convert nitrogen in the soil back to an atmospheric form

32. **A**—When there are more animals in an area than an area can support, the animals overconsume the plants and overcrowd one another. This can lead to disease and famine.

33. **B**—The 10 percent rule is the idea that as usable energy moves up the pyramid much of it is "lost" to the laws of thermodynamics. So if there were 1,000 kcal available at the producer level, there will be 100 available at the herbivore level.

34. **C**—70/3 = 23 years

35. **B**—In years 1–3 the grasses begin to move back in.

36. **C**—Laws that say how many fish or how big a fish can be when caught would help lessen overfishing problems.

37. **D**—During an El Niño–Southern Oscillation (ENSO), upwellings from the sea bed occur in normal years, bringing nutrients up for the plankton to feed on, and the plankton is food for the marine life up the food chain. In an El Niño year, that upwelling does not occur so the quantity of plankton is reduced, and in turn, so are the fish stocks.

38. **A**—The ocean provides a lot of moisture to the area. As the moist air rises, it cools and a lot of rain falls on the windward side of the mountain. However, because the air loses its moisture on the windward side of the mountains, it is dry on the other side.

39. **B**—The stratosphere is where the protective ozone layer is found.

40. **C**—Seventy-eight percent of the troposphere is made up of nitrogen.

41. **C**—The pyramid is stable.

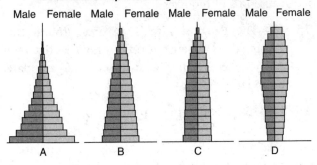

Generalized Population Age-Structure Diagrams

42. **A**—The primary productivity in water is dependent on how clear the water is and how deep the red and blue light can penetrate.

43. **A**—Cultural ecosystem services are not "things" we tangibly benefit from but rather interactions with nature, such as taking a walk and enjoying what you see or art that comes from looking at nature, etc.

44. **D**—The Montreal Protocol is an international treaty designed to protect the ozone layer by phasing out the substances, such as CFCs, that are responsible for ozone depletion.

45. **C**—Stratospheric ozone depletion allows more UV light to get through the stratosphere and to the surface of the Earth. UV light is dangerous because it damages the DNA in skin cells, and leads to skin cancer, eye damage such as cataracts, premature aging, and can suppress the immune system.

46. **B**—Decomposers are not pictured in the food web but are a vital component of food webs.

47. **D**—Since marmots are shown to eat grasses, if you remove the marmot, the grasses would increase since you are removing the animal that eats them.

48. **A**—Carbon dioxide is a greenhouse gas that traps heat close to the Earth, increasing temperatures on Earth. As Earth gets warmer, thermal expansion of the oceans occurs and land-based ice melts and runs off into the ocean. All of this contributes to sea levels rising.

49. **D**—When we burn fossil fuels, we emit carbon dioxide. As carbon dioxide levels in the atmosphere increase, so do temperatures on Earth.

50. **B**—Coal-burning power plants release nitrogen oxides (NO_x) and sulfur oxides (SO_2) into the atmosphere. When these chemicals go into the atmosphere and mix with the rain, snow, fog, hail or dust, they can become acid rain and fall to the Earth. By requiring power plants to remove the SO_2, the problem of acid rain is diminished.

51. **B**—Similar to how electricity is generated from coal, oil or natural gas, we can also split atoms of uranium-235, a process known as fission, to generate a lot of heat. The heat can be used to boil water to make steam to turn a turbine to generate electrical energy.

52. **D**—Thermal pollution is often from a nuclear power plant where large amounts of heated water are dumped into a body of water.

53. **A**—Photochemical smog is formed when volatile organic hydrocarbons and nitrogen oxides, along with heat and sunlight, mix and pollution occurs.

54. **C**—According to the graph, 34 percent of deaths from indoor air pollutants are caused by stroke, the highest percentage of all categories.

55. **D**—Coal burning power plants, vehicles, manufacturing, and even volcanoes release nitrogen oxides (NO_x) and sulfur oxides (SO_2) into the atmosphere. When these chemicals go into the atmosphere and mix with the rain, snow, fog, hail or dust, they can become acid rain and fall to Earth.

56. **C**—Generalists can live in many different places and eat many different things. Generalists are less likely to be impacted by an environmental event.

57. **A**—Since the mussel has 1,000,000 offspring it is most likely a r-strategist.

58. **B**—Furrow irrigation is where trenches are dug between rows of crops and that area is flooded with water. This allows the farmer to flow water down these trenches and the water is absorbed by the roots of the plants. The advantages and disadvantages are similar to flood irrigation with about 35 percent being lost to evaporation.

59. **D**—The graph shows that as countries develop their annual consumption of electrical power increases.

60. **D**—Natural gas is the fossil fuel that burns the cleanest and can be used for energy. It is made up mostly of methane but contains other things like carbon dioxide, nitrogen, etc.

61. **A**—Fracking is an extraction method in which liquid is forced at very high pressures down into the rock to cause the oil or gas to be released. This can lead to groundwater contamination because the water that is used to release the oil or natural gas can contain contaminates that then run off into waterways. In addition, this process releases volatile organic compounds during the natural gas production process.

62. **C**—If people checked their boats for zebra mussels and removed any before moving on to a new lake or river, we would greatly reduce the numbers that are being introduced to new areas.

63. **B**—As oceans become more acidic, this acidity doesn't allow animals like clams and mussels to make protective shells. Coral are also impacted similarly because of a loss of calcium carbonate from their shells.

64. **A**—In March the sea ice has gone from approximately 6.5 to 5.5 million square miles and in September from 3 to 2 million square miles. So, there is a loss of about 1 million square miles in both months.

65. **C**—The primary reasons that oceans (and land) are warming is from global climate change as a result of an increase in greenhouse gases from burning fossil fuels and agriculture.

66. **D**—Species diversity is the number of species and abundance of each species that live in a particular community. Species diversity helps to contribute to the health of an ecosystem because each species has an important role in this heath. In addition, an area with a higher species diversity is an area that can recover faster from a disaster.

67. **B**—Humans and kangaroos are examples of Type I. According to the graph, almost 100 percent of kangaroos survive childhood and most survive a long time and into many years. These are often k-selected species.

68. **C**—A species with a Type III survivorship curve have very few who make it to adulthood. Think of frog eggs—most get eaten, dry out, and never mature, or they never hatch at all. Then, tadpoles are also a major food source for many species so lots of young frogs are also killed. However, a few make it to old age and become adult frogs. These are often r-selected species.

69. **C**—Hydroelectric power cons are that building dams is expensive, and when you build a dam you change the river ecosystem. You flood an area above the dam, which was once a land habitat, and you reduce the flow of water downstream, reducing the amount of nutrients available and changing the ecosystems.

70. **A**—If the farmer uses genetically modified/engineered crops that the bugs don't like and won't eat, then he won't have to spray a large quantity of pesticides on his crop.

71. **D**—Ranchers began to use concentrated animal feeding operations (CAFOs) rather than free-range cattle farming. In CAFOs, the cattle reach market weight faster than in free-range cattle farming, resulting in fewer cattle than previously in the United States.

72. **D**—Switching to renewable resources would lower our dependence on mining and the environmental problems that are associated with mining.

73. **D**—One problem with urbanization is that large areas of soil have concrete or asphalt put down on them for parking lots, streets, etc. and water can't seep into aquifers. If we use paving stones for parking lots, then water can seep in between the stones rather than running off.

74. **C**—Nonrenewable resources are replaced slowly or not at all. These include things like coal, oil, natural gas, and nuclear energy resources.

75. **A**—Geothermal energy uses heat from deep in the Earth to create steam to turn a turbine to create electrical energy.

76. **D**—To calculate the percentage increase you take the new (solar) and subtract the old (coal) and divide by the old (coal) and then multiply by 100 to make it a percent. 13 for solar minus 2 for coal equals 11 divided by 2 equals 5.5. 5.5 times 100 percent = 550 percent. Or $(13-2)/2 \times 100 = 550\%$.

77. **C**—Passive solar systems do not collect or store energy but can be used to heat or cool homes, etc. An example of this would be to build a home with large windows that face where the sun shines the most. Then, the sun will come in through the windows and heat the home. During the summer the homeowner could put thick curtains on the windows to prevent the heat from coming in.

78. **C**—The problem with hydrogen fuel cells is that to create the hydrogen gas through a process called electrolysis requires energy, possibly produced from nonrenewable sources such as coal. Partly because of this it is very expensive.

79. **A**—Every time you exhale, you add CO_2 to the atmosphere. CO_2 is also formed as things decompose and when volcanoes erupt. We measure CO_2 in parts per million (ppm). Natural sources of particulates are dust, sea salt, pollen, and also particles from volcanic eruptions.

80. **B**—The author states "How does our noise affect the animals around us? Unlike us, they can't put in some earplugs, close a window or turn off the stereo. Recent studies are showing that our increasingly loud world is having negative effects on a range of animals, across a variety of habitats." So, the best answer would be that the noise is causing stress and possibly changes to the migration of animals.

Explanations for the Free-Response Questions

1.

(a) (1 point possible) One point for correctly identifying one possible reason for the increase in nitrogen and phosphorus. Some possible responses may be fertilizers, sewage leakage, and runoff from CAFOs.

(b) (3 points possible) One point for correctly stating a hypothesis. A correct hypothesis includes a relationship between nitrates/phosphates and the item identified in (a) above. The prediction needs to show how the increase in nitrates/phosphates is linked to the identified item. Two points for correctly identifying the method you would use to test your hypothesis. A correct method would show how you would manipulate an independent variable. You will need at least three experimental groups and one control group.

(c) (2 points possible) One point for identifying a step that could be taken and one point for explaining an environmental consequence. It depends on what you said above, but possible answers could be planting plants to catch fertilizer runoff, fixing the sewage leak, not having as many animals on one plot of land, or allowing free-range grazing.

(d) (4 points possible) One point for each human activity and one point each for a thorough explanation of how this activity could lower biodiversity in the park.

There are many possible answers including cars, trash, foot traffic, fishing, and so on. Some possible explanations include habitat loss, invasive species, pollution, climate change, and over exploitation.

2.

(a) (2 points possible) One point for identifying that r-selective species have many offspring, expend minimal energy caring for offspring, mature early, have short life spans, and may reproduce only once in their lifetime. Another point for explaining that they often can outcompete native species because they are generalists.

(b) (2 points possible) One point for correctly naming another invasive species and one point for explaining because an invasive species is a nonnative species, any species that moves into an environment where it doesn't naturally occur could become a problem. The negative impact will depend on the species named. However, usually the impact is threatening native species.

(c) (2 points possible) One point for correctly identifying an example of a strategy that has been implemented in the past and one point for a thorough response of the negative problem that occurred from this. Again, there are many possible answers but some famous examples include the cane toad whose toxin kills native wildlife, rats who eat birds' eggs, the snakehead fish that feeds on native fish, and the Kudzu vine that smothers other plants.

(d) (2 points possible) One point each for correctly describing characteristics of an endangered species that would cause it to be slow to recover. For example, endangered species have specific habitat requirements, such as a limited diet, being wanted by humans for horns, tusks, and meat.

(e) (2 points possible) One point for an example of the economic incentive and one point for the explanation of how this would work. There are many possible examples but some include buying Tegu lizards (dead or alive), making the Tegu a food source for humans, or finding a use for their hide such as a leather-like product. All of these would make people want to capture Tegus in the wild.

3.

(a) (3 points possible) One point for the calculation in 1543–1803 and one point for the calculation in 1803–1928. No points are awarded if work is not shown.

The formula is: 70/growth rate = doubling time

70/growth rate = 260 years, so a .27 percent growth rate from 1543–1803

70/growth rate = 125 years, so a .56 percent growth rate from 1803–1928

An additional point for explaining that the general trend in the graph is that it is taking fewer years for the population to double. Only recently (since 1987) has the years it takes to double been increasing slightly.

(b) (3 points possible) One point for explaining the difference between a density-independent and a density-dependent factor. A density-independent factor exerts its influence regardless of the population's density and a density-dependent factor intensifies as the population increases in size. One point for identifying a density-independent factor and one point for describing a density-dependent factor. Density-independent factors are a storm, fire, heat wave, or drought and density-dependent factors are access to clean water and air, food availability, disease transmission, or territory size.

(c) (2 points possible) One point for an action a government could do that would affect the growth or decline of a population. Governments could provide access to family planning, to education and employment opportunities, etc. They could also encourage postponement of marriage and guarantee the availability of pensions. One point for identifying if that action would lower or raise the population size.

(e) (2 points possible) One point for identifying a way human population impacts biodiversity. There are many possible answers such as habitat destruction, invasive species, pollution, climate change, and over exploitation. Then another point for explaining a strategy that could combat the problem you identified. The correct answer will depend on the problem you identified and there are many ways to combat the problem.

AP Environmental Science Practice Exam 1
Score Approximation

You can get a rough approximation of what your score on the AP Environmental Science Exam would be. Use this worksheet to compute an approximation of your score.

Section I: Multiple Choice

Determine the number of multiple-choice questions you got right then enter that number below.

Number of questions answered correctly (80 possible)   _____

                                                                    × 1.125

This is your **Weighted Section I** Score   _____

Section II: Free Response

Award yourself points as determined by the scoring guide given in the explanation for each question.

Question 1 (10 points possible)   _____
Question 2 (10 points possible)   _____
Question 3 (10 points possible)   _____

Add the three scores for the free-response section   _____

                                                                    × 2

This is your **Weighted Section II** Score   _____

Add your Weighted Section I Score and your Weighted Section II Score.   _____

This is your **Composite Score.**

Score Conversion Chart

COMPOSITE SCORE RANGE	APPROXIMATE AP SCORE
110–150	5
89–109	4
77–88	3
63–76	2
0–62	1

AP Environmental Science Practice Exam 2
Multiple-Choice Questions

ANSWER SHEET

1 (A) (B) (C) (D)	31 (A) (B) (C) (D)	61 (A) (B) (C) (D)
2 (A) (B) (C) (D)	32 (A) (B) (C) (D)	62 (A) (B) (C) (D)
3 (A) (B) (C) (D)	33 (A) (B) (C) (D)	63 (A) (B) (C) (D)
4 (A) (B) (C) (D)	34 (A) (B) (C) (D)	64 (A) (B) (C) (D)
5 (A) (B) (C) (D)	35 (A) (B) (C) (D)	65 (A) (B) (C) (D)
6 (A) (B) (C) (D)	36 (A) (B) (C) (D)	66 (A) (B) (C) (D)
7 (A) (B) (C) (D)	37 (A) (B) (C) (D)	67 (A) (B) (C) (D)
8 (A) (B) (C) (D)	38 (A) (B) (C) (D)	68 (A) (B) (C) (D)
9 (A) (B) (C) (D)	39 (A) (B) (C) (D)	69 (A) (B) (C) (D)
10 (A) (B) (C) (D)	40 (A) (B) (C) (D)	70 (A) (B) (C) (D)
11 (A) (B) (C) (D)	41 (A) (B) (C) (D)	71 (A) (B) (C) (D)
12 (A) (B) (C) (D)	42 (A) (B) (C) (D)	72 (A) (B) (C) (D)
13 (A) (B) (C) (D)	43 (A) (B) (C) (D)	73 (A) (B) (C) (D)
14 (A) (B) (C) (D)	44 (A) (B) (C) (D)	74 (A) (B) (C) (D)
15 (A) (B) (C) (D)	45 (A) (B) (C) (D)	75 (A) (B) (C) (D)
16 (A) (B) (C) (D)	46 (A) (B) (C) (D)	76 (A) (B) (C) (D)
17 (A) (B) (C) (D)	47 (A) (B) (C) (D)	77 (A) (B) (C) (D)
18 (A) (B) (C) (D)	48 (A) (B) (C) (D)	78 (A) (B) (C) (D)
19 (A) (B) (C) (D)	49 (A) (B) (C) (D)	79 (A) (B) (C) (D)
20 (A) (B) (C) (D)	50 (A) (B) (C) (D)	80 (A) (B) (C) (D)
21 (A) (B) (C) (D)	51 (A) (B) (C) (D)	
22 (A) (B) (C) (D)	52 (A) (B) (C) (D)	
23 (A) (B) (C) (D)	53 (A) (B) (C) (D)	
24 (A) (B) (C) (D)	54 (A) (B) (C) (D)	
25 (A) (B) (C) (D)	55 (A) (B) (C) (D)	
26 (A) (B) (C) (D)	56 (A) (B) (C) (D)	
27 (A) (B) (C) (D)	57 (A) (B) (C) (D)	
28 (A) (B) (C) (D)	58 (A) (B) (C) (D)	
29 (A) (B) (C) (D)	59 (A) (B) (C) (D)	
30 (A) (B) (C) (D)	60 (A) (B) (C) (D)	

AP Environmental Science Practice Exam 2
Section I: Multiple-Choice Questions

Time: 90 minutes

Directions: For the multiple-choice questions to follow, select the best answer and fill in the appropriate letter on the answer sheet.

1. A plant is found in an environment that receives very little rain and very high temperatures most of the year. The plant has special ways of storing and conserving water, has little to no leaves, and has extremely long roots. Which of the following biomes is this plant most likely found in?

   (A) Taiga
   (B) Desert
   (C) Boreal forest
   (D) Grassland

Use the information below to answer questions 2–4.

According to NOAA, most reef-building corals contain photosynthetic algae called zooxanthellae that live in their tissues. The coral provides the algae with a place to live and the algae produce oxygen for the coral and remove wastes. In addition, zooxanthellae are responsible for the beautiful colors of many corals. Sometimes when corals become stressed, as is the case when ocean temperatures become too warm, the polyps expel their algae cells and the colony looks white in appearance. This is known as "coral bleaching."

2. Which of the following best identifies the author's claim?

   (A) Zooxanthellae can become parasitic to coral in stressful environments.
   (B) Coral reefs are structures that can protect the estuaries from natural disasters such as hurricanes.
   (C) Zooxanthellae is an organism worthy of scientific study.
   (D) If a large area of coral reef is colored white, zooxanthellae have left the coral tissues because ocean temperatures are above the optimal growth range.

3. Zooxanthellae and coral are in which type of symbiotic relationship?

   (A) Mutualism
   (B) Commensalism
   (C) Parasitism
   (D) Predator-prey

4. Crown-of-thorns sea stars are a predator on coral reefs. Which of the following would be true of the crown-of-thorn sea stars?

   (A) Crown-of-thorn sea stars are herbivores.
   (B) Ten percent of the energy from the coral will go to the crown-of-thorn sea star when it eats the coral.
   (C) The crown-of-thorn sea star and the coral are in a commensalism relationship.
   (D) Crown-of-thorn sea stars return nitrogen in the form of atmospheric nitrogen back to the atmosphere.

Use the information below to answer questions 5–6.

Soil erosion costs the world billions of dollars every year. One reason for this economic cost is the number of pollutants washing into the streams and rivers and the loss of farmland due to erosion. A group of students decides to set up an experiment to see if they can reduce the amount of soil that is eroded after a rainfall.

5. Which of the following would the students discover as the best way to remediate the problem of soil erosion?

(A) Allow animals to graze near the river/stream.
(B) Clearcut the trees around the river/stream.
(C) Plant plants near the river/stream.
(D) Begin construction projects near the river/stream.

6. A large dam is built above the river, which changes the flow of the stream/river and prevents fish from migrating upstream. What would be a way to solve this environmental problem?

(A) Build fish ladders to allow fish to bypass the dam and get upriver.
(B) Construct new dams to replace older ones.
(C) Dredge the river below the dam to move sediment back upstream.
(D) Bring in nonnative species help repopulate the animals displaced by the dam.

Use the graph below to answer questions 7–8.

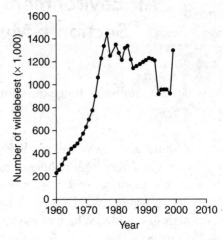

Serengeti Wildebeests

7. Based on the graph above, what would be the best estimate of the carrying capacity of the Serengeti wildebeests?

(A) 50,000
(B) 400,000
(C) 800,000
(D) 1,200,000

8. Which of the following factors might lower the carrying capacity of the herbivore wildebeests?

(A) A significant amount of rainfall increases the grasses the wildebeests eat.
(B) The predators of the wildebeests are culled to protect the local sheep population.
(C) The Serengeti goes through a severe drought impacting local plant life.
(D) A virus moves through the wildebeest predators killing 50 percent of the adult population.

Use the data table below to answer questions 9–10.

An ecological footprint compares resource demands and waste production for a person or for a society. The table below is a sample of an ecological footprint for five people in an office. Each number represents the amount of land, measured in hectares (10,000 square meters).

	FOOD (MEAT)	CARBON EMISSIONS	HOUSING	GOODS AND SERVICES	TOTAL
Person 1	1.8	2.9	2.4	1.6	8.7
Person 2	3.2	3	1.6	1.2	9
Person 3	1.4	2.7	2.2	2.0	8.3
Person 4	2.7	3	1.5	2.9	10.1
Person 5	2.8	3	3.4	1.9	11.1

9. If person 5 wanted to lower his ecological footprint to be more like person 3, what two activities would help the most?

   (A) Take mass transit and buy fewer shoes and less clothing.
   (B) Eat less meat and move to a smaller apartment.
   (C) Eat less meat and buy fewer shoes and less clothing.
   (D) Take mass transit and/or bike to work.

10. Person 1 and person 3 have the lowest ecological footprint when it comes to the food they eat. What is one reason why eating lower on the food chain can help lower your ecological footprint?

    (A) Eating lower on the food chain takes approximately 20 times less land to produce the same number of calories as from meat.
    (B) Eating lower on the food chain helps to lower your A1C and prevent diabetes.
    (C) Eating lower on the food chain increases the amount of methane released into the atmosphere.
    (D) Eating lower on the food chain uses more carbon helping to increase photosynthesis of land plants.

11. Which of the following would be a nonpoint source pollutant that would affect the health of a local forest?

    (A) Smoke from a power plant in the area
    (B) Wastewater from a drainage pipe
    (C) Fire started from an irresponsible camper
    (D) Acid rain

12. A doctor tells his patient that she is exhibiting the effects of an endocrine disrupter on her body. What part of the body would the endocrine disruptor be impacting?

    (A) Cardiovascular system
    (B) Skin
    (C) Hormones
    (D) Nervous system

Use the graph below to answer questions 13–14.

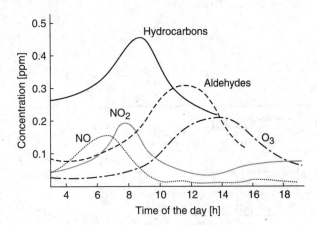

13. Looking at the graph, what time of the day would photochemical smog be at its worst?

(A) 4–6 h
(B) 8–10 h
(C) 12–14 h
(D) 16–18 h

14. What is the human health impact of photochemical smog?

(A) Respiratory problems and eye irritation
(B) Cancer
(C) Skin irritation and eczema
(D) Nervous system problems

15. A family has an average utility use of 1,000 kWh per month. The family has a refrigerator that uses 40 kWh per month. Which of the following is the percentage of the family's total monthly electricity use to run the refrigerator?

(A) 4%
(B) 10%
(C) 40%
(D) 25%

16. Which of the following is the correct order from cleanest and most heat generated to least clean and least heat generated when burned?

(A) Anthracite – lignite – bituminous
(B) Bituminous – lignite – anthracite
(C) Lignite – anthracite – bituminous
(D) Anthracite – bituminous – lignite

17. Bird, butterfly, and bat migration have been a concern among many people when it comes to wind farms. What would be one way to minimize the impact of wind farms on these migrations?

(A) Move wind farms offshore rather than on land.
(B) Slow the speed or turn off the turbines during migration periods.
(C) Lower the height of the wind turbine to 50 meters.
(D) Paint the wind farms a bright color so birds and bats will see and avoid them.

Use the graph below to answer questions 18–20.

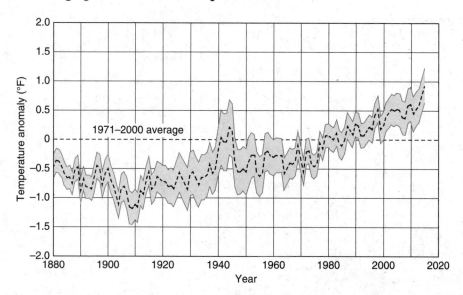

18. What would be the most likely cause of the trend in the graph above?

   (A) Global migration of mammal species
   (B) A severe El Niño year off the coast of South America
   (C) The effects of climate change
   (D) A normal fluctuation in hurricane activity

19. The trend in the graph will most likely lead to what environmental concern?

   (A) Increased air pollution
   (B) Overexploitation of marine species
   (C) Habitat loss along coastlines
   (D) Increased human population growth

20. What would be the best way to slow the cause of the trend in the graph?

   (A) Slow the expansion of nuclear energy
   (B) Limit the use of fossil fuels
   (C) Stop construction in coastal areas
   (D) Limit the use of pesticides and fertilizers on farmland

Use the image below to answer questions 21–23.

Eutrophication

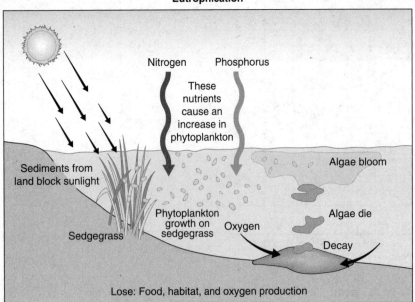

21. What would be the environmental consequence of the additional nitrogen and phosphorus entering the lake?

    (A) A decrease in dissolved oxygen and a large die-off of fish and other aquatic organisms
    (B) Temperature increase due to the algae bloom
    (C) Increased lake levels from the algae decay
    (D) An increase in pathogens and infectious diseases from local industry

22. A student is trying to find the source of the nitrogen and phosphorus that is causing eutrophication. Where should the student first begin her investigation?

    (A) The local coal-burning power plant
    (B) The large multi-use construction project in the neighboring city
    (C) The pesticide plant producing organophosphates
    (D) The runoff from agricultural land

23. What is one suggestion the student could give the city to mitigate the problem of eutrophication?

    (A) Take large nets and scoop out the algae that is blocking the sunlight.
    (B) Introduce fish such as the Bristlenose Plecostomus that eat algae.
    (C) Plant plants around the lake known as a riparian buffer.
    (D) Encourage herbivores like cattle to graze near the river.

Farmed Fish is the most Resource Efficient Protein on the Planet.
[The Perfect Protein]

	Feed	Fresh water
	1.2 Pounds	1 Gallons
	2.3 Pounds	2,000 Gallons
	6 Pounds	3,500 Gallons
	13 Pounds	2,500 Gallons

24. The graphic above shows how aquaculture or farming fish is the most efficient form of animal protein saving millions of gallons of water and needing much less food to feed the fish. However, which of the following is an environmental consequence of aquaculture?

    (A) The surrounding water can be contaminated with organic waste.
    (B) Fish are inexpensive and therefore do not generate economic profits.
    (C) Soil erosion can occur trapping light and preventing photosynthesis.
    (D) Pesticides must be sprayed to stop fish disease which contaminates the water.

25. Which of the following environmental problems are associated with burning fossil fuels, vehicle emissions, and deforestation?

    (A) Eutrophication
    (B) Island biogeography
    (C) Ocean acidification
    (D) Thermal pollution

26. Which of the following best describes the greenhouse effect?

    (A) Acid rain can cause a positive feedback loop further heating the Earth.
    (B) Gases in Earth's atmosphere trap heat from the sun.
    (C) The principal greenhouse gases are hydrogen, nitrogen, and helium.
    (D) The greenhouse effect is the Earth's ability to mitigate the rising sea levels.

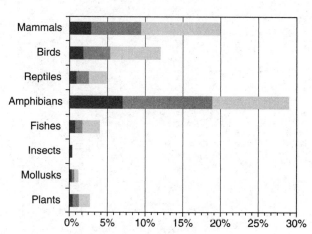

27. A student was researching endangered species. What should she conclude from the data above?

    (A) There are no insects on the vulnerable list.
    (B) Fish and reptiles both have the same environmental stressors.
    (C) Mollusks and insects should not be an environmental concern.
    (D) Amphibians have the greatest impact from changes to their environment.

Use the image below to answer questions 28–29.

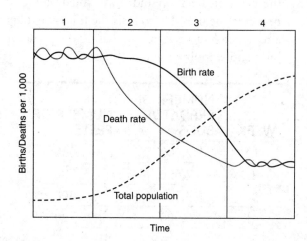

28. In the graph above, at which phase does the population stay relatively stable?

    (A) 1 and 4
    (B) 1 and 2
    (C) 2 and 3
    (D) 3 and 4

29. In which phase above would the country's population be growing exponentially?

    (A) 1 and 4
    (B) 2 and 4
    (C) 2 and 3
    (D) 1 and 2

30. A farmer purchases wasps and ladybugs to eat the pests on his crop and lower the amount of pesticides he uses. He collects the following data after just a few weeks of purchasing the predator bugs and stopping the use of pesticides.

WEEK	NUMBER OF PREDATOR BUGS	NUMBER OF PESTS
1	2,000	1,000
2	2,500	700
3	3,500	300
4	5,000	20

What can we conclude from the data on the farm and what benefit does that pose to the environment?

(A) The farmer is adding a new pest to the farm that could potentially damage local wildlife.

(B) The farmer is using integrated pest management and reducing the risk of pesticides to the wildlife in the area.

(C) The farmer's method is not working and he will need to switch to a new form of the pesticide.

(D) The predator bugs are overpopulating the farm which will lead to devastating financial problems in the future.

31. What type of biome would we expect to find at 30°N and 30°S?

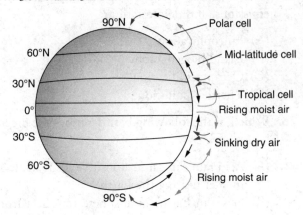

(A) Rainforest
(B) Savannah
(C) Tundra
(D) Desert

32. What relationship can we assume about phosphorus from the diagram below?

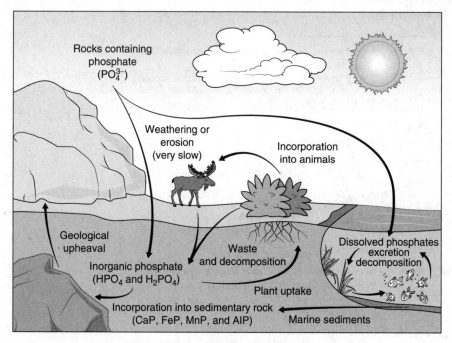

Phosphorus Cycle

(A) Rocks and soil contain phosphorus and, since there is no atmospheric form, the phosphorus cycle is slow.

(B) The atmosphere and soil contain phosphorus so we can assume phosphorus is also prevalent and abundant in aquatic ecosystems as well.

(C) The rocks and the atmosphere contain phosphorus that comes directly from animals as they undergo cellular respiration and decompose after death.

(D) Lakes and the atmosphere contain phosphorus so we can assume the phosphorus cycle is a fast cycle that replenishes very quickly.

33. If the population of a country grows at a rate of approximately 4 percent per year, how many years will it take for the population to double?

(A) 280 years
(B) 17.5 years
(C) 175 years
(D) 5.7 years

34. The pesticide dichlorvos, an insecticide used in household pesticide strips, is determined to have an LD_{50} of 61 mg/kg. If a typical mouse weighs .30 kg, which of the following would be the appropriate dose to kill mice?

(A) 61 mg/kg × 50% × 0.30 kg
(B) 61 mg/kg × 0.30 kg
(C) 61 mg/kg × 0.30 kg/50%
(D) 61 mg/kg/50%

Use the graph below to answer questions 35–36.

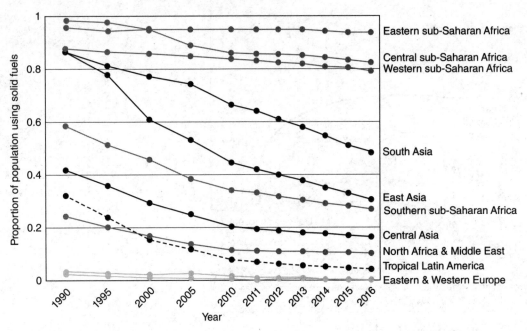

Proportion of Population Subject to
Indoor Air Pollution, 1990–2016

35. According to the graph above, much of the world is subjected to indoor air pollution from burning solid fuels for cooking or heating. Which of the following would be correct according to the trend in the graph?

(A) East Asia is going through the demographic transition process.
(B) Western sub-Saharan Africa is seeing the greatest decrease in indoor air pollutants over the past 30 years.
(C) The number of people exposed to indoor air pollution is dropping.
(D) Western Europe has never had an indoor air pollution problem.

36. What can you conclude from the graph about Eastern sub-Saharan Africa?

(A) This is a developed country.
(B) Indoor air pollution is being addressed in this country.
(C) Industrial smog is a problem in this country.
(D) There is widespread use of solid fuels for cooking and heating.

37. The graph below shows the development of primary energy consumption worldwide and makes projections until 2030. Which of the following can you conclude from the graph?

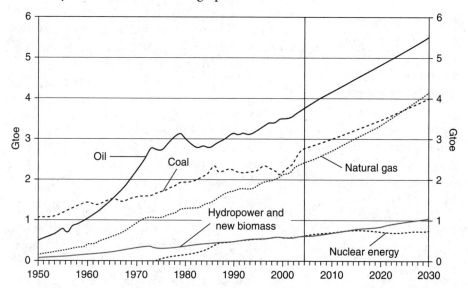

(A) Oil will increase by 5 Gtoe from 1950 to 2030.

(B) Hydropower will not increase at all from 1950 to 2030.

(C) Nuclear has the greatest slope and therefore the greatest potential for future use.

(D) Natural gas will increase exponentially from 1950 to 2030.

38. Based on the data in the graph below, how many million tons of paper was sent to MSW before recycling in 2008?

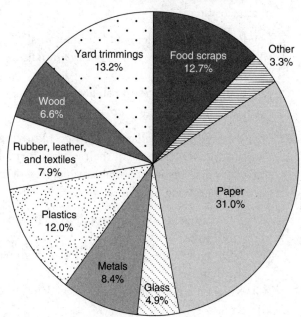

Total MSW Generation (by material), 2008
250 Million Tons (before recycling)

(A) 172.5 million tons

(B) 77.5 million tons

(C) 31 million tons

(D) 310 million tons

39. A scientist is studying the effects of DDT, a synthetic organic compound banned worldwide in 2001. Which of the following best identifies a testable hypothesis for his study?

(A) DDT is a persistent organic pollutant and will show up in the tissues of top predators for many decades.
(B) DDT is unlikely to show up in the tissues of top predators since it was banned almost 20 years ago.
(C) DDT will not be found in the tissues of plants because it was banned almost 20 years ago.
(D) DDT will not be linked to human health impacts in the year 2030.

40. Which of the following should be studied to see if a geologic feature is causing increases in CO_2 and particulate matter?

(A) Plant pollen
(B) Burning of fossil fuels
(C) Respiration from local wildlife
(D) Volcanoes

41. Which of following would be an effect of an endocrine disruptor chemical on the biodiversity of an ecosystem?

(A) Respiratory problems in land mammals
(B) Stress and anxiety in migratory animals due to the noise
(C) Gender imbalances in fish and other species
(D) Birth defects in the human population

42. Many environmentalists propose removing dams from rivers because of their environmental impact. What environmental advantage would occur by removing old dams?

(A) The habitat would be restored to its original condition.
(B) Sediment would be allowed back to above the dam.
(C) Nutrient flow would be reduced below the dam.
(D) Hydroelectric power could now be generated.

43. A family's electricity bill is $160 using 1,600 kWh at the cost of $0.10/kWh. The family is considering ways to lower this cost by replacing their old electric furnace with a newer, more energy efficient one. Their current furnace uses 9,000 watts per hour and runs for three hours each day and the new one uses only 5,000 watts per hour. How much money per month (30 days) will the family save assuming the time the furnace will run stays the same?

(A) $15 per month
(B) $36 per month
(C) $360 per month
(D) $150 per month

44. The stratospheric ozone layer is approximately 30 miles above the Earth and is responsible for protecting the Earth from harmful UV-C radiation. What is the human health benefit from the protective stratospheric ozone layer?

(A) Cases of asthma and emphysema are reduced.
(B) Cases of insect vector diseases are reduced.
(C) Cases of nervous system poisonings are reduced.
(D) Cases of skin cancer are reduced.

45. In 1996 leaders from around the world met in Montreal, Canada, and banned chlorofluorocarbons (CFCs). Why did these world leaders want to ban CFCs?

(A) CFCs are known carcinogens.
(B) CFCs destroy ozone in the stratosphere.
(C) CFCs are mined in fragile ecosystems and destroy habitats.
(D) CFCs are harmful organophosphates that bioaccumulate up the food web.

46. The greenhouse effect is a process that occurs when gases in Earth's atmosphere trap the sun's heat. This is important to life on Earth. Which of the following is one of the main greenhouse gases?

(A) Nitrogen
(B) Argon
(C) Water vapor
(D) Hydrogen

47. The map below shows where huge floods may be normal by 2050. Which of the following would be an expected effect of climate change?

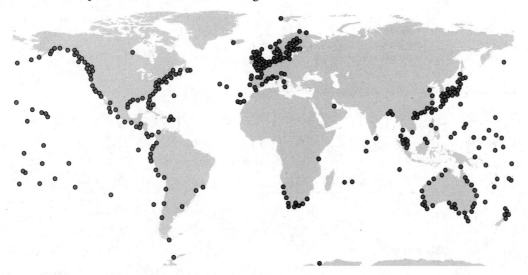

(A) Coastal populations will be displaced.
(B) Greenland will have extensive habitat loss.
(C) Invasive species will become a larger concern in Africa.
(D) Island nations will need to switch to renewable energy.

48. A local forest has had a large wildfire go through it with many plant species burned. A scientist goes back three years later to discover grasses, bushes, and even small trees are thriving. What can the scientist determine about the forest?

(A) The forest was a former tree farm with one monocrop.
(B) The forest had a high species diversity before the fire.
(C) The forest had a low species diversity before the fire.
(D) The forest was part of a coniferous forest biome.

49. The graph below shows the population density, deforestation, and soil erosion associated with long-term Maya settlement in the Peten lowlands.

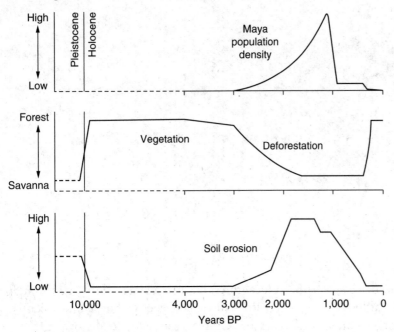

Which of the following can you determine from the data?

(A) The Mayans were hunter/gatherers.
(B) Soil erosion is directly proportional to deforestation.
(C) As the Mayan population increased, they planted large areas of forests.
(D) As the Mayan population increased, environmental damage occurred.

50. The graph below shows the effects of climate change on birds. Which of the following can you derive from the graph that demonstrates how birds have adapted to their environment from 1966 to 2013?

Change in Latitude of Bird Center of Abundance, 1966–2013

(A) Birds have begun breeding with different species.

(B) Birds have bred and increased in number.

(C) Birds have moved an average of 20 to 60 miles north.

(D) Birds have reacted to climate change by eating different food sources.

51. A scientist is studying the number of species on a particular island chain. Island A is 20 km from the mainland, island B is 50 km from the mainland, island C is 75 miles from the mainland, and island D is 150 km from the mainland. The scientist notices that there are many fewer species on island D than on any of the other islands. What could the scientist conclude as the reason for this?

(A) Island D was hit by a large hurricane in the last century.

(B) Island D had less species able to travel the 150 km from the mainland.

(C) Island D is a larger island.

(D) Island D has no native plants on it.

52. A group of students notice that the playground near the local elementary school is experiencing a large amount of runoff, which is not allowing the rainfall to soak into the soil. They design an experiment to test the best ways to increase infiltration and limit runoff. Which of the following would be the likely results of this experiment?

(A) Covering the land with nonporous asphalt will increase infiltration.

(B) Covering the playground with an impermeable rubber mat will decrease injury and increase infiltration.

(C) Covering the playground with permeable pavement like gravel will increase infiltration.

(D) Removing all plants, trees, and shrubs that use water will increase infiltration.

53. Chinese farmers have been using rice terraces since ancient times. This method of growing rice on hilly and mountainous land has continued into modern day. What is one environmental benefit of this practice of rice terracing?

(A) Terracing limits soil erosion.
(B) Terracing allows for larger profits.
(C) Terracing increases overgrazing.
(D) Terracing decreases the need for pesticides.

54. The image below shows how floods will increase and impact coastal areas over the next 50–100 years. What is the environmental cause of this increase in coastal flooding?

Amplification of Moderate Floods

(A) Deforestation
(B) Habitat loss
(C) Overharvesting
(D) Climate change

55. According to the U.S. National Oceanic Atmospheric Administration (NOAA), the temperature in the upper few meters of the ocean has increased by approximately 0.13°C per decade over the past 100 years. Which of the following is the primary reason for this increased ocean temperature?

(A) Increased El Niño–Southern Oscillation events in the past century
(B) Increased greenhouse gas emission causing global temperatures to rise
(C) Decreased albedo effects
(D) Decreased solar activity in the form of solar flares

56. Kudzu is an invasive vine plant to North America that is native to eastern Asia, Southeast Asia, and some Pacific Islands. Kudzu smothers other plants and trees under a blanket of leaves, blocking all sunlight and eventually killing the native plants. Some environmentalists have suggested looking at economic means of controlling the kudzu. Which of the following would be an example of an economic means of solving this environmental problem?

(A) Spray kudzu with a nonpersistent pesticide to avoid the pesticide treadmill.
(B) Encourage chefs to find new ways to harvest and cook kudzu for profit.
(C) Slash and burn large areas to destroy the kudzu and allow native plants to regrow.
(D) Import a predator from Asia that eats kudzu and release it to areas where kudzu is found.

57. According to the U.N., about 61 percent, or 1,393,000 hectares, of Belize is forested but between 1990 and 2010, Belize lost an average of 9,650 hectares, or 0.61 percent, per year, adding up to 12.2 percent of its forest cover, or 193,000 hectares, being lost to deforestation. Which of the following methods would most benefit the Belizean environment and help to mitigate the human impact on forests?

(A) Use and buy wood only from sustainable forestry techniques.
(B) Build large networks of roads through the forest and encourage replanting.
(C) Import fast-growing trees from other countries that can repopulate the forest.
(D) Spray broad-spectrum pesticides to limit damage to trees from pests.

58. Clear-cutting forests can have many environmental effects. Which of the following would be the most immediate environmental effect of clear-cutting a forest?

(A) Decreased stream temperatures around the forest
(B) Decreased flooding around the forest
(C) Increased profits for the lumber industry
(D) Increased soil erosion around the forest

59. A farmer is noticing an increased loss of her crops to a pest. She wants to solve this problem without using even more pesticide, which causes environmental problems. Which of the following would be a good solution for the farmer to employ?

(A) Switch to a less toxic pesticide
(B) Plant monocrops
(C) Plant trees to provide shade to her crops
(D) Plant genetically engineered crops resistant to pests and disease

60. The diagram below shows a thermal inversion over the UK.

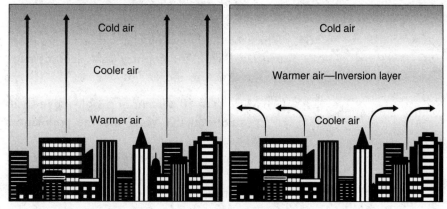

Which of the following would be the most likely result from this temperature inversion?

(A) Sunlight would be diminished for many days.
(B) Temperatures would decrease during the day.
(C) Smog and particulates would be trapped close to the ground.
(D) Tornadoes will form due to the difference in temperatures above the city.

61. Living fences are used in many places as a permanent hedge that is tight enough and tough enough to serve the same functions as a manufactured fence. What would be the environmental benefits of a living fence?

(A) Living fences are cheaper to build than using manufactured wood.
(B) Living fences provide edge habitat that support ecological diversity.
(C) Living fences are never eaten and destroyed by livestock.
(D) Living fences can be invasive.

Use the image below to answer questions 62.

Carbon Cycle

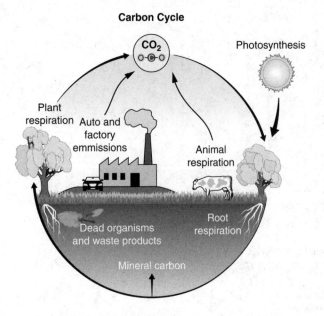

Use the diagram below to answer questions 64–65.

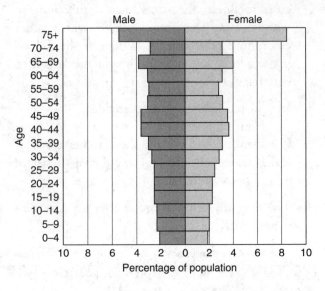

62. Which of the following is true and seen in the image above?

(A) Carbon cycles between cellular respiration and photosynthesis.

(B) Carbon does not have an atmospheric component.

(C) Carbon is found only nonanthropogenically.

(D) Carbon makes up the majority of our atmosphere.

63. Coyotes are native to North America and are highly versatile in their choice of food. Their diet consists of 90 percent meat including bison, rodents, birds, lizards, and snakes. Koalas on the other hand are herbivores with most of their diet consisting of eucalyptus leaves, which are found mainly in Australia. Which of the following best describes these two species?

(A) Koalas are herbivores and coyotes are detritovores.

(B) Koalas are specialists and coyotes are generalists.

(C) Koalas are prey to the predator coyotes.

(D) Koalas and coyotes live in a mutualistic relationship with one another.

64. Which of the following characteristics are most associated with the country that demonstrates the age structure above?

(A) More than 50 percent of people are in their postreproductive years and the population will shrink.

(B) A company looking to profit in this country would want to invest in baby diapers and baby formula.

(C) This country is in the first stage of the demographic transition.

(D) This country lacks universal health care, governmental food benefits, and other support systems for a struggling, poverty-stricken country.

65. Which of the following might be true of the country that demonstrates the age structure above?

(A) There are high infant mortality rates in this country.

(B) A baby boom has increased population size for generations.

(C) Access to education and health care is low in this country.

(D) Women are putting careers before thoughts of marriage and children.

66. Identify the type of plate boundary shown in the image below.

Strike-Slip

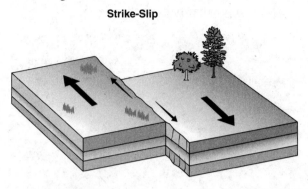

(A) Transform boundary
(B) Divergent boundary
(C) Convergent boundary
(D) Ring of fire

67. Using the diagram below, which area receives the most solar radiation during any time of the year and why?

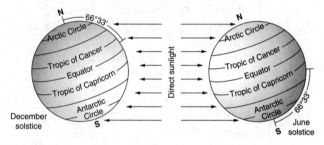

(A) The Arctic Circle because it is located at the North Pole.
(B) The Tropic of Cancer because it is tilted toward the sun during the June solstice.
(C) The equator because it receives the most direct sunlight during all seasons.
(D) The Tropic of Capricorn because it is titled toward the sun during the December solstice.

68. Which of the following is true during an El Niño–Southern Oscillation event in the United States?

(A) It will be colder and drier in Canada.
(B) It will be rainier in California.
(C) The East Coast will experience extreme rainfall events.
(D) There is no relationship between weather and El Niño in the United States.

69. A housing developer has decided to cut down a large part of a forested area to build a neighborhood. A group of students discovers that the plan is to clearcut the entire area to make it cheaper and easier to build homes on. The students want to prove to the developer that clearcutting is going to cause extensive soil erosion. What would be the best way for the students to prove their point to the housing developer?

(A) Take soil samples and test for the amounts of nitrogen, phosphorus, and potassium.
(B) Set up an erosion experiment to show that plants and trees help prevent soil runoff.
(C) Take temperature data around the planned housing area and provide that data to the developer.
(D) Take soil samples to find the amount of sand, silt, and clay and provide that information to the developer.

70. The image below shows the different layers of the atmosphere.

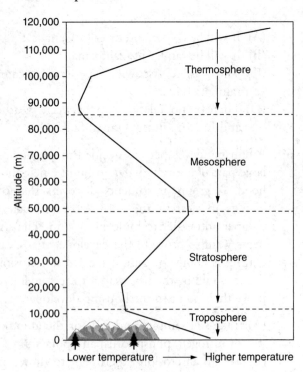

Which layer is where all weather on Earth occurs?

(A) Troposphere
(B) Stratosphere
(C) Mesosphere
(D) Thermosphere

71. What kind of weather pattern would you expect in the circled region below and why would you expect to see that pattern there?

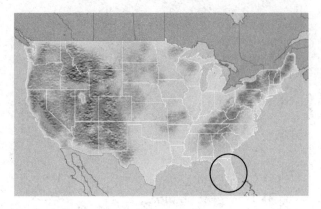

(A) Warm and dry because it is in the southern United States
(B) Cool and wet because of the ocean's impact on all sides
(C) Cool and dry because of the wind patterns from the Coriolis effect
(D) Warm and wet because of the ocean's impact on all sides

72. Which of the following graphs would be indicative of a k-selected species?

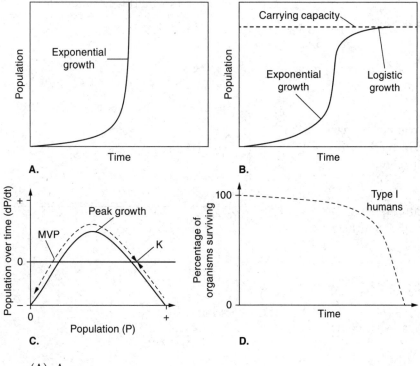

A.

B.

C.

D.

(A) A
(B) B
(C) C
(D) D

73. The image below shows a nuclear power plant. What is the environmental concern that occurs at the area labeled A?

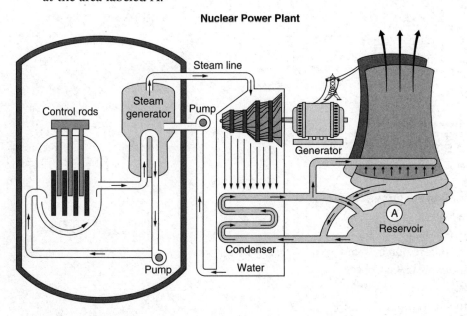

(A) Release of carbon dioxide
(B) Nuclear radiation leaks
(C) Thermal pollution
(D) Production of soot

74. Humans have impacted biodiversity in many ways. For example, by building roads and inhabiting wild areas. Which of the following is the biggest impact of this human activity on biodiversity?

(A) Habitat fragmentation
(B) Overexploitation
(C) Water turbidity in local streams
(D) Climate change

75. Ocean acidification is a local and regional human activity that has global impacts. Which of the following is the cause of ocean acidification?

(A) Generation of nuclear energy
(B) Increased CO_2 levels in the atmosphere
(C) Invasive oceanic species in the Southern Hemisphere
(D) Expansion of the Green Revolution

76. If the graph below showed the numbers of lionfish found in the Western Atlantic Ocean, Caribbean Sea, and Gulf of Mexico, what could we conclude from the data?

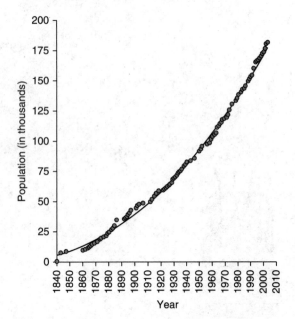

(A) The resources needed for lionfish growth are abundant.
(B) Lionfish are k-strategists.
(C) Lionfish eat phytoplankton, a resource abundant in the Western Atlantic Ocean, Caribbean Sea, and Gulf of Mexico.
(D) Lionfish have reached their carrying capacity.

77. Many fish have many offspring at one time that they do not take care of. Which of the following survivorship curves would fish represent?

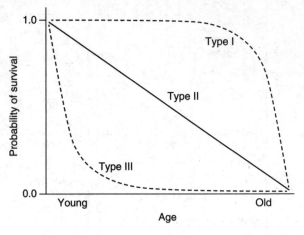

(A) Type I
(B) Type II
(C) Type III
(D) Types I and III

78. A student is on a walk and decides to test some of the soil he finds. After testing he discovers it is 40 percent sand, 30 percent silt, and 30 percent clay. Which of the following soil types would the student classify the soil as?

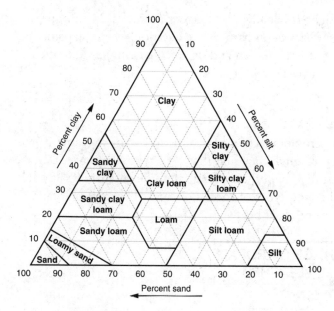

(A) Silty clay
(B) Clay loam
(C) Sandy clay loam
(D) Clay

79. Which of the following would be classified as a provisioning ecosystem service?

(A) Food
(B) Carbon sequestration
(C) Habitats for species
(D) Tourism

80. Which of the following explains why ecosystems have very few tertiary consumers compared to the numbers of primary and secondary consumers?

(A) The net primary productivity levels in areas with tertiary consumers is low.
(B) Ecological tolerance demonstrates less tertiary than primary consumers.
(C) Bioaccumulation of persistent pesticides up the food chain limit the numbers and distribution of tertiary consumers.
(D) Energy is lost as heat as you move upward to higher trophic levels and therefore cannot support as many tertiary consumers.

STOP. End of Section I.

AP Environmental Science Practice Exam 2
Section II: Free-Response Questions

Time: 70 minutes

Directions: Answer all three questions, which are weighted equally; the suggested time is 23 minutes for answering each question. Your answers should completely answer all parts of the question. Where explanation or discussion is needed, support your answers with relevant information and/or specific examples. If a calculation is required, clearly show all your work and how you arrived at your answer.

1. **Design an investigation.**

   A group of students have a concern about coral bleaching and want to know if it is linked to climate change. In their research they find that coral typically grows at 27°C. They set up an experiment to test their hypothesis. To do this, they prepare 6 salt water tanks to include the same number and types of species of coral. They set each tank at a different temperature as seen in the chart below:

TEMPERATURE	PERCENTAGE OF CORALS THAT ARE BLEACHED
26°C	0%
27°C	0%
28°C	10%
29°C	22%
30°C	45%
31°C	80%
32°C	82%

   (A) Propose a testable hypothesis for this experiment.
   (B) **Identify** the control in this experiment.
   (C) **Identify** the dependent and independent variables in this experiment.
   (D) What could the students do to improve the validity of the experiment?
   (E) An increase in atmospheric temperatures is one reason oceans are warming. Identify ONE cause of higher atmospheric temperatures and for that describe a way we could stop or slow atmospheric warming.
   (F) Identify TWO renewable energy resources and for one that you identify describe either a positive or a negative effect of that resource.

2. **Analyze an environmental problem and propose a solution.**

Science Daily published an article titled "U.S. and Canada Have Lost More Than 1 in 4 Birds in the Past 50 Years." The article states "A study published today in the journal *Science* reveals that since 1970, bird populations in the United States and Canada have declined by 29 percent, or almost 3 billion birds, signaling a widespread ecological crisis. The results show tremendous losses across diverse groups of birds and habitats—from iconic songsters such as meadowlarks to long-distance migrants such as swallows and backyard birds including sparrows."

(A) **Identify** ONE factor that could have led to an almost 30 percent decline of bird populations in the United States and Canada and **explain** how that factor might impact bird populations?

(B) While bird populations are declining, there have been some success stories. **Identify** ONE example of a bird species whose population has recovered and explain what was done to protect that species.

(C) **Identify** THREE characteristics of an organism that would make them particularly vulnerable to becoming threatened or endangered.

(D) Make ONE economic or ecological argument for protecting endangered/threatened species and make ONE economic or ecological argument against protecting them.

(E) **Identify** ONE ecological service that animals provide.

3. **Analyze an environmental problem and propose a solution using calculations.**

The average American produces 4.3 pounds of waste per day, adding up to a total amount of waste by Americans of 220 million tons per year. Much of the waste produced in the United States ends up in landfills, which can generate large amounts of methane. In fact, landfills are the third-largest source of anthropogenic methane in the United States, accounting for approximately 14.1 percent of methane emissions. One ton of methane causes 72 times more warming than does one ton of carbon dioxide.

One way to lower the environmental impact of landfill methane is to capture the methane to produce electricity. One million tons of landfill waste per day can generate .78 MW of electricity.

(A) How many pounds of waste would an average family of 4 produce per year?

(B) If all trash produced in a year in the United States were put in landfills and converted into electricity, how much electricity could be generated?

(C) Methane has a high warming potential. **Identify** TWO environmental problems associated with a warmer environment and for each **explain** how that could cause harm to biodiversity.

(D) **Identify** ONE gas other than methane and carbon dioxide that contributes to climate change and for the one you identified **describe** a human activity that leads to its release.

STOP. End of Section II.

Answers and Explanations for the Multiple-Choice Questions

1. **B**—Desert. This biome covers about 20 percent of the land on our planet and is characterized by less than 50 cm of rain a year. Trees are usually absent and there is little vegetation.

2. **D**—According to the author, "Sometimes when corals become stressed, as is the case when ocean temperatures become too warm, the polyps expel their algae cells and the colony looks white in appearance."

3. **A**—Mutualism is when both species benefit from the relationship. The coral provides the algae with a place to live and the algae produce oxygen for the coral and remove wastes.

4. **B**—The 10 percent rule is the idea that as usable energy moves up the pyramid much of it is "lost" to the laws of thermodynamics.

5. **C**—Plant roots hold in soil and prevent erosion, so by planting plants you would help remediate the problem of soil erosion.

6. **A**—Fish ladders would allow fish to bypass the dam that would otherwise be blocking their migration path.

7. **D**—Carrying capacity is the number of organisms an ecosystem can support over time. This is often shown in a graph like the one below. The population of wildebeests, once established, fluctuates around the 1,200,000 mark. The carrying capacity of wildebeests is about 1,200,000.

Population Changes and Carrying Capacity

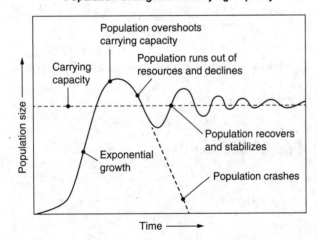

8. **C**—Herbivores eat grass. If there were a severe drought that killed off all the grass, we would have a loss of the herbivore, among them the wildebeests.

9. **B**—Person 5's greatest ecological footprint is in food and housing, so by lowering both of these he would lower his ecological footprint the most.

10. **A**—Eating less meat has some big environmental advantages. It takes almost 20 times less land to get the same number of calories from growing plants rather than animals.

11. **D**—Nonpoint source pollution is pollution that can't point to just one particular source. Acid rain on a forest is caused by numerous things.

12. **C**—Endocrine disruptors are chemicals that can mimic hormones in organisms and can come from a variety of things, such as pesticides, food, and pharmaceuticals.

13. **B**—This type of smog occurs in warm places that have a lot of people, cars, factories, power plants, etc. It is formed when volatile organic hydrocarbons and nitrogen oxides, along with heat and sunlight, mix, causing pollution. The hydrocarbons and nitrogen oxides peak on the chart between hours 8 and 10.

14. **A**—Photochemical smog can cause eye irritation and respiratory illness. It also produces ground-level ozone.

15. **A**—40 kW/1000 × 100% = 4%

16. **D**—See picture below.

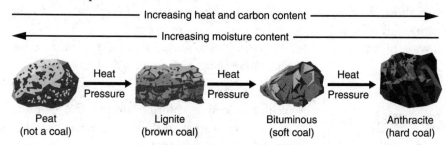

17. **B**—If you slow the speed or turn off the turbines during migration periods, you would harm fewer birds, butterflies, and bats because they could fly through the blades without being harmed.

18. **C**—The graph is showing the increase in temperatures on Earth due to climate change.

19. **C**—As temperatures increase, sea levels are rising, a fact that would harm the organisms living in the estuaries and coastlines.

20. **B**—Burning fossil fuels emits carbon dioxide, and carbon dioxide increases global temperatures. To stop the increase of global temperatures, we could limit the burning of fossil fuels.

21. **A**—*Eutrophication* is the term used to describe a body of water that has so many nutrients (fertilizers like nitrogen and phosphorus) that the nutrients have "fertilized" the algae that live in the water. Then, when the algae die, microbes like bacteria and fungi that live in the water eat the algae and in doing so use nearly all of the dissolved oxygen in the water. This creates what is called a dead zone.

22. **D**—Agriculture uses a great deal of nitrates and phosphates to fertilize crops so that they grow faster, larger, etc. If the student is trying figure out who is causing the eutrophication, then starting by looking at farming would make the most sense.

23. **C**—Since plants use nitrates and phosphates, if the student wants to limit the amount of nitrates and phosphates going into the lake, she could plant plants around the lake. The plants could take up the nutrients before they enter the lake.

24. **A**—The environmental problem of aquaculture is that the large numbers fish or shellfish can produce huge quantities of waste (fish poop, excess fish food, etc.), which can pollute the river, lake, or ocean.

25. **C**—The oceans absorb almost a quarter of global CO_2 emissions we create from burning fossil fuels and deforestation. As the CO_2 enters the ocean, it causes the ocean to become more acidic (lower pH), causing ocean acidification.

26. **B**—In the greenhouse effect, solar radiation (infrared) from the sun is absorbed by Earth's surface. It warms the surface, and some is reflected back to space. The main gases that are in our atmosphere that absorb the solar radiation are carbon dioxide, methane, water vapor, nitrous oxide, and chlorofluorocarbons.

27. **D**—The chart shows that nearly 30 percent of amphibians are listed as endangered, critically endangered, or vulnerable. So, they must have the greatest threats to their environment.

28. **A**—During both stages 1 and 4, births and deaths are the same, so the population is not growing.

29. **C**—In stages 2 and 3, births are greater than deaths, so the population is growing.

30. **B**—Biological methods like predator bugs that a farmer buys to eat the pests (biocontrol) or rotating crops to reduce pests are examples of integrated pest management.

31. **D**—Rising, moist air that goes off in both directions and sinks at 30° north and south. This sinking, dry air is where Earth's major deserts are found.

32. **A**—The phosphorus cycle is a slow cycle and it does not have an atmospheric form. Phosphorus is only found on the land and in the water.

33. **B**—70/4 = 17.5 years to double

34. **B**—The LD_{50} is 61 mg/kg × 0.30 kg (the weight of the mouse).

35. **C**—In almost every region listed, the proportion of the population using solid fuels is going down. So, indoor air pollution is dropping.

36. D—In eastern sub-Saharan Africa the line has stayed relatively flat over the years shown in the graph and it still above 90 percent. This tells us that the use of solid fuels is still widespread.

37. A—Oil rises from .5 Gtoe to 5.5 Gtoe, or a difference of 5 Gtoe.

38. B—250 million tons × .31 = 77.5 million tons

39. A—DDT (dichlorodiphenyltrichloroethane) is a synthetic organic chemical used as an insecticide and PCBs (polychlorinated biphenyls) are used as dielectric and coolant fluids in electrical equipment. POPs do not break down in the environment very quickly and can build up in the tissues and fat of animals. This bioaccumulation of POPs in an organism's tissues can be toxic. Because POPs don't break down, and because animals migrate long distances, and because these chemicals can travel very far in wind and water, there are POPs in almost all parts of our planet.

40. D—Volcanoes are geologic features that emit CO_2 and particulates.

41. C—Endocrine disruptors have been linked to developmental, reproductive, neural, immune, and other problems in animals. A gender imbalance would be a reproductive example.

42. A—Since dams can cause habitat damage by flooding an area that used to be land and lowering the water flow downstream, by removing the dam you could begin to restore the natural habitat.

43. B—

9000 Watts	1 kW	$.10	3 hours	30 days
	1000 Watts	1 kWh	1 day	1 month

= $81 month

5000 Watts	1 kW	$.10	3 hours	30 days
	1000 Watts	1 kWh	1 day	1 month

= $45 month

$81 − $45 = $36 per month savings

44. D—More UV light is able to get through the stratosphere and to the surface of the Earth. UV light is dangerous because it can damage the DNA in skin cells, lead to skin cancer, cause cataracts, cause premature aging, and suppress the immune system.

45. B—The sun's UV energy breaks up CFC molecules, releasing chlorine atoms. The chlorine atoms then react with the O_3 molecules breaking up the O_3 and taking one oxygen atom to form chlorine monoxide and O_2. Ozone absorbs UV light, so CFCs lower the stratosphere's ability to absorb UV light.

46. C—The main gases in our atmosphere that absorb the solar radiation are carbon dioxide, methane, water vapor, nitrous oxide, and chlorofluorocarbons.

47. A—Sea levels are rising, which can flood coastal communities, displace coastal populations, and impact ocean organisms that are subsequently too deep to photosynthesize.

48. B—Species diversity is the number of species and abundance of each species that live in a particular community. Species diversity helps to contribute to the health of an ecosystem because each species has an important role in this heath. Since the area rebounded quickly, it can be concluded that it has a high species diversity.

49. D—As the Mayan population increased, so did soil erosion and deforestation.

50. C—The bottom line shows that birds have moved 20 miles and the top line shows they have moved 60, so they have moved somewhere between 20 and 60 miles north.

51. B—Island biogeography is the study of the species and the distribution that would occur on each of these islands. The theory states that islands closer to the mainland (where the animals/plants have moved from) and/or larger islands will have more species than islands farther away or smaller.

52. C—Covering the playground with permeable pavement like gravel will increase infiltration and allow more water to seep into the soil.

53. A—Terracing is similar to contour plowing, but when an area is very hilly or mountainous, the farmer will make step-like rows and plant the crops on these rows. This helps to reduce soil erosion.

54. **D**—As climate change is melting the ice caps and causing thermal expansion of ocean waters, coastal cities could have increased flooding.

55. **B**—Our oceans get warmer because of climate change from greenhouse gases.

56. **B**—If invasive species could become profitable, such as becoming a form of food, then people would make sure to collect them, helping lower their numbers.

57. **A**—If we stopped clear-cutting forests and instead used sustainable forestry methods, we would decrease the problem of deforestation.

58. **D**—Trees have roots that hold in the soil. When we clear-cut areas of land, we expose this soil, leaving it vulnerable to erosion and/or flooding. Furthermore, this soil may end up in a river, lake, or stream, leading to problems there.

59. **D**—Genetically engineered crops are grown so the pests don't or can't harm them. This has pros and cons. The pros are increased profits for farmers, helping to keep the cost of food afford-able, and reduced need for pesticides. Reduced use of pesticides is good for the environment since pesticides can often harm other organisms that they weren't designed to harm. However, the con is loss of diversity in the crop.

60. **C**—This is a weather condition when warm, less dense air moves over dense, cold air. Because of the thermal inversion, the dense air traps pollu-tion, particularly smog and particulates, near the ground and it can't "escape" to space.

61. **B**—Living fences are used instead of regular fences. These trees or hedges can become a bio-logical corridor for animals to use as a habitat or a means of travel.

62. **A**—Photosynthesis and cellular respiration are how carbon cycles in living things and is known as short-term cycling.

63. **B**—Specialists are organisms that require par-ticular habitats, food, etc. An example of a specialist species would be a koala who can only eat eucalyptus. If the habitat where koalas live is damaged and their specific food source is gone, this could be particularly devastating to the pop-ulation of koalas. Generalists are the opposite.

They can live in many different places and eat many different things. Generalists are less likely to be impacted by an environmental event.

64. **A**—The population will shrink. Countries like Germany, Bulgaria, and Russia are considered negative- or declining-growth countries because more than 50 percent of the population is past the age of reproduction.

65. **D**—In these countries, parents may only be having one child, so when mom and dad die the family (and the country) get smaller. Often, this is because women are working and putting off having children until they are older. This limits the number of children women can have because their reproductive age is limited.

66. **A**—Transform boundaries are where the plates slide side-by-side one another. The most common example you will be familiar with is California's San Andreas fault. Earthquakes are common along these faults as the plates move past each other and stored energy is released as energy of motion.

67. **C**—The equator is always nearly directly facing toward the sun.

68. **B**—The impact of El Niño includes changes to rainfall, wind, and ocean circulation patterns. It is particularly rainy during an El Niño year on the West Coast of the United States and South America.

69. **B**—Since trees have roots that hold in the soil, when we clear cut large areas of land we expose this soil, leaving it vulnerable to erosion and/or flooding. This soil may end up in a river, lake, or stream leading to problems there.

70. **A**—All weather on our planet is found in the troposphere. No weather phenomenon happens in any other layer of the atmosphere.

71. **D**—The area circled is Florida, which is sur-rounded on all sides by the ocean. This regulates the temperature and keeps it relatively warm and wet all year.

72. **D**—Humans are an example of a k-selected species. The graph shows a Type I survivorship curve, which is indicative of a k-selected species. Almost 100 percent of humans survive child-hood and most humans survive for many years.

73. **C**—Nuclear energy generation produces so much heat that it must be "dumped" into a water source. Thermal pollution is often the result of a nuclear power plant where large amounts of heated water are being dumped into a body of water. The heated water doesn't have to have any pollutants in it, but just being warm can cause problems. This is because warm water can't hold as much oxygen as cold water. The oxygen diffuses out of the water and into the air.

74. **A**—The greatest reason for loss of biodiversity is habitat loss. We harm habitats by cutting down forests, by building roads, and by inhabiting areas where there used to be large areas of uninhabited land (habitat fragmentation).

75. **B**—The ocean absorbs carbon dioxide from the atmosphere. This is caused by the wind producing waves and turbulence, resulting in the water absorbing the carbon dioxide. The oceans absorb almost a quarter of global CO_2 emissions we create from burning fossil fuels and deforestation. As the CO_2 enters the ocean it causes the ocean to become more acidic (lower pH).

76. **A**—The lionfish are growing exponentially, which means that there must be plenty of food and habitat for them so they can keep reproducing until they reach their carrying capacity.

77. **C**—Type III. If they have many babies and don't take care of them, they are indicative of Type III.

78. **B**—To do this, start with sand and find the percentage along the bottom of the triangle, in this case 40 percent, and follow the line that goes up and to the left for sand. Then, move to the right side of the triangle and find the line for silt, in this case 30 percent. Follow this line down and to the left until it intersects the line you found for sand. Then, where they cross, draw a straight line to the left, where you find clay. You should be at the 30 percent line, which is your percentage of clay. Where these three lines intersected is the type of soil you have. In this case, clay loam.

79. **A**—Provisioning ecosystem services are things like food and clean water.

80. **D**—The 10 percent rule is the idea that as usable energy moves up the pyramid much of it is "lost" to the laws of thermodynamics. The first law of thermodynamics states that energy cannot be created or destroyed but the second law states that it can be transferred or transformed. So, there can't be as many top predators as there are primary and secondary consumers.

Explanations for the Free-Response Questions

1.

(A) (1 point possible) One point for correctly proposing a testable hypothesis. This could have many answers such as an increase in temperature will increase coral bleaching. One testable hypothesis would be that water temperature differences will not affect mortality rates of corals.

(B) (1 point possible) One point for identifying the control would be the temperature coral typically grows at, so the control is the tank at 27°C.

(C) (2 points possible) One point for identifying the independent variable in this experiment is the change in temperature. One point for identifying the dependent variable is the mortality (bleaching) of the coral.

(D) (1 point possible) One point for stating that the students could repeat the experiment many times at each temperature or they could take multiple measurements on an actual coral reef.

(E) (2 points possible) One point for identifying a cause of higher atmospheric temperatures. There are many possible answers, such as burning of fossil fuels, methane release from cattle and landfills, and so on. Another point for describing a way to slow atmospheric warming. Your answer must be a way to stop or slow what you identified as a cause of higher atmospheric temperatures. Ways to slow atmospheric warming include switching to renewable energy sources and eating less meat.

(F) (3 points possible) One point each for identifying two sources of renewable energy and one point for describing a positive or negative effect of one of the sources you identified. Possible answers include:

RENEWABLE ENERGY SOURCE	POSITIVE EFFECTS	NEGATIVE EFFECTS
Biomass	Low cost	Produces carbon dioxide, carbon monoxide, particulates, and volatile organic compounds, can lead to deforestation
Solar	No combustion, no air pollution or waste	Expensive, can damage ecosystems
Hydroelectric	No combustion, no air pollution or waste	Destruction of habitats
Geothermal	No combustion, no air pollution	Expensive, not available everywhere, can release hydrogen sulfide
Wind	No combustion, no air pollution or waste	Can disrupt bird and bat migrations

2.

(A) (2 points possible) One point for identifying a factor that could have led to the decline in bird populations. Some answers could include habitat loss, invasive species, pollution, overexploitation, overpopulation of humans, cats, glass windows, and pesticide use. One point for an explanation of how that factor might impact bird populations. A complete explanation of the factor must be included. Answers will vary depending on the factor chosen.

(B) (2 points possible) One point for identifying an example of a bird species whose population has recovered. Possible answers include waterfowl and raptors such as the bald eagle. Other possible answers include piping plovers, purple martin, golden-winged warblers, California condor, whooping crane, brown pelicans, and the Florida scrub-jay.

One point for explaining what was done to protect the species you selected. Answers will depend on the bird chosen but possible answers would be banning DDT and other persistent pesticides, habitat restoration, creating protected areas, using habitat corridors, and promoting sustainable land use practices.

(C) (3 points possible) One point for each characteristic identified, up to three points. There are many reasons but answers could include that endangered species often have specialized feeding behaviors, need specialized food sources, require a large territory, or have limited geographic range or habitat. Some endangered species prey on livestock or people, or compete with humans for space or food—factors which might cause them to be hunted. If a species is exploited for economic value or it has no natural defenses against introduced species, it might be endangered. Other reasons a species could be endangered are it has a limited range of tolerance or it has a small population linked to the lack of genetic diversity. Finally, if the species feeds at high trophic levels or if pollution has caused biomagnification of chemicals in the species, it could be endangered.

(D) (2 points possible) One point for an economic argument FOR protecting a species. One possible answer for protecting threatened or endangered species is the importance of one species to the survival of other species. Other arguments for protecting species are to further genetic diversity, to get products that only the species can provide, and to provide tangible and intangible benefit to humans.

One point for an economic argument AGAINST protecting a species. Arguments against protecting a species is that it is expensive to protect species, that it may protect an animal that preys on livestock, that it may block economic development of a region, and that by protecting one species it might harm other species.

(E) (1 point possible) One point for an ecological service that animals provide. Some answers include food for other species or for humans; pollinators for many types of plant species; detritivores that recycle nutrients; beauty, education, entertainment for humans; and nutrient cycling of things like carbon, nitrogen, and phosphorus.

3.

(A) (2 points possible) One point for a correct setup and one point for the correct answer. $4 \times 4.3 \times 365 = 6,278$ pounds per year

(B) (2 points possible) One point for a correct setup and one point for the correct answer. 220 million $\times$ .78 MW/1 million = 171.6 MW of electricity

(C) (4 points possible) One point each for the two environmental problems identified and one point for a correct explanation of how that problem could harm biodiversity. There are many possible answers. Some answers might include sea level rising, causing a loss of habitat for species living in coastal regions; melting permafrost, which encourages erosion and leads to further methane release; invasive species, who could take over and outcompete with native species; and stronger storms, which can cause a loss of habitat.

(D) (2 points possible) One point for identifying a gas that causes climate change and one point for describing the human activity that leads to the release of the gas. Gases other than methane and carbon dioxide that cause climate change are listed below along with information about human activities that release them.

- Ozone (O_3): Released by vehicle exhaust from internal combustion engines
- Nitrous oxide (N_2O): Released by burning of petroleum products, biomass, and nitrogen-rich fuels (particularly coal); also released by feedlots (CAFO and/or CAFL) and dairy farms
- CFCs (freons), HFCs, and HCFCs: Released through their usage in refrigerators and air conditioners, in foam production, to clean electronics, and formerly as propellants

AP Environmental Science Practice Exam 2
Score Approximation

You can get a rough approximation of what your score on the AP Environmental Science Exam would be. Use this worksheet to compute an approximation of your score.

Section I: Multiple Choice

Determine the number of multiple-choice questions you got right then enter that number below.

Number of questions answered correctly (80 possible)   _____

$\times 1.125$

This is your **Weighted Section I** Score   _____

Section II: Free Response

Award yourself points as determined by the scoring guide given in the explanation for each question.

Question 1 (10 points possible)   _____
Question 2 (10 points possible)   _____
Question 3 (10 points possible)   _____

Add the three scores for the free-response section   _____

$\times 2$

This is your **Weighted Section II Score**   _____

Add your Weighted Section I Score and your Weighted Section II Score.   _____

This is your **Composite Score**.

Score Conversion Chart

COMPOSITE SCORE RANGE	APPROXIMATE AP SCORE
110–150	5
89–109	4
77–88	3
63–76	2
0–62	1

5 Minutes to a 5

180 Activities and Questions in

5 Minutes a Day

Check off each activity as it is completed.

1. ❏	46. ❏	91. ❏	136. ❏
2. ❏	47. ❏	92. ❏	137. ❏
3. ❏	48. ❏	93. ❏	138. ❏
4. ❏	49. ❏	94. ❏	139. ❏
5. ❏	50. ❏	95. ❏	140. ❏
6. ❏	51. ❏	96. ❏	141. ❏
7. ❏	52. ❏	97. ❏	142. ❏
8. ❏	53. ❏	98. ❏	143. ❏
9. ❏	54. ❏	99. ❏	144. ❏
10. ❏	55. ❏	100. ❏	145. ❏
11. ❏	56. ❏	101. ❏	146. ❏
12. ❏	57. ❏	102. ❏	147. ❏
13. ❏	58. ❏	103. ❏	148. ❏
14. ❏	59. ❏	104. ❏	149. ❏
15. ❏	60. ❏	105. ❏	150. ❏
16. ❏	61. ❏	106. ❏	151. ❏
17. ❏	62. ❏	107. ❏	152. ❏
18. ❏	63. ❏	108. ❏	153. ❏
19. ❏	64. ❏	109. ❏	154. ❏
20. ❏	65. ❏	110. ❏	155. ❏
21. ❏	66. ❏	111. ❏	156. ❏
22. ❏	67. ❏	112. ❏	157. ❏
23. ❏	68. ❏	113. ❏	158. ❏
24. ❏	69. ❏	114. ❏	159. ❏
25. ❏	70. ❏	115. ❏	160. ❏
26. ❏	71. ❏	116. ❏	161. ❏
27. ❏	72. ❏	117. ❏	162. ❏
28. ❏	73. ❏	118. ❏	163. ❏
29. ❏	74. ❏	119. ❏	164. ❏
30. ❏	75. ❏	120. ❏	165. ❏
31. ❏	76. ❏	121. ❏	166. ❏
32. ❏	77. ❏	122. ❏	167. ❏
33. ❏	78. ❏	123. ❏	168. ❏
34. ❏	79. ❏	124. ❏	169. ❏
35. ❏	80. ❏	125. ❏	170. ❏
36. ❏	81. ❏	126. ❏	171. ❏
37. ❏	82. ❏	127. ❏	172. ❏
38. ❏	83. ❏	128. ❏	173. ❏
39. ❏	84. ❏	129. ❏	174. ❏
40. ❏	85. ❏	130. ❏	175. ❏
41. ❏	86. ❏	131. ❏	176. ❏
42. ❏	87. ❏	132. ❏	177. ❏
43. ❏	88. ❏	133. ❏	178. ❏
44. ❏	89. ❏	134. ❏	179. ❏
45. ❏	90. ❏	135. ❏	180. ❏

Day 1

When two species have a close long-term interaction with one another, it is known as a symbiotic relationship. Identify and describe the three types of symbiosis.

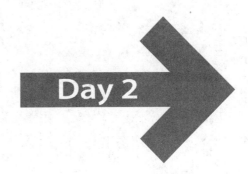

Day 2

Identify the nine major terrestrial biomes, and describe the characteristics of each.

Which of the following is true of aquatic biomes?

    (A)   There are five major types of aquatic biomes.

    (B)   Freshwater biomes make up the majority of the water on our planet.

    (C)   The majority of freshwater on Earth is found in aquifers.

    (D)   Marine biomes take in a large amount of carbon dioxide from our atmosphere.

Day 4

Sketch a rough drawing of the carbon cycle, making sure to include all sources and sinks and adding arrows to show movement of carbon.

Sketch a rough drawing of the nitrogen cycle, making sure to include all sources and sinks and adding arrows to show movement of nitrogen.

Day 6

Sketch a rough drawing of the phosphorus cycle, making sure to include all sources and sinks and adding arrows to show movement of phosphorus.

Day 7

Sketch a rough drawing of the hydrologic (water) cycle, making sure to include all sources and sinks and adding arrows to show movement of water.

Day 8

Define primary productivity, and describe why it is important.

Explain the 10 percent rule and why about 90 percent of the energy in a system is "lost" as heat.

Day 10

Use the following image to answer the following questions:

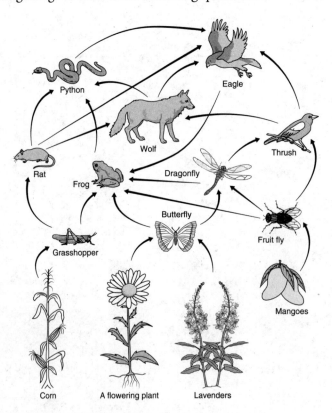

1. Identify a primary producer.
2. Identify a secondary consumer.
3. Identify two organisms that would compete for a common food source.
4. Describe what would happen to the food web if the rat was removed.

Day 11

Using the image of the food web from Day 10, if the flowering plant has 15,000 kilocalories available, identify the kilocalories available for the butterfly, dragonfly, and thrush, and then explain why these organisms would have the amount you identified.

Most apple snails are not native to the United States and can become problems because of how fast they reproduce. In fact, apple snails lay 200 to 600 eggs every four to seven days. However, not all those eggs will become adult snails. List as many reasons as you can think of why these eggs might not become adult snails.

Day 13

Describe the difference between genetic, species, and habitat diversity and give an example of each.

Define specialist and generalist species and explain which would be at a greater risk due to habitat loss.

Day 15

Define each of the four categories of ecosystem services.

Day 16

Describe and give examples of how human activity can harm the different ecosystem services.

One island is 100 kilometers away from the mainland, and another is 500 kilometers away. Both are virtually the same size. Which of the following would be correct about the number of species living on the islands?

(A)   The numbers would be generally the same, but neither island would have species from the mainland.

(B)   There would be more species on the island farther away and fewer species on the island closer to the mainland.

(C)   There would be fewer species on the island farther away and more species on the island closer to the mainland.

(D)   The numbers would be generally the same and would include species from the mainland.

Day 18

What role in evolution does island biogeography play?

The *Monstera* plant has broad, thin leaves. The plant was planted in an arid desert climate. After three days, the leaves started to wilt and turn brown. Describe how the ecological tolerance of the plant made it unsuited for a desert climate.

Day 20

Below is a chart of biomass per hectare in Sequoia National Park. What kind of natural disruption to the ecosystem might have happened in 2012?

2010	2011	2012	2013	2014
380 metric tons per hectare	385 metric tons per hectare	200 metric tons per hectare	220 metric tons per hectare	230 metric tons per hectare

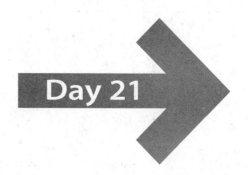

Day 21

Based on the event you described on Day 20, what might be the long-term impact on the ecosystem?

(A) Biodiversity never recovers, and the national park goes from a deciduous forest to a desert climate.

(B) Biodiversity is affected for approximately 18 years but eventually returns to homeostasis.

(C) The climate in the park becomes 2° cooler.

(D) Erosion decreases because of increased sunlight to the forest floor.

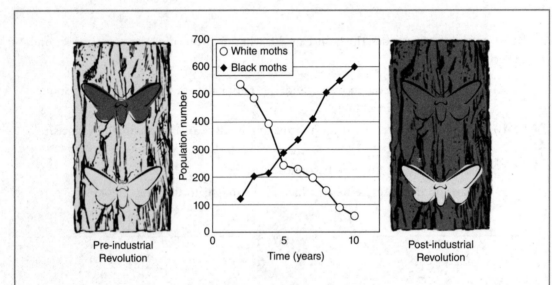

Pre-industrial
Revolution

Post-industrial
Revolution

Describe what happened to moths before, during, and after the Industrial Revolution.

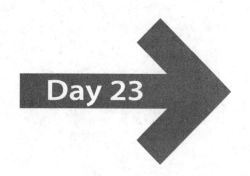

Day 23

In 1500, the Portuguese colonized Brazil. They began deforesting the Amazon rainforest in order to settle the land and grow crops. Below is a graph of the poison dart frog population from 1500 to 1700.

YEAR	1500	1550	1600	1650	1700
No. of poison dart frog species in Amazon rainforest	427	415	370	314	298

According to the data, the poison dart frog is a(n)

(A)   indicator species.

(B)   keystone species.

(C)   generalist species.

(D)   pioneer species.

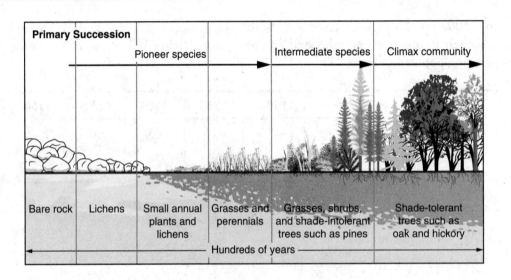

Primary Succession

Pioneer species

Intermediate species

Climax community

| Bare rock | Lichens | Small annual plants and lichens | Grasses and perennials | Grasses, shrubs, and shade-intolerant trees such as pines | Shade-tolerant trees such as oak and hickory |

Hundreds of years

Look at the figure above. Describe what has occurred over time during primary succession and the positive or negative effect it has had on the ecosystem.

Identify the characteristics of generalist species, and give one example of a generalist species.

Day 26

Identify the characteristics of k-selected species, and then give one example of a k-selected species.

YEAR	2016	2017	2018	2019
Population of rabbits	2	12	64	140
Population of kangaroos	2	4	8	12

Identify which is the k-selected species and which is the r-selected species.

Day 28

Which of the following species would not provide extensive parental care to its offspring?

(A)

SPECIES	NUMBER OF FERTILIZED EGGS PER YEAR
Dog	6

(B)

SPECIES	NUMBER OF FERTILIZED EGGS PER YEAR
Cat	8

(C)

SPECIES	NUMBER OF FERTILIZED EGGS PER YEAR
Fish	8,000

(D)

SPECIES	NUMBER OF FERTILIZED EGGS PER YEAR
Koala	2

5 Minutes to a 5

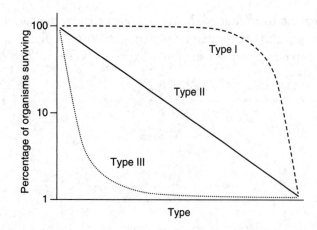

Songbirds have a constant death rate throughout their life. They die at early ages, middle ages, and old age. Using the above figure, what type of survivorship curve do songbirds fit, and are they r-selected or k-selected species?

Day 30

Very few frogs make it to adulthood. Many eggs are eaten by predators, and those that hatch to tadpoles are also often eaten by predators. Using the figure in Day 29, what type of survivorship curve do frogs fit, and are they r-selected or k-selected species?

Almost 100 percent of humans survive to adulthood, and most humans survive many years. Using the figure in Day 29, what type of survivorship curve do humans fit, and are they r-selected or k-selected species?

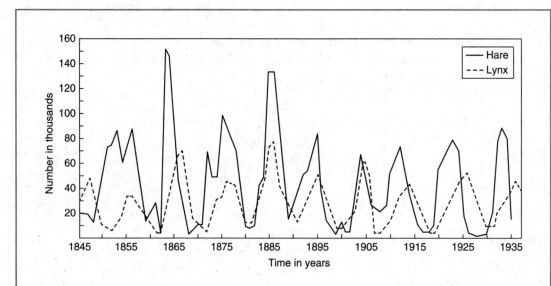

Using the graph above, what is most likely the carrying capacity of the lynx?

(A)   20,000

(B)   50,000

(C)   100,000

(D)   140,000

Using the graph in Day 32, describe what would happen if the lynx went over its carrying capacity.

In 1940, the hare population saw a sudden decline. Using the graph in Day 32, predict what happened next to the lynx population.

Day 35

Using the graph in Day 32, calculate the percent change in population growth of hares from 1860 to 1865.

Using the graph in Day 32, calculate the percent change in population growth of hares from 1885 to 1890.

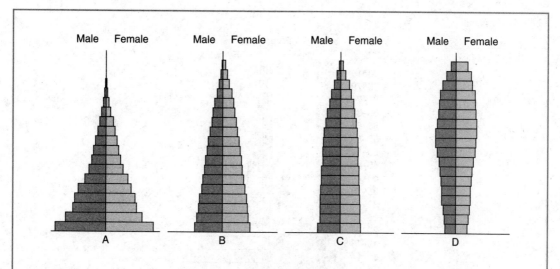

Explain the type of population growth occurring in each of the countries above.

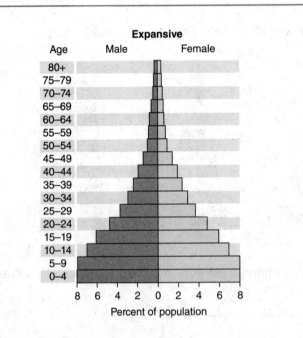

Approximately what percentage of the population consists of children under the age of 15?

COUNTRY	POPULATION (MILLIONS)	BIRTHS PER 1,000 INDIVIDUALS	DEATHS PER 1,000 INDIVIDUALS	TOTAL FERTILITY RATE	INFANT MORTALITY RATE PER 1,000 INDIVIDUALS	LIFE EXPECTANCY AT BIRTH (YEARS)
A	1 billion	12	6	1.6	—	70
B	300 million	11.6	8.5	1.9	6	79
C	25 million	42	22	2.1	25	74
D	79.4 million	90	25	6.4	85	56

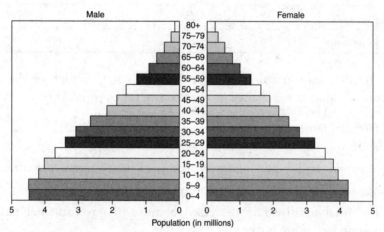

Source: U.S. Census Bureau, International Data Base.

Which of the following countries best represents the population pyramid above?

(A)   Country A
(B)   Country B
(C)   Country C
(D)   Country D

Population Statistics in 2020

COUNTRY	POPULATION (MILLIONS)	BIRTHS PER 1,000 INDIVIDUALS	DEATHS PER 1,000 INDIVIDUALS	TOTAL FERTILITY RATE	INFANT MORTALITY RATE PER 1,000 INDIVIDUALS	LIFE EXPECTANCY AT BIRTH (YEARS)
A	1 billion	12	6	1.6	—	70
B	300 million	11.6	8.5	1.9	6	79
C	25 million	42	22	2.1	25	74
D	79.4 million	90	25	6.4	85	56

The total fertility rate in country A for 1980 was 3.4. Which of the following statements best supports the change in fertility rate for country A?

(A) The total fertility rate remained constant despite the increased access to arable land.

(B) The total fertility rate increased because of better access to contraception.

(C) The total fertility rate decreased because of better access to contraception.

(D) The total fertility rate decreased because of governmental policies that incentivized more births.

Day 41

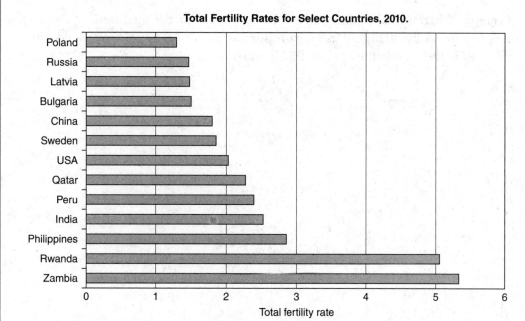

Total Fertility Rates for Select Countries, 2010.

(Bar chart showing Total fertility rate on the x-axis from 0 to 6)

- Poland
- Russia
- Latvia
- Bulgaria
- China
- Sweden
- USA
- Qatar
- Peru
- India
- Philippines
- Rwanda
- Zambia

Total fertility rate

Source: UN World Population Prospects, 2008.

Which of the following statements best describes the chart above?

(A) Countries that are geographically closer to the equator have lower total fertility rates.

(B) Countries that are more developed have higher total fertility rates.

(C) Countries that are in an earlier stage of the demographic transition have higher total fertility rates.

(D) Countries with access to clean water have higher total fertility rates.

Day 42

Country X had a total fertility rate of 4.2 in 1970, but the total fertility rate had dropped to 3.4 by 2020. List as many reasons as you can think of that would cause the drop in the total fertility rate in this country.

Day 43

A country has a population growth rate of 6 percent. How long will it take this country's population to double?

According to some sources, the Earth has lost a third of arable land in the past 40 years. If this trend were to continue, how might this impact the human population?

(A)   More humans occupying arable land would increase farming.

(B)   Infant mortality rates will decline because of better nutrition to pregnant mothers.

(C)   Per capita land consumption will lead to a population growth increase as set forth by the Malthusian theory.

(D)   Less land to grow crops will lead to less food and increased starvation.

CHARACTERISTIC	COUNTRY A	COUNTRY B
Population size	300 million	25 million
Land area	345,000 square miles	600,000 square miles
Infant mortality rate	1.5/1,000	246/1,000
Net immigration rate	0.7/1,000	−1.2/1,000

Describe the characteristics of each country that would tell a scientist if the country was developed or developing.

Sketch a rough draft of the demographic transition model, making sure to label all four stages, and include births, deaths, and population size.

Sketch a picture of a convergent, divergent, and transform plate boundary. After each sketch, provide a summary of what is happening at each plate boundary.

Day 48

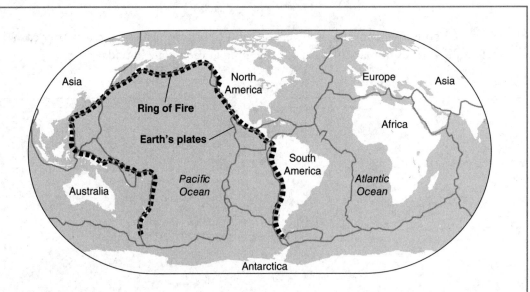

Look at the image above. Describe what is happening at the Ring of Fire, and sketch a sideways view of what this plate boundary would look like both above and below the Earth's surface.

Day 49

Describe what is meant by the term **hot spot**, draw a sketch of a hot spot, and give an example of where we would find a hot spot.

A student wants to test the soil around a riverbank to see if the cattle in the area are leading to the soil being eroded from overgrazing. Design an experiment to test for soil erosion around the riverbank. Make sure to include the dependent variable, the independent variable, the control, the hypothesis, and the method you will use to test your hypothesis (procedure).

A student wants to create an experiment to test the amount of soil contamination caused by a power plant that was built in the 1940s. She needs to collect soil samples from different areas around the power plant to test the amount of lead that leached into the soil. What would be a good control sample for this experiment?

(A)   Soil taken from under a tree on the north side of the power plant

(B)   Soil taken from the south side of the power plant

(C)   Soil taken from the same ecosystem that is away from the power plant

(D)   Soil taken at three different times, once in January, once in June, and once in October

A student wants to create an experiment to test the amount of soil contamination caused by a power plant that was built in the 1940s. She needs to collect soil samples from different areas around the power plant to test the amount of lead that leached into the soil. What would be a good dependent variable for this experiment?

(A) Soil taken from the same ecosystem that is away from the power plant

(B) Soil that is taken from the north side of the power plant

(C) A lead sample

(D) A different type of soil from a different ecosystem

Day 53

A student wants to create an experiment to test which type of soil is best for growing a succulent plant. Which of the following would be the dependent variable for this experiment?

(A)   The soil

(B)   The succulent

(C)   The amount of sunlight

(D)   The container the student puts the succulents in

Create a hypothesis for which type of soil you think will be the best for growing a succulent that is found in a desert climate.

(A)   Humus
(B)   Clay
(C)   Sand
(D)   Silt

Look at the following chart. What type of soil would have a high water-holding capacity and low permeability?

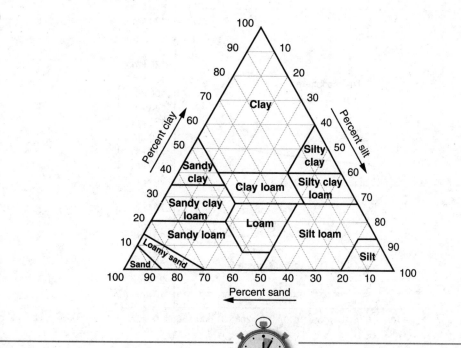

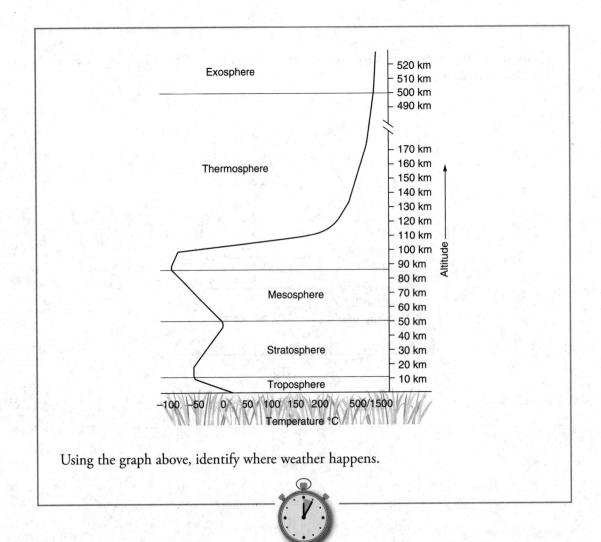

Using the graph above, identify where weather happens.

Day 57

Using the graph in Day 56, between what altitudes does the ozone layer exist?

Look at the following figure. What type of biome would you expect to find at 0° and at 30°? What drives all the global wind patterns?

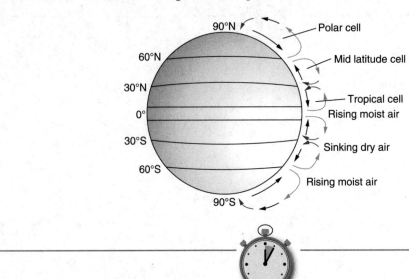

Day 59

Using the figure in Day 58, explain the Coriolis effect.

A housing developer is trying to determine if nonpoint-source pollution will be a problem in the new neighborhood. He is encouraged to study a map of the area to see the characteristics of the watershed. List as many characteristics of a watershed that he should be looking for.

5 Minutes to a 5

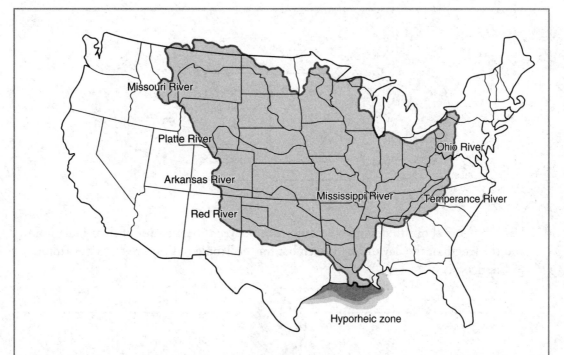

Hyporheic zone

This is a picture of the Mississippi River watershed draining into the Gulf of Mexico. This watershed covers about 40 percent of the United States and impacts the Gulf of Mexico in many ways. Describe some ways this watershed is negatively impacting the Gulf of Mexico, including what is causing the impact and what is occurring in the gulf because of the impact.

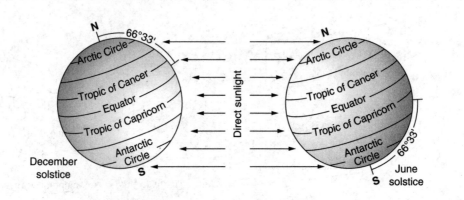

Use the figure above to describe the difference between the amount of solar radiation and the length of the day during December for the Tropic of Cancer versus the Tropic of Capricorn.

Use the figure in Day 62 to describe the difference between the amount of solar radiation and the length of the day during June for the Tropic of Cancer versus the Tropic of Capricorn.

Describe the difference between the amount of solar radiation that is received at the north and south poles compared with the amount of solar radiation that is received at the equator, and explain why this is so.

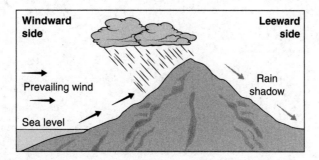

Describe the type of climate you would expect to find on the leeward side of the mountain range in the figure above, and explain why this occurs.

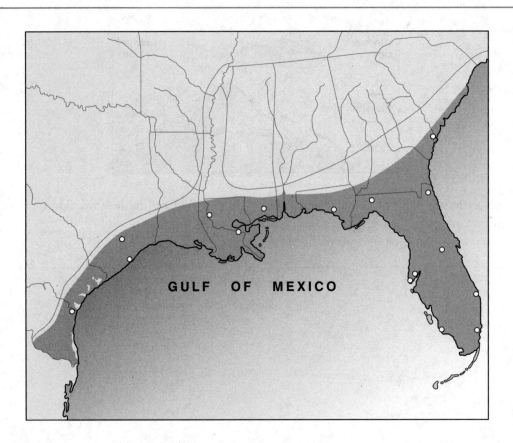

GULF OF MEXICO

Describe the type of climate you would find in the area shown on the map above, and for this area, explain what would be the cause of this climate type.

Describe the kind of weather you would expect to find off the Pacific Coast of South America, such as off the coast of Peru and Ecuador, during an El Niño event, and explain why.

Day 68

Describe the kind of weather you would expect to find in Indonesia during an El Niño event, and explain why.

The ocean is a shared resource. Explain the concept of the tragedy of the commons.

Explain the possible consequences of clear-cutting a forest.

"Private agribusiness has spent billions of dollars in research on pesticide- and herbicide-resistant crops. Much of this new seed technology is protected under U.S. patent law. These laws allow a firm to be the single supplier of these crops. This can come into conflict with traditional farming practices when genetically modified seeds are stored with unmodified seeds in storage silos. Farmers who have traditionally used some of these seeds to plant the next year's crop end up planting seeds owned by the large agribusiness firms and receive the benefit of the technology without paying for it. The agribusiness firms have sued small farmers for this practice at great personal cost to the farmers. The cost to these farmers, however, is far less than the benefit to the firms and consumers. Seed storage and traditional farming practices have to change in order to prevent further conflicts of interest." Which of the following best describes the author's perspective on the conflict between farmers and agribusiness firms?

(A) Farmers should transition from traditional seeds to genetically modified seeds.

(B) Private agribusiness should leave farmers alone so that they can provide food to American homes.

(C) The privatization of U.S. patents has destroyed American farming practices and traditional farming communities.

(D) Seed storage and traditional farming practices need to change in order to promote continued research and development in seed technology.

Describe one characteristic of each agricultural practice, and for that practice, list the environmental damage the practice could cause.

Day 73

Complete the following chart:

IRRIGATION METHOD	ADVANTAGE	DISADVANTAGE
Drip		
Flood		
Furrow		
Spray		

The Ogallala Aquifer is suffering from human impact. Which of the following would be an environmental solution to the problems occurring to this aquifer?

(A) Switch to genetically modified crops that don't require as much pesticide use

(B) Switch to better irrigation methods that conserve water in this region

(C) Increase in the number and area of paved surfaces in the area to increase runoff of groundwater

(D) Addition of CAFOs to help increase plant fertilization by natural processes

A farmer is trying to weigh the benefits and costs of spraying pesticides on his crop. Describe both the benefit and costs of pesticide use for pest control.

Look at the following image from the U.S. Department of Agriculture, and describe the environmental impact of the increase in U.S. per capita availability of beef, pork, chicken, and fish/shellfish from 1910 to 2017.

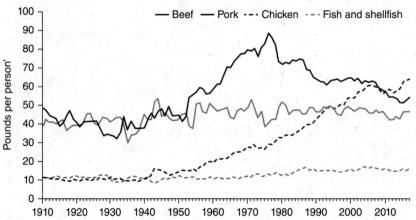

U.S. Per Capita Availability of Beef, Pork, Chicken, and Fish/Shellfish, 1910–2017

'Calculated on the basis of raw and edible meat in boneless, trimmed (edible) weight. Excludes edible offals, bones, viscera, and game from red meat. Includes skin, neck, and giblets from chicken. Excludes use of chicken for commercially prepared pet food.
Source: USDA, Economic Research Service, Food Availability Data.

Look at the following image. Compared with 2008, in 2018, which of the following happened?

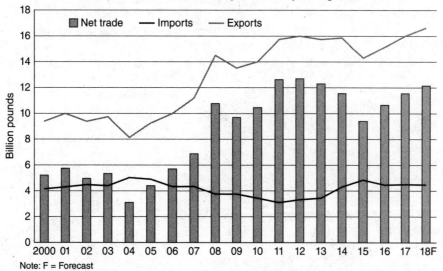

U.S. Production of Meat and Poultry Is Fueled by Strong Global Demand

Note: F = Forecast

Source: USDA, Economic Research Service, Livestock and Meat International Trade and Domestic data.

(A) Imports increased, exports increased, net trade increased.

(B) Imports increased, exports increased, net trade decreased.

(C) Imports decreased, exports increased, net trade increased.

(D) Imports increased, exports decreased, net trade decreased.

Look at the image in Day 77. Explain why net trade decreased in 2015.

Day 79

A family goes down to the beach on a fishing trip and purchases a fishing license. The license has the number of each type of fish that can be caught, the lengths and species of fish that can be caught, etc. What problems is the state trying to solve by issuing such licenses and requirements?

Explain the two ways that mineral ore from the ground is removed through mining, and describe both the positive and negative environmental impacts of each.

What would be some human health concerns of mining practices?

Day 82

Describe the advantages of urbanization.

Day 83

Describe the disadvantages of urbanization.

An ecological footprint compares resource demands and waste production for a person or for a society. The following table is a sample of an ecological footprint for five people in an office. Each number represents the amount of land, measured in hectares (10,000 square meters).

	FOOD (MEAT)	CARBON EMISSIONS	HOUSING	GOODS AND SERVICES	TOTAL
Person 1	1.8	2.9	2.4	1.6	8.7
Person 2	3.2	3	1.6	1.2	9
Person 3	1.4	2.7	2.2	2.0	8.3
Person 4	2.7	3	1.5	2.9	10.1
Person 5	2.8	3	3.4	1.9	11.1

Which of the office workers has the largest ecological footprint, and what change could this person make to lower his or her footprint the greatest?

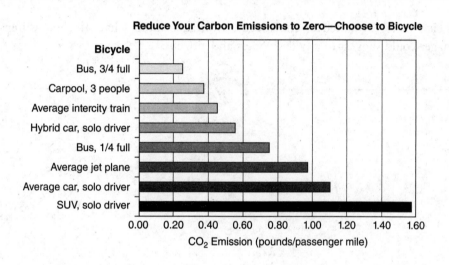

Reduce Your Carbon Emissions to Zero—Choose to Bicycle

Bicycle

Bus, 3/4 full

Carpool, 3 people

Average intercity train

Hybrid car, solo driver

Bus, 1/4 full

Average jet plane

Average car, solo driver

SUV, solo driver

0.00   0.20   0.40   0.60   0.80   1.00   1.20   1.40   1.60

CO_2 Emission (pounds/passenger mile)

Which of the following is best supported by the graph above?

(A) Carpooling with three people emits 1.20 pounds of CO_2 per passenger mile more than an SUV solo driver.

(B) A bus that is a quarter full emits more pounds of CO_2 per passenger mile than the average intercity train and hybrid car solo driver combined.

(C) A bicycle emits 160 percent less CO_2 emissions than an SUV solo driver.

(D) Flying in a jet plane uses less oxygen than driving an SUV alone.

Day 86

If a city manager wanted to encourage less urban runoff, what are some things the manager could suggest to city developers and citizens?

What are the benefits and costs of using integrated pest management?

List as many examples of integrated pest management as you can think of.

Day 89

List as many examples of sustainable agriculture as you can think of.

List the benefits and costs of aquaculture.

Describe why a forestry manager might want to do a prescribed burn in a forest.

Which of the following would be the best example of a way to help mitigate the problems humans have caused for a forest?

(A)   Buy wood products from native forest ecosystems

(B)   Use large amounts of pesticides to control pest species

(C)   Implement reforestation methods in areas where the forest has been harvested

(D)   Allow undergrowth such as shrubs and small trees to grow so that the forest is native and wild

Day 93

Identify what is a renewable and a nonrenewable resource.

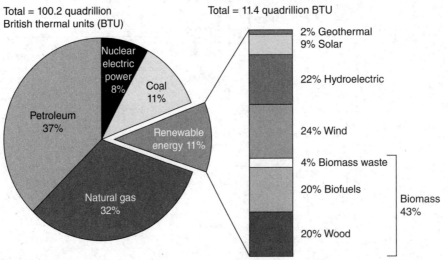

U.S. Primary Energy Consumption by Energy Source, 2019

Total = 100.2 quadrillion
British thermal units (BTU)

Total = 11.4 quadrillion BTU

2% Geothermal
9% Solar

22% Hydroelectric

24% Wind

4% Biomass waste
20% Biofuels
20% Wood

Biomass 43%

Nuclear electric power 8%

Coal 11%

Petroleum 37%

Renewable energy 11%

Natural gas 32%

Note: Sum of components may not equal 100% because of independent rounding.

Source: U.S. Energy Information Administration, *Monthly Energy Review*, Table 1.3 and 10.1, April 2020, preliminary data

How many quadrillion British thermal units (BTUs) of nonrenewable resources were used in the United States in 2019?

(A) 11.022 BTUs

(B) 32.064 BTUs

(C) 88.176 BTUs

(D) 100.2 BTUs

Day 95

A large office building uses 2 million kilowatt-hours of electricity per year. During June, July, and August, the building uses 50 air conditioners to cool the building. Each air conditioner uses 1,000 kilowatt-hours per month. How many kilowatt-hours are used on cooling during June, July, and August? What percent of the annual kilowatt-hour electricity usage is used for cooling during the summer?

A family living in a developing country would probably use which of the following to heat their home or cook their food?

(A) Wood

(B) Natural gas

(C) Oil

(D) Cogeneration

Describe the three types of coal plus peat, and in your description, include the amount of heat and carbon that are produced and the moisture content found in each.

Look at the following diagram and describe what you see in regard to where we would find natural energy resources.

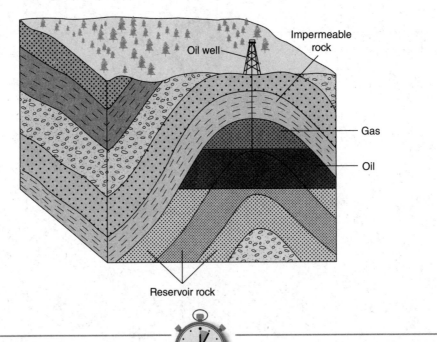

Describe how fossil fuels are used to generate energy. In your description make sure to include all steps from burning the fuel to generating the electricity.

Identify as many environmental problems that result from using fossil fuels to get energy as you can think of.

Look at the following figure. Describe in detail the process of generating energy from nuclear power.

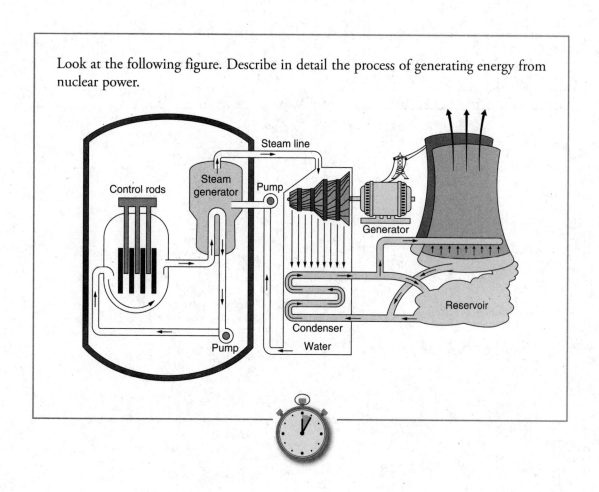

What are the benefits and costs of using nuclear resources to generate electricity?

What are some of the human health and environmental concerns from burning biomass in a home for heat or to cook food?

Describe active and passive solar energy.

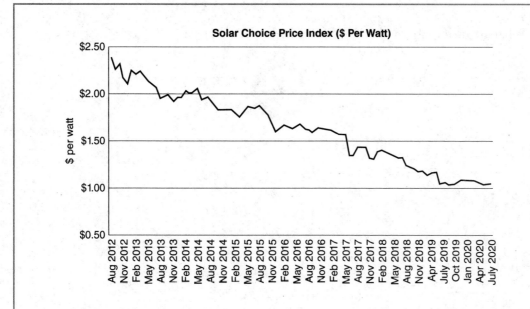

Solar Choice Price Index ($ Per Watt)

Compared with the price per watt in August 2013, the price per watt in July 2020 was

(A)   100 percent less.

(B)   75 percent less.

(C)   50 percent less.

(D)   25 percent less.

What are the benefits and costs of using hydroelectric power?

Explain how a river can be used to generate electricity.

Why would geothermal energy not be useful in all parts of the world?

Explain how geothermal energy can generate electricity.

Describe how a hydrogen fuel cell would power a vehicle.

Day 111

What are the benefits and costs of using hydrogen fuel cells?

Explain how a wind turbine generates electricity.

Day 113

What are the benefits and costs of using wind to generate electricity?

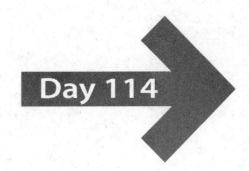

A local utility supplies electricity to households at $0.15 per kilowatt-hour. A family seeking to conserve electricity and save money decides to purchase a more efficient refrigerator. They calculate that both refrigerator compressors run 33 percent of the day. Their original refrigerator used 200 watts of electricity, and their new refrigerator uses only 120 watts of electricity. How much money will the family save in electricity cost per day?

(A) $0.80 per day

(B) $0.60 per day

(C) $0.45 per day

(D) $0.10 per day

The family decides to switch from grid-supplied power from the local utility at $0.15 per kilowatt-hour to active solar power by installing solar panels on their roof and by adding a bank of storage batteries and an inverter in their garage. They calculate that this will cost them an average of $0.10 per kilowatt-hour per year. The initial cost of the active solar power equipment and the labor cost for installation is $20,000. If the family uses an average of 30 kilowatt-hours of electricity per day, about how many years will it take for the family to recoup the cost of the active solar power system?

(A)   400,000 years

(B)   37 years

(C)   13 years

(D)   12 years

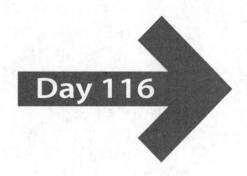

Day 116

Identify all the chemicals that are released when you burn fossil fuels, and for each chemical, identify a way to successfully remove it before it is released from the power plant.

A coal-burning power plant is located in a large city. The citizens of the city are concerned that the power plant might be doing harm to the air. Which would be the best way to test whether the citizens' concerns are valid?

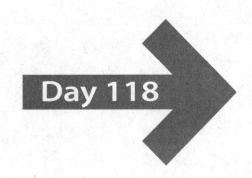

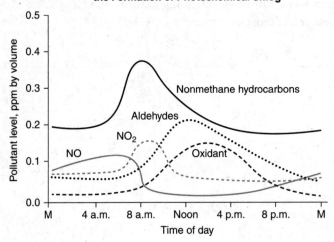

Look at the figure above. Between 4 a.m. and 8 a.m., the amount of nonmethane hydrocarbons present in the atmosphere increases by about

(A)   10 percent.
(B)   33 percent.
(C)   50 percent.
(D)   100 percent.

Day 119

Look at the figure in Day 118. Between 8 a.m. and 4 p.m., the amount of nonmethane hydrocarbons in the atmosphere decreases by about

(A)   10 percent.

(B)   33 percent.

(C)   50 percent.

(D)   100 percent.

Use the following image to describe what happens during a thermal inversion in regard to air pollution.

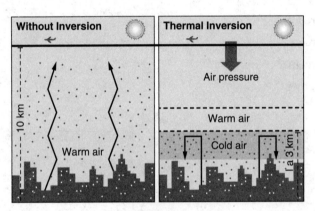

Look at the image in Day 120 and describe what topographic or geographic areas would be more likely to have thermal inversions occur.

A city council is investigating what is causing the high amounts of particulate matter seen in the air. They call in a scientist to set up an experiment to see what could be the sources of the air pollutant. What are all the sources you can think of, both natural and human made, that the scientist might find are causing this problem?

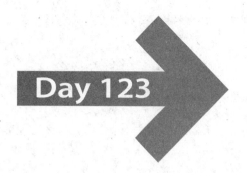
List the sources of carbon dioxide found naturally in our atmosphere.

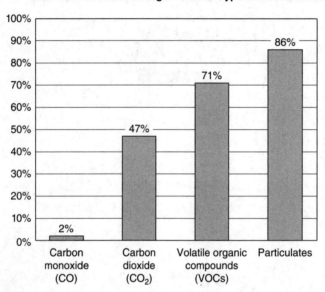

AirAdvice 2004 IAQ Findings: Problem Type and Occurrence

Carbon monoxide (CO): 2%
Carbon dioxide (CO₂): 47%
Volatile organic compounds (VOCs): 71%
Particulates: 86%

Volatile organic compounds (VOCs) have been known to cause eye, nose, and throat irritation, shortness of breath, headaches, fatigue, nausea, dizziness, and skin problems. VOCs also can cause lung problems and damage the liver, kidneys, and central nervous system. The graph above shows the findings for different air pollutants. Where would VOCs most commonly be found in homes and buildings?

(A)   VOCs come from dust from human skin.

(B)   VOC's come from radon gas.

(C)   VOC's come from computer equipment.

(D)   VOC's come from furniture, paneling, and carpets.

5 Minutes to a 5

Day 125

Using the graph in Day 124, what household pollutants would be classified as particulates?

Day 126

For each of the following methods, identify the pollutant that it is targeted to remove.

- Vapor recovery nozzle
- Catalytic converter
- Wet and dry scrubber
- Electrostatic precipitators

Catalytic converters were introduced to the United States in 1975 as a result of Environmental Protection Agency (EPA) rules on toxic emission reductions. The U.S. Clean Air Act required a 75 percent decrease in emissions of all new-model vehicles after 1975, to be carried out with catalytic converters. Which of the following pollutants would be expected to be removed from a vehicle by using a catalytic converter?

(A) Lead

(B) NO_x

(C) Particulates

(D) Soot

Explain how a coal-burning power plant could be causing acid deposition on a lake that is downwind from the plant.

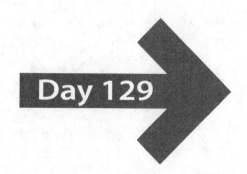

Identify the environmental effects of acid deposition to an area.

"Noise from human activities like planes, machinery, and traffic is thought to be 'a major global pollutant' for many animals. Animals' hearts can beat faster, they might have fewer offspring, and their ability to navigate, to find food, to find mates, and to survive predation are all things that have been linked to noise pollution. This unintended result of human urbanization is having a dramatic effect on the animals we must coexist with, and these noise levels need to be limited." Which of the following would be the author's claim about noise pollution?

(A) Humans should try to limit the amount of noise pollution to lessen the impact on animals.

(B) Human noise has increased over the past 30 years to unreasonable levels.

(C) Animals have learned to adapt to the noise coming from planes, machinery, and traffic.

(D) Animals and humans can't live together in harmony because of human noise levels.

Describe and give an example of a point and a nonpoint source of pollution.

Which of the following is an example of a nonpoint source of pollution that would affect the air quality in a city?

(A)   A person smoking a cigarette

(B)   A coal-burning power plant

(C)   A concentrated animal feeding operation (CAFO)

(D)   Car exhaust coming from cars on highways and city streets

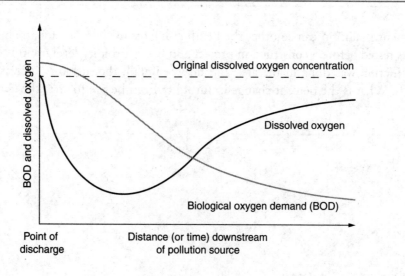

Using the graph above, describe what happens when sewage is discharged into a body of water. Make sure to refer to the graph as you describe what is happening at each point in the graph.

Sediment pollution can smother the benthic organisms living in aquatic habitats. An area is tested before a construction project and has a turbidity level of 50 NTUs. After construction was done in the area and heavy rainfall, the turbidity increased to 350 NTUs. What is the percent change in turbidity from before to after the change?

Day 135

Explain endocrine disruptors and what they can do to animals.

Wetlands and mangroves are being threatened from construction of homes and businesses. Which of the following would be the best way to help minimize this threat?

(A) Plant new mangrove trees along coastlines to prevent further erosion.

(B) Enforce laws that construction projects must include solar panels to meet electricity demands in the area.

(C) Ensure that secondary sewage treatment projects meet U.S. Clean Water Act requirements.

(D) Monitor ocean acidification to prevent further damage to coral reefs.

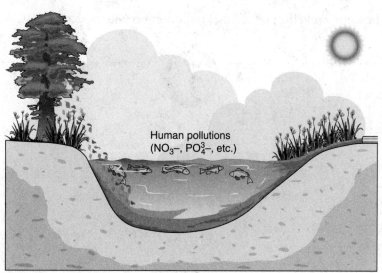

Human pollutions
(NO_3^-, PO_4^{3-}, etc.)

Eutrophic stage

Use the image above to describe what happens to an aquatic ecosystem that is undergoing eutrophication, and explain what can be the environmental result of this.

Day 138

Describe the cause and effect of thermal pollution on aquatic ecosystems.

Day 139

Describe how persistent organic pollutants (POPs) can harm organisms and why they can be a problem far away from where they were generated.

A scientist is studying the effects of persistent substances in predatory birds. He uses the birds as biomonitors of environmental contamination. These predatory birds sit high on the food chain, and the persistent substances accumulate in their bodies and can lead to eggshell thinning and developmental deformities. Which of the following would best identify a testable hypothesis for his study?

(A)   Tissue samples from eagles will have more persistent substances in them than tissue samples from falcons.

(B)   Environmental concentrations of persistent substances are responsible for hormonal disruptions of breeding birds and abnormalities in their offspring.

(C)   Persistent substances are acutely toxic to predatory birds and other species.

(D)   Persistent substances can leak out of dairy farms and agricultural practices, getting into the groundwater and becoming feed for predatory birds.

Describe the difference between bioaccumulation and biomagnification.

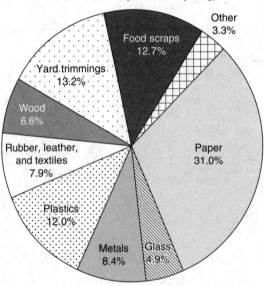

Total MSW Generation (By Material), 2008
250 Million Tons (Before Recycling)

According to the graph above, what three items, if recycled or composted, would prevent the most waste from ending up in a landfill?

(A)   Food scraps, wood, metals

(B)   Paper, yard trimmings, plastics

(C)   Rubber, leather, textiles, yard trimmings, food scraps

(D)   Food scraps, yard trimmings, paper

5 Minutes to a 5

Describe the different methods of solid waste disposal, and for each method, identify an environmental problem of that particular disposal method.

A typical landfill can accept 2,800 tons of trash per day. Typically, 1 million tons of landfill waste can emit approximately 432,000 cubic feet of landfill gas per day, enough to produce 0.78 megawatt of electricity. How many kilowatts of electricity can 2,800 tons of trash produce?

Describe ways we could lower the amount of waste we create.

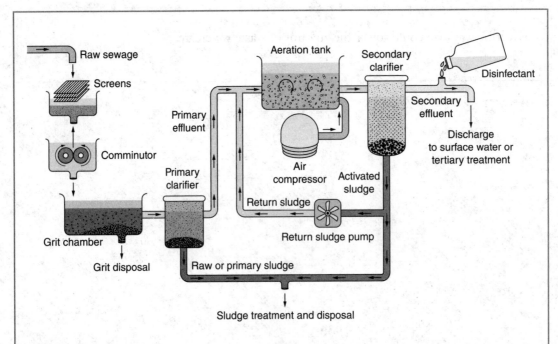

On the diagram above of a sewage treatment plant, label primary, secondary, and tertiary treatments.

The LD$_{50}$ for salt in humans is approximately 12,000 mg/kg. If a person weighs 180 lb and 1 kg = 2.2 lb, how many grams of salt would it take to reach the LD$_{50}$ for a human?

Day 148

Use the following dose-response curve to identify what dose it takes for 50 percent of the organisms to see the pharmacologic response?

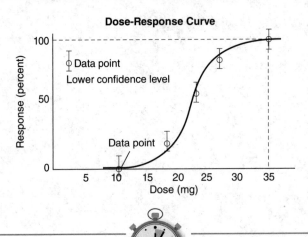

A hospital notices a large number of people coming in and being diagnosed with mesothelioma. The doctor begins investigating and discovers that all the patients worked at the same factory during the same time period. What material would the doctor discover the workers were most likely exposed to during their time at the factory?

Below is a diagram of how the bubonic plague was transmitted. It is estimated that more than 100,000 people died from the bubonic plague in London from 1665 to 1666, and the plague is famous for having killed millions in Europe during the Middle Ages. Using the following diagram as reference, explain how the plague was able to spread so quickly during these times.

How the Bubonic Plague Was Transmitted

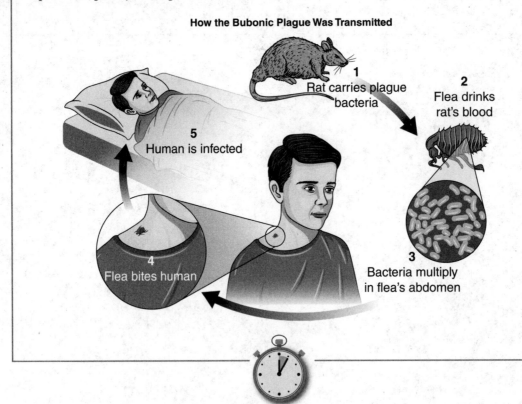

Explain why tropical diseases are spreading into subtropical and temperate areas.

Describe why ozone in the stratosphere is important to life on our planet.

5 Minutes to a 5

Day 153

Identify the human health and environmental effects of too much ultraviolet (UV) light hitting our planet.

Explain, using chemical formulas, the process of how chemicals such as chlorofluoro-carbons break down stratospheric ozone.

Describe the purpose of the Montreal Protocol.

How can we lower the impact of ozone-depleting chemicals?

Identify the gases/chemicals that are the major greenhouse gases.

Describe the greenhouse effect, and explain why it is important for life on Earth.

Why would chlorofluorocarbons (CFCs) be a bigger concern to some scientists who study climate change than CO_2?

Identify the environmental effects of increased greenhouse gases.

Identify the human health threats of increased greenhouse gases.

What impact do greenhouse gases have on the ocean?

Use the following graph to answer the following question.

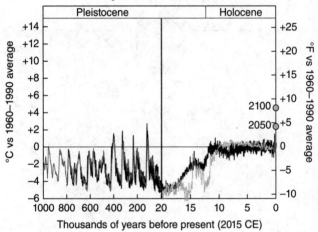

Temperature of Planet Earth

According to the graph, how many degrees above normal are temperatures expected to be in 2100?

According to the graph in Day 163, what have temperatures done from 1,000 years before the present to now?

Day 165

What are some environmental consequences of the change in climate data as seen on the graph in Day 163?

Day 166

Explain why polar regions are seeing a greater effect from climate change than equatorial regions.

Day 167

Describe coral bleaching, including what causes it and what happens to the corals to make them "bleached."

Day 168

What are the environmental effects of a warmer ocean?

Identify the human activities that cause ocean acidification.

Day 170

Describe the environmental effects of ocean acidification.

Day 171

Does increased CO_2 in the atmosphere make the ocean more or less acidic? Explain.

Describe the three ways to control invasive species.

Day 173

Which of the following would more likely pose a threat of becoming an invasive species?

(A)   A keystone species

(B)   A generalist

(C)   A predator

(D)   A k-selected strategist

5 Minutes to a 5

The following chart shows the numbers of a particular species. Which of the following would be true of this species?

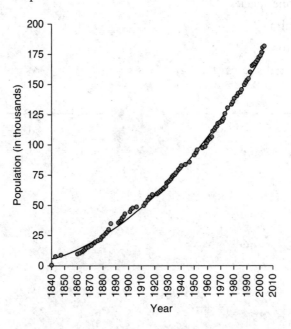

(A)   The species has a predator that is keeping it in check.

(B)   The species is a k-strategist.

(C)   The species is most likely an invasive species.

(D)   Biogeography has occurred on an island.

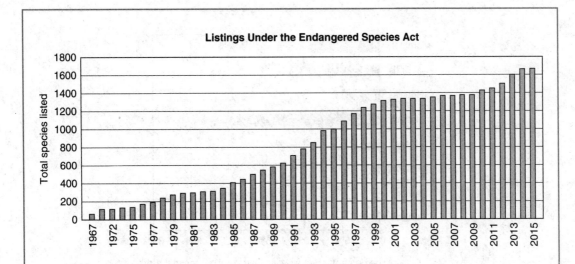

Listings Under the Endangered Species Act

Using the graph above, provide three environmental and/or anthropogenic reasons why the number of species identified has increased since 1967.

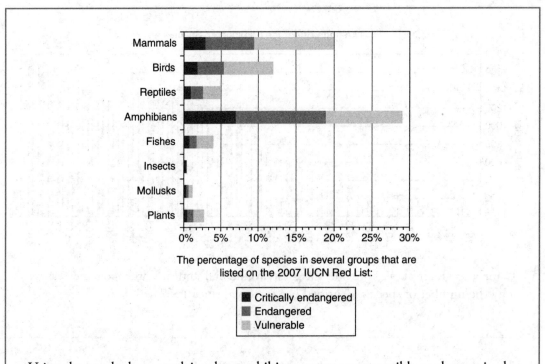

The percentage of species in several groups that are
listed on the 2007 IUCN Red List:

- ■ Critically endangered
- ■ Endangered
- ■ Vulnerable

Using the graph above, explain why amphibians are more susceptible to changes in the environment than other species?

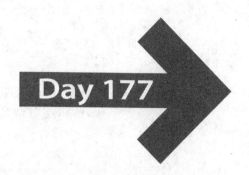

Using the graph in Day 176, explain how species are classified as vulnerable, endangered, or critically endangered?

Day 178

Identify what each letter stands for in the acronym HIPPCO, which shows reasons why we are seeing a decrease in biodiversity.

Day 179

Describe ways that humans can stop the loss of biodiversity we are seeing on Earth.

5 Minutes to a 5

Describe habitat fragmentation, and give an example of ways we are causing this.

Answers

Day 1

In **mutualism**, both species benefit from the relationship. The example you are probably most familiar with is the clownfish and anemone. Thank you, Disney, for *Finding Nemo!* In this common example, the anemone has stinging tentacles that allow it to sting and eat its prey—usually small fish like the clownfish. However, the clownfish has slimy mucus that protects it from the anemone. The clownfish benefits by eating the algae and leftover fish from the anemone, and the anemone benefits by getting more oxygen to its tentacles as the clownfish swims through it.

Commensalism is another relationship between species when one organism benefits and the other neither benefits nor is harmed. One example you might be familiar with is the remora and the shark. The remora uses the shark for both food and transportation. It eats food that is left over from the shark and also has a sucking disk that allows it to adhere to the body of the shark and get a free ride. The shark is not helped or harmed. Another example is cattle egrets and cattle. Cattle egrets eat the insects that the cattle disturb as they forage. The cattle are not helped or harmed, but the cattle egrets benefit.

Parasitism is the final example of symbiosis. In this relationship, one species benefits, while the other is harmed. The common examples here are fleas, mosquitoes, and tapeworms. All these organisms feed off a host and benefit while the host is harmed, some more than others.

Day 2

BIOME	CHARACTERISTIC
Taigas	A coniferous forest (pine trees), with permafrost soil, usually found between the tundra and temperate forests. This is the world's largest land biome.
Temperate rainforests	Found on the coast and consists of both coniferous and broadleaf trees. This biome is characterized by a lot of rain.
Temperate seasonal forests	These forests have all four seasons and are characterized by trees that are green in the spring and summer and turn bright colors of yellow, orange, and red in the fall, losing their leaves in the winter. This biome has warm, wet summers and cold winters.
Tropical rainforests	These forests are found near the equator and stay warm all year long. They are characterized by extreme amounts of rainfall all year. More than half the world's species live in this biome.
Shrubland	This biome is typically found near coasts and has hot, dry summers and cool, moist winters. Shrubland consists of shrubs and short trees with grasses. Some plants are adapted to little rainfall, such as cacti.
Temperate grassland	This biome has many different types of grasses and very few trees because of the low levels of rainfall. The climate varies during the seasons from very cold to very warm.
Savanna	This biome consists of grassland with widely scattered trees found in tropical regions, usually between the desert and rainforest. Wildfires are common, and there are wet and dry seasons.
Desert	This biome covers about 20 percent of the land on our planet and is characterized by less than 50 centimeters of rain per year. Trees are usually absent, and there is little vegetation.
Tundra	This is an extremely cold climate characterized by no trees, little precipitation, short growing seasons for plants and grasses, and poor nutrients.

Day 3

D—Marine biomes take in a large amount of carbon dioxide from our atmosphere.

Marine biomes cover about 75 percent of the Earth's surface and are very important in climate control. They produce large quantities of oxygen and remove carbon dioxide, a major contributor to climate change, from the atmosphere.

Day 4

Here is an example of the carbon cycle. Did you get all the major parts on your sketch?

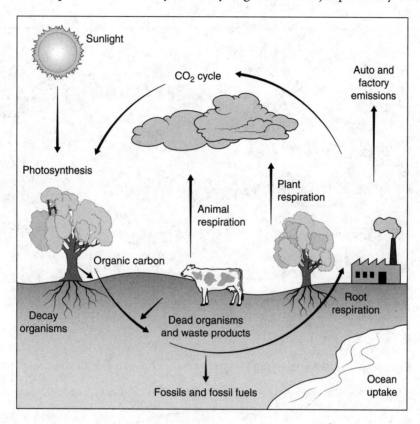

Day 5

Here is an example of the nitrogen cycle. Did you get all the major parts on your sketch?

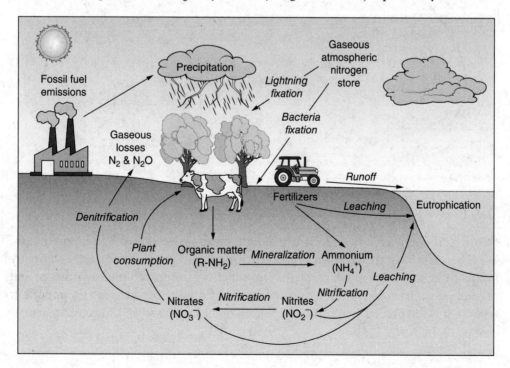

Answers

Day 6

Here is an example of the phosphorus cycle. Did you get all the major parts on your sketch?

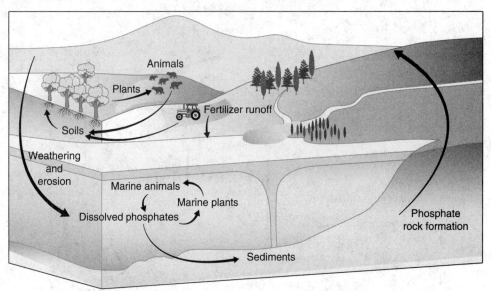

Day 7

Here is an example of the hydrologic (water) cycle. Did you get all the major parts on your sketch?

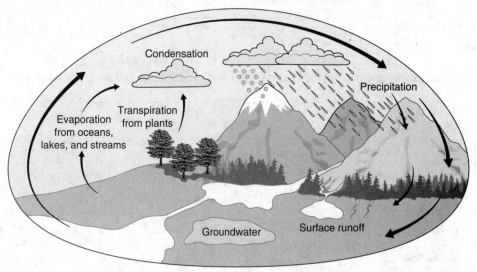

Day 8

Primary productivity is the rate at which food energy is generated by photosynthesis. We can look at both gross and net productivity to see how productive an area is. Primary productivity is the rate at which plants and other organisms can photosynthesize and produce organic compounds in an ecosystem. Primary productivity is important because it is the process that forms the foundation of food webs in most ecosystems.

Day 9

Energy is taken in by the producers in the environment from the sun. This energy decreases as you move up the energy pyramid because the organisms use this energy and release it as heat. As the animal (primary consumer) eats the plant (producer), the primary consumer uses up about 90 percent of the energy it received from the plant. So, when another animal (secondary consumer) eats the primary consumer, it only gets about 10 percent of the energy that was available at the plant level.

Day 10

1. Corn, flowering plant, lavenders, and mangoes are all primary producers.

2. Grasshoppers, butterflies, and fruit flies are all secondary consumers.

3. Frogs and rats both compete for grasshoppers; pythons and wolves both compete for rats; and so on.

4. If the rat was removed, we could have many things happen. For example, because rats eat grasshoppers, then grasshopper numbers might increase because the predator is gone. Because pythons eat rats, python numbers might decrease because the food they eat is gone, etc.

Day 11

If the flowering plant has 15,000 kilocalories available, the butterfly will have 1,500 kilocalories available, the dragonfly will have 150 kilocalories available, and the thrush will have 15 kilocalories available. A plant or primary producer has 100 percent of the energy from the sun. But once a primary consumer eats that plant, it only gets 10 percent of the original energy from the producer, so, in this case, the butterfly will get 1,500 kilocalories. Then the butterfly goes about its day flying around, heating his body, etc., and it uses up 90 percent of the energy it received from the flowering plant, leaving only 150 kilocalories for the dragonfly. Next, the thrush will only get 15 kilocalories because it gets only 10 percent of the energy from the dragonfly.

Day 12

Possible answers include competition between or within species, predators that feed on the eggs or the snails, not enough resources (food, water, etc.), parasites, etc.

Day 13

Genetic diversity—the diversity within a species; example: how you are genetically different from every other human (unless you are an identical twin!). Species diversity—the different species and abundance in a community; example: the deer and bears and grass and trees in a forest. Habitat diversity—the different habitats found in a region; examples are different forests, deserts, grasslands, etc.

Day 14

Specialists are organisms that require particular habitats, food, and so on. Generalists can live in many different places and eat different things. A specialist would be at a greater risk from habitat loss than a generalist because of its narrow niche.

Day 15

Provisioning—services such as food and clean water.

Regulating—services such as plants cleaning the air, bees pollinating flowers, plants holding soil in place to prevent erosion, and the regulation of climate by natural processes.

Cultural—services that are not tangible things that benefit us but rather interactions with nature, such as taking a walk and enjoying what you see or art that comes from looking at nature, and so on.

Supporting—these are harder to understand but are the ecosystem services that support all others, such as producing oxygen, water cycling, and so on.

Day 16

Humans can impact ecosystems in many ways. Things such as climate change, pollution, resource exploitation, introducing species into nonnative environments, mining, loss of habitat, and so on can harm ecosystem services. If something a human does impacts the economic or ecological service that is gained from the ecosystem, it can harm the biodiversity of the area.

Day 17

C—The theory states that islands closer to the mainland (where the animals/plants have moved from) and/or larger islands will have more species than islands farther away or smaller. The size of the island in theory matters because larger islands can support more and different species, whereas smaller ones would be more limited.

Day 18

Island biogeography impacts evolution because an island is isolated and species can't move around easily. Because of this, the island reacts to environmental pressures differently from species on the mainland. Islands have limited resources such as food and habitats and often have specialists living on them that can be impacted by human and/or natural events such as invasive species being introduced.

Day 19

The *Monstera* plant is adapted to have more water, less heat, and less sunlight than a desert environment provides. The *Monstera* plant is outside of its ecological tolerance zone. It would be better suited in a wetter, cooler, shadier environment.

Day 20

Because of the drastic loss of biomass between 2011 and 2012, we can conclude that some sort of natural disruption to the ecosystem occurred, such as a forest fire, flood, or drought.

Day 21

B—Biodiversity would be affected in the short term because of a natural disruption, but the ecosystem is recovering at approximately 10 metric tons per hectare per year. Therefore, in about 18 years, the ecosystem would return to homeostasis.

Day 22

Before the industrial revolution, white moths camouflaged better with the light-colored trees. During the Industrial Revolution, the barks on the tree darkened due to soot, so white moths no longer camouflaged as well with the darker bark. Therefore, they were at greater risk of being hunted. Black moths were better suited to camouflage with the darkened bark, so their population increased. Their darker coloring adaptation made it so that they weren't as visible to predators.

Day 23

A—The poison dart frog is an indicator species, a species that **indicates** an environmental condition and is used to diagnose the health of the ecosystem. Some common examples of indicator species are plants, lichens, and many amphibians such as frogs.

Day 24

Over time, the ecosystem goes from bare rocks to a full-grown forest after a disturbance, such as a forest fire. As seen, lichens come in first, then small annual plants, then grass and perennials, then shrubs and shade-intolerant trees, and then, finally, shade-tolerant trees. This has a positive effect on the ecosystem by creating more biodiversity, habitats, and oxygen.

Day 25

- They can live in many different places.
- They can eat many different things.
- Generalists are less likely to be impacted by an environmental event.
- An example: cockroach.

Day 26

- They require particular habitats, food, and so on. If the habitat where a specialist species lives is damaged and its specific food source is gone, this could be particularly devastating to the population.
- An example: koalas.

Day 27

Rabbits are r-selected species; they reproduce exponentially and quickly. Kangaroos are k-selected species; they reproduce slowly and steadily.

Day 28

C—Fish do not have to provide extensive parental care to their offspring; they are r-selected species and have many offspring at once.

Day 29

Songbirds fit the Type II survivorship curve; they have a steady death rate. They are also k-selected species.

Day 30

Frogs fit the Type III survivorship curve; most die at a young age, and few live to old age. They are also r-selected species.

Day 31

Humans fit the Type I survivorship curve; most survive to adulthood and live to old age. They are k-selected species.

Day 32

B—50,000, because the lynx population hovers around 50,000. Anytime it gets far above this number, it is followed by a drastic decline, and the population will rebound to about this number once the conditions are appropriate for a rebound.

Day 33

If the lynx went above its carrying capacity, it would eat all the hare and run out of food; then there would be a decline in population from starvation, as seen multiple times in the graph.

Day 34

If the hare population declined, the lynx would follow the hare decline because its food source would run out, and it would then starve and die.

Day 35

$$\text{Percent change} = \frac{\text{New value} - \text{Old value}}{\text{Old value}} \times 100\%$$

If the result is positive, it is an increase.
If the result is negative, it is a decrease.

Percent change = $150 - 10/10 \times 100 = 1{,}400\%$

The population changed by 1,400 percent.

Day 36

Percent change = $20 - 140/140 \times 100 = -85.7\%$

The population changed by −85.7 percent.

Day 37

In population A, the population is experiencing rapid growth, shown by the large numbers of younger people compared with older people. In population B, the population is experiencing slow and steady growth, represented by the slow but steady increase in younger people. In population C, the population is experiencing no growth, shown by the steady number of younger, middle-aged, and older people. In population D, the population is showing a decline.

Day 38

Forty-six percent of the population is under age 15.

Day 39

Country D.

Day 40

C—Total fertility rates decrease when women have better access to contraception because they are less likely to get pregnant.

Day 41

C—The total fertility rate is higher in countries in earlier stages of the demographic transition because they do not have as much access to healthcare and contraception.

Day 42

Any of the following would lower the total fertility rate in a country:

- Women having greater access to family planning
- Women having greater access to education
- Women having better nutrition
- Women postponing marriage until the couple was older
- Women having lower birth rates
- Women having lower infant mortality rates
- Women having more clean food and water

Day 43

The population growth rate formula is 70/growth rate = doubling time. Thus, 70/6 = 11.7 years.

Day 44

D—If a third of the arable land has been lost and this continues, we will run out of land to grow food, and there will not be enough food to feed the ever-growing human population.

Day 45

Country A has a large population size with a low infant mortality rate and a low migration rate. This tells me that this is a developed country. Country B has a small population size in a large land area, but there is very high infant mortality per 1,000 babies born and a negative migration rate (people are leaving this country). This tells me that country B is most likely a developing country.

Day 46

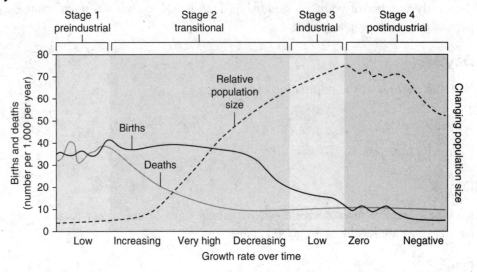

Stage 1 preindustrial | Stage 2 transitional | Stage 3 industrial | Stage 4 postindustrial

Births and deaths (number per 1,000 per year)

Relative population size

Births

Deaths

Changing population size

Low | Increasing | Very high | Decreasing | Low | Zero | Negative

Growth rate over time

Day 47

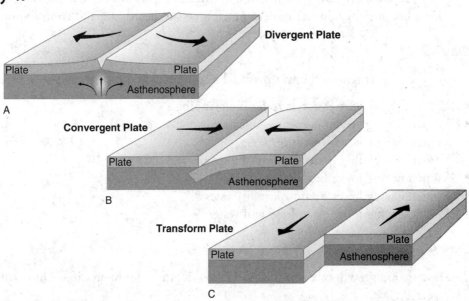

Divergent Plate

Plate — Plate

Asthenosphere

A

Convergent Plate

Plate — Plate

Asthenosphere

B

Transform Plate

Plate — Plate

Asthenosphere

C

The first way plates move is away from each other at **divergent plate boundaries**. When plates move apart, we get seafloor spreading, rift valleys, volcanoes, and earthquakes. Along these boundaries, earthquakes are common, and magma (molten rock) rises from the Earth's mantle to the surface. Once this magma solidifies, we get new oceanic crust. The most common example of a divergent plate boundary is the Mid-Atlantic Ridge found in the middle of the Atlantic Ocean on the bottom of the seafloor.

The second way plates move together is at **convergent plate boundaries**. When two land (continental) plates come together, the land buckles, and mountain ranges are formed. The Himalayan Mountains are an example of this. When a land plate and a sea (oceanic) plate collide, we get deep seafloor trenches with lines of volcanoes and earthquakes near them. As the ocean plate subducts, or is forced below the continental plate, the ocean plate melts and rises. As the ocean plate melts because of the heat in our Earth, it begins to rise, forming a volcano.

The final way plates move is at **transform boundaries**, where two plates moving in opposite directions slide by one another. The most common example you may be familiar with is California's San Andreas fault. Earthquakes are common along this fault as the plates move past each other and the stored energy is released as energy of motion.

Day 48

The **Ring of Fire** (Figure 8.4) is an area around the Pacific plate where a "ring" of volcanoes and earthquakes can be found because of convergent plate boundaries. The side view of what would be happening at this plate boundary (convergent plate boundary) would look like this:

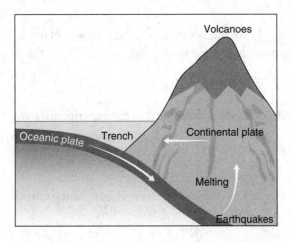

Day 49

Hot spots are areas where the magma from the mantle rises through the lithosphere, creating a volcano (Figure 8.6). If the lithosphere is moving over a stationary hot spot, you can get a line of volcanic islands. The Hawaiian Islands are an example of hot spot volcanism.

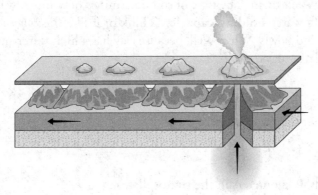

Day 50

This will depend on the experiment you design. However, remember the parts of an experiment and what they mean.

Dependent variable—this is the variable being tested and measured in an experiment and is "dependent" on the independent variable.

Independent variable—this is the variable the experimenter changes and is assumed to have a direct effect on the dependent variable.

Control—the part of the experiment that happens when you don't introduce the variable.

Method—the procedure or steps the experimenter takes when doing the experiment.

Day 51

C—A control has to be soil that is not from the power plant and has not been contaminated but is of the same makeup as the power plant's soil.

Day 52

B—Soil that is taken from the north side of the power plant is the best dependent variable. The experiment is created to test soil samples from the power plant.

Day 53

A—The soil is the dependent variable because the experimenter will be testing different types of soil.

Day 54

C—Sand is what is found in desert climates and has good drainage; therefore, it is the best soil for the succulent that is from a desert climate.

Day 55

Clay—Different types of soil allow water through at different rates, or not at all. For example, water goes easily through sand because the water particles are smaller than the sand particles. Water can go through silt slower because silt particles are smaller. Water can't go through clay at all because the particles of clay are so small that water can't squeeze between them. The type of soil determines how much water the soil can hold, or the soil's **water-holding capacity**. Think of it like this: clay is used to make things like pots and bowls. Why? Well, because clay has a high water-holding capacity. It can hold water for days.

Day 56

Weather occurs in the troposphere.

Day 57

Between 10 and 50 kilometers in the stratosphere.

Day 58

0—Rain forests; 30—Deserts. The sun, or solar radiation, drives all global wind patterns.

Day 59

As the Earth spins on its axis, winds and water veer to the right, and storms such as hurricanes spin counterclockwise in the Northern Hemisphere and veer to the left and spin clockwise in the Southern Hemisphere. The Coriolis effect is all about the Earth's rotation. The Earth rotates faster at the equator than it does at the poles. Because the Earth is wider at the equator, it makes a rotation in one 24-hour period and moves much faster in equatorial regions (1,000 miles per hour). Near the poles, the Earth rotates at about 0.00005 miles per hour.

Day 60

The characteristics of a watershed are area, length, slope, soil type, vegetation type, and the area that divides one watershed from another.

Day 61

The Gulf of Mexico has an annually recurring "hypoxic" zone caused by excess nutrient pollution from human activities such as agriculture, mining, and urbanization from the Mississippi River watershed. A hypoxic zone is a zone where oxygen levels are too low for most aquatic organisms to survive because of an overgrowth of algae from excess nutrients (mainly nitrogen and phosphorus) entering the gulf. Sediment is also deposited in the gulf from the river.

Day 62

In December, the Tropic of Cancer has shorter days and less solar radiation than does the Tropic of Capricorn because of the direct sunlight on the Tropic of Capricorn during this time of the year.

Day 63

In June, the Tropic of Cancer has longer days and more solar radiation than does the Tropic of Capricorn because of the direct sunlight on the Tropic of Cancer during this time of the year.

Day 64

More solar radiation is received at the equator than at the poles because the sun's rays strike the Earth's surface more directly (and all year) at the equator than they do at the poles. The sun's radiation hits the poles at a more oblique angle, which causes long periods of darkness and low radiation.

Day 65

You would expect to find a drier, warmer climate because as the warm, wet moisture from the ocean rises on the windward side, it dumps most of its moisture as rain on that side, so by the time it reaches the leeward side, it has lost most of its moisture, and therefore, there is much less rain.

Day 66

You would expect to find a humid subtropical to tropical climate because of the impact of the Gulf of Mexico. The Gulf of Mexico's water temperatures are warm throughout the year, and the south winds from the Gulf of Mexico lead to a warm and muggy climate in the area surrounding the gulf.

Day 67

You would expect to find increased precipitation and rainfall. This is because the westward-blowing trade winds begin to weaken near the equator, and this causes warm water on the surface of the ocean to move eastward. The warmer water in the ocean brings in increased rainfall because of convection currents.

Day 68

You would expect to find drought-like conditions in Indonesia because of the shift in rainfall that is usually over Indonesia moving eastward into the central Pacific, leaving Indonesia in a drought.

Day 69

The tragedy of the commons is the idea that individuals tend to overexploit shared resources until the resource becomes unavailable to all.

Day 70

Clear-cutting can lead to a release of carbon dioxide stored in the trees if the trees are burned; climate change; less pollutants being removed from the atmosphere and from water and soil; the occurrence of soil erosion; less carbon dioxide being absorbed; flooding; soil that erodes ending up in the rivers, lakes, and streams; increased ground temperatures due to less shade; etc.

Day 71

D—Seed storage and traditional farming practices need to change in order to promote continued research and development in seed technology. The author clearly states this in the last sentence, which is his argument.

Day 72

Tilling—this is how farmers dig, stir, and turn the soil so that they can plant new crops. This aerates the soil and allows for seedlings to be established. However, when we till the soil, it leaves the soil vulnerable to erosion.

Slash-and-burn farming—taking wild or forested land and converting it to farmland by cutting and burning the existing trees. This devastates habitats and species, causes deforestation, and can lead to climate change.

Fertilizer and pesticide use—fertilizers can run off into the water, causing eutrophication, and pesticides can contaminate the soil and water and be toxic to organisms that they were not intended to harm, such as birds, fish, "good" insects, and plants.

Day 73

IRRIGATION METHOD	ADVANTAGE	DISADVANTAGE
Drip	Saves water because only about five percent of the water is lost to evaporation	Expensive
Flood	Produces more food (therefore increasing profits for the farmer) and incurs less loss of crops from drought	Loss of a lot of water to evaporation and can lead to increased salinization of the soil
Furrow	Produces more food (therefore increasing profits for the farmer) and incurs less loss of crops from drought	Loss of about 35 percent of water to evaporation and can lead to increased salinization of the soil
Spray	Less water loss than flood or furrow	Expensive

Day 74

B—Switch to better irrigation methods that conserve water in this region.

The Ogallala Aquifer in the middle of the United States, where much of our food is grown, is being severely depleted because of massive overuse of water in the past century. The underground layers of water have been tapped for irrigation and other uses. The water has been severely depleted because of the demand for the water. If we used better irrigation methods, we would lessen demand for water coming from the aquifer.

Day 75

One problem with pesticides is that the organism that the pesticide is designed to kill builds up resistance over time. Pesticides are designed to prevent crop damage and increase crop profits, but if pesticide resistance becomes a problem, the pesticide will no longer work (or will not work as well). The farmer will have to either use more pesticide or stronger doses or switch to a new type, and this can impact both the profits and the environment. This is known as the pesticide treadmill. One method to help stop this is by genetically engineering crops so that the pests don't or can't harm them. This has pros and cons. A pro is that there is less need for pesticides, which is good for the environment because pesticides can often harm other organisms that they weren't designed to harm. Other pros are increased profits for farmers and helping keep the cost of food affordable. However, on the negative side is the loss of diversity in the crop.

Day 76

Increase in CO_2, methane, and N_2O emissions; increased water use; increased use of antibiotics and growth hormones; and overgrazing leading to deforesting and desertification would be some environmental impacts.

Day 77

A—Imports increased, exports increased, net trade increased.

If you look at the year 2008, imports were a little under 4 billion pounds, exports were a little over 14 billion pounds, and net trade was about 11 billion pounds. In 2018, imports were a little over 4 billion pounds, exports were almost 17 billion pounds, and net trade was 12 billion pounds, so everything increased.

Day 78

Net trade decreased in 2015 because exports decreased while imports increased that year.

Day 79

The state is worried about the problem of overfishing, which can lead to lower bio-diversity in the ocean, can lead to less food supply for humans if too many fish are captured, and can lead to not enough of certain sought-after types of fish.

Day 80

When the mineral resource is found on the surface of the Earth and we extract this mineral resource, it is called **surface mining**, and when the resource is found deep underground, it is called **subsurface mining**, which is more expensive.

There are many methods of surface mining, such as strip mining, open-pit mining, and mountaintop removal. Each of these has its own set of environmental impacts. In order to get to these resources, miners must first remove the soil, plants, and rock known as **overburden**. After mining, the wastes from mining, called **slag** and **tailings**, are left behind to be dealt with. Mining removes plant life, opens the soil up to erosion and runoff, harms habitats, can contaminate aquifers, releases methane from the soil, and causes fine particles of dust to be released. The process can also be expensive. However, each of these allows us to get to resources that are needed for energy use and other materials.

Day 81

Some possible human health issues could be dust particles causing respiratory problems (especially in students with asthma and other similar health problems), possible contamination of drinking water from the mining runoff, and contamination of food if the runoff from the mining came in contact with crops used for human consumption.

Day 82

Advantages of urbanization include less driving, leading to lower carbon emissions and other impacts of transportation; access to clean water, healthcare services, and other opportunities provided by cities; and the economic benefits of living in cities.

Day 83

Disadvantages of urbanization include saltwater intrusion because of overdrawing of water resources, increases in carbon dioxide from burning fossil fuels and from landfill emissions, flooding and soil erosion from pavement and buildings, and increased disease spread from people living in closer proximity to one another.

Day 84

Person 5 has the largest ecological footprint, with a total footprint of 11.1. Because his or her housing has the greatest footprint of all, making changes to the housing situation would help to lower person 5's footprint the greatest, followed by lowering the amount of meat he or she eats because this is the second-highest amount for this person.

Day 85

C—A bicycle emits 0 pounds of CO_2 per passenger mile. An SUV solo driver uses 1.60 pounds of CO_2 per passenger mile. Therefore, a bicycle uses 160 percent less CO_2 than an SUV solo driver.

Day 86

The city manager might suggest any way that would allow more water to sink into the soil and not run off. Some examples would be to lessen the number of parking lots or to add pavers instead of asphalt or concrete to the parking lot. Also, adding more trees would help water to absorb into the soil. The city manager might suggest taking public transportation to lessen the amount of oil and gasoline that runs off or build high-rise buildings or two-story homes rather than buildings/homes that take up lots of land area. There could be other answers here that you might think of that would also allow water to infiltrate into the ground rather than run off it.

Day 87

The benefits of integrated pest management (IPM) include using fewer pesticides that are linked to human health and environmental problems (land and water). The cost of IPM is usually financial because these are oftentimes more expensive and time consuming.

Day 88

Examples include predator insects, crop rotation, pest tolerant/resistant varieties of crops, planting crops to avoid pest times, using pheromones to attract bugs away from crops, intercropping, and limiting the amount of chemical pesticides you use on the crops.

Day 89

Rotational grazing, crop rotation, composting, using natural manure, contour plowing, terracing, not tilling the soil or tilling less, strip cropping, perennial crops, cover cropping, integrated pest management (IPM), hydroponics/aquaponics, permaculture, crop diversity, etc.

Day 90

The benefits of aquaculture are feeding more people; taking up very little space, water, or energy, and the ability to be implemented in places where fish are not normally found. The costs of aquaculture are that disease can spread because of so many fish living so close together, some fish may escape the enclosure and become invasive, large amounts of food fed to the fish can pollute the ground or surface waters, etc.

Day 91

Prescribed burns help to stop large crown fires from occurring. A forester would take an area of the forest and set a small fire to it that is controlled to burn away the under-growth such as shrubs, small trees, etc. This also opens up light to the forest floor that is healthy for the forest. The prescribed burns are done under very safe conditions so that the fire doesn't get out of control. Then, without the extra fuel, the forest is less likely to have a larger fire that might burn out of control.

Day 92

B—The best way to help mitigate the problems humans cause to a forest is to implement reforestation methods in areas where the forest has been harvested. By planting native trees in the area, you help to reestablish the forest ecosystem after trees have been cut down for sale or for human habitation.

Day 93

Renewable energy resources are resources that can be replaced over a relatively short time scale. These include such things as solar, wind, hydroelectric, geothermal, and biomass resources. Nonrenewable energy resources are not replaced quickly or not at all. These include things such as coal, oil, natural gas, and nuclear energy resources.

Day 94

C—88.176 BTUs because natural gas, petroleum, nuclear electric power, and coal made up for 88 percent of the U.S. energy consumption. $100.2 \div 100 = 1.002 \times 88 = 88.176$.

Day 95

150,000 kWh are used to cool during the summer months: 1,000 kWh $\times$ 50 units $\times$ 3 months = 150,000 kWh.

Seven point five percent of the annual electricity usage is used on cooling during the summer months.

$$\frac{100\%}{x\%} = \frac{2000000}{150000}$$
$$\frac{x\%}{100\%} = \frac{150000}{2000000}$$
$$\Rightarrow x = 7.5\%$$

Day 96

A family in a developing country would most likely use wood to heat their homes or cook their food because this would be something readily available that they could cut down or buy relatively cheap. This often leads to problems of deforestation and habitat destruction to the area.

Day 97

Peat is partially decomposed plant matter that burns relatively quickly and not very hot. It has a large amount of moisture. The other three can be seen in the following graphic:

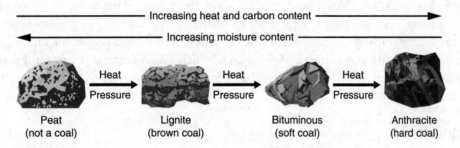

Day 98

If we look at Figure 10.2, we can see where oil and gas energy sources are found. You will be given a diagram similar to this on the test and asked to draw some conclusions. First, the oil is found in a layer below the gas. This is because gas bubbles up from the oil and floats on top. The rock reservoir is the layer that has the rich organic matter from millions of years ago. This has then been subjected to heat and pressure. The oil has risen up through the next permeable layer but stopped at the layer that is impermeable. We then drill down through the impermeable layer and get the gas and oil.

Day 99

Let's take coal as an example. First, coal is pulverized into a very fine powder, which is then burned to make heat. This heat is used to boil water and produce steam. This steam is then pumped through a pipe at extremely high pressure and is focused on a giant **turbine**, causing the turbine to spin (similar to blowing on a pinwheel and causing it to spin). This turbine is connected to an electrical generator that generates electricity. The same process occurs when oil or natural gas is burned.

Day 100

Burning fossil fuels produced carbon dioxide and other greenhouse gases (which lead to climate change), groundwater contamination can happen from hydraulic fracturing, mining can destroy habitats and be dangerous to the humans doing the mining, volatile organic compounds can be released, sulfur dioxides are released that can lead to acid rain, etc.

Day 101

We can also split atoms of uranium-235 in a process known as **fission** to produce extremely high heat. Similar to how electricity is generated from coal, oil, or natural gas, the heat is used to boil water to make steam to turn a turbine to generate electrical energy.

Day 102

The benefit of nuclear energy is that because we aren't actually burning anything, no air pollution is produced, and therefore, this energy source does not cause climate change. There are several costs of nuclear energy. First, when we use uranium, the waste that is left over must be stored for a very long time. This waste is radioactive and must be very carefully disposed of. In addition, uranium-235 is a nonrenewable resource that must be mined. Also, nuclear energy generation creates so much heat that it must be "dumped" into a water source, which causes thermal pollution. Finally, release of radiation if there is a nuclear accident can have impacts on humans and the environment.

Day 103

Openly burning wood in a closed home or hut produces carbon dioxide, carbon monoxide, nitrogen oxides, particulates, and volatile organic compounds. None of these is good to be breathing for long periods of time, and many lead to climate change. In addition, if a country is doing this on a large scale, there are problems of deforestation and habitat destruction.

Day 104

Active solar systems collect, store, and convert solar energy to electrical power. They do this by using heat from the sun to heat a liquid and store the energy. Passive solar systems do not collect or store energy but can be used to heat or cool homes and other structures. An example is building a home with large windows that face where the sun shines the most. Then the sun will come in through the windows and heat the home. During the summer, the homeowner could put thick curtains on the windows to prevent the heat from coming in. Another option is planting shade trees to help keep a house cooler in summer.

Day 105

C—50 percent less. Percent change: $(\$1.00 - \$2.00)/\$2.00 \times 100 = -50$ percent.

Day 106

The benefit of hydroelectric power is that it doesn't produce any air pollution because nothing is burned. The costs are that building dams is expensive, and when you build a dam, you change the river ecosystem. You flood an area above the dam, which was once a land habitat. If some of the water is diverted to irrigation, you reduce the flow of water downstream, reducing the amount of nutrients available and changing the ecosystems. In some cases, the flow is so reduced that the water never reaches the sea. This can damage habitats and cause loss of biodiversity.

Day 107

This can be done by building a dam across a river; the dam has a turbine that the water passes over as it goes downstream. This turbine turns and is connected to a generator that converts energy of motion into electrical energy.

Day 108

In many places in the world, the heat from geothermal sources is too deep, doesn't have the high-temperature resources necessary, and/or would be too expensive to acquire.

Day 109

Geothermal energy generates energy by taking heat from the Earth to heat water to create steam to turn a turbine that is connected to a generator that converts energy of motion into electrical energy.

Day 110

A hydrogen fuel cell uses hydrogen gas (H_2) and oxygen gas (O_2), and the products are water, heat, and electricity. Hydrogen is oxidized at the anode and flows to the cathode, where oxygen reacts with hydrogen to make water. This then converts potential energy into electrical energy for transportation.

Day 111

The benefit of hydrogen fuel cells is that they produce no carbon dioxide as they make electricity. The costs are that they are still very expensive and, in order to create the hydrogen gas, a process called **electrolysis** is used, which requires energy possibly produced from nonrenewable sources such as coal.

Day 112

Wind is used to turn a turbine that is connected to a generator to turn energy of motion into electrical energy.

Day 113

The benefits of wind energy include that it is clean, it is free, and it can be used in areas where you are doing other things, such as ranching or growing crops; the costs are that migrating birds, butterflies, and bats have been known to get caught in the turbines and killed.

Day 114

200 − 120 = 80 watts saved.

(80 watts × 8 hours)/1 day = 640 watts/day × 1 kilowatt/1,000 watts = 0.640 kilowatt-hour/day.

(0.640 kilowatt-hour × 0.15 cents)/1 day × 1 kilowatt-hour = 0.096, or 9.6 cents.

Day 115

(30 kilowatt-hours × 365 days)/(1 day × 1 year) = 10,950 kilowatt-hours.

0.15 cent − 10 cents = 0.5 cent saving.

(10,950 kilowatt-hours × 0.05 cent)/1 kilowatt-hour = $547.50/year.

(1 year × 20,000)/$547.50 = 36.5 or 37 years.

Day 116

CHEMICAL	REMOVAL TECHNIQUE
Sulfur dioxide	Gas scrubbing or fluidized-bed combustion
Nitrogen oxides	Catalytic converters
Toxic metals	Catalytic reduction or electrostatic precipitators
Particulates	Baghouse filters or electrostatic precipitators

Day 117

You would want to test the air for ozone, nitric acid, sulfur dioxide, particulates, and other toxic metals. If these tested at higher than normal levels, the citizens should be concerned.

Day 118

D—100 percent. 4 a.m. = 0.2 ppm and 8 a.m. = 0.4 ppm. Percent change: (0.4 ppm − 0.2 ppm)/0.2 ppm = 100 percent.

Day 119

C—50 percent. 8 a.m. = 0.4 ppm and 4 p.m. = 0.2 ppm. Percent change: (0.2 ppm − 0.4 ppm)/0.4 ppm × 100 = −50 percent.

Day 120

During a thermal inversion, warm, less dense air moves over dense, cold air. The dense air traps pollution, particularly smog and particulates near the ground, and the pollutants can't escape to space.

Day 121

Thermal inversions would most likely occur near coastal areas because of the upwelling of cold water decreasing surface temperatures or areas where there are mountains, and the cold air from the mountains flows down into the valleys and the cold air pushes under the warm air.

Day 122

There are many causes of particulate matter both natural and human made. These include but are not limited to

- Volcanic eruptions
- Soil erosion/dirt
- Sea salt
- Desert sand
- Dust
- Pollen
- Traffic
- Agriculture
- Industry
- Power plants
- Smoke
- Soot
- Construction sites
- Burning fossil fuels

Day 123

Some sources include respiration (both animal and plant), decomposition, volcanic eruptions, wildfires, and decomposing biomass, among many others.

Day 124

D—VOCs come from furniture, paneling, and carpets. In addition, VOCs can come from formaldehyde, plywood, particleboard, glues, drapes and fabrics, foam insulation, gas, wood and kerosene, tobacco products, perfume, hair spray, cleaning agents, dry cleaning fluid, paints, lacquers, varnishes, hobby supplies, and copy machines, among others.

Day 125

Some household pollutants that would be classified as particulates include asbestos, dust, smoke, pollen, skin flakes and dander, mold spores, etc.

Day 126

- Vapor recovery nozzle: fumes from gasoline pumps
- Catalytic converter: CO, NO_x, hydrocarbons
- Wet and dry scrubber: particulates and/or gases from industrial exhaust streams
- Electrostatic precipitators: fine particles like dust, smoke, soot, and ash

Day 127

B—NO_x. Catalytic converters remove CO, NO_x, and hydrocarbons.

Day 128

Coal-burning power plants release nitrogen oxides (NO_x) and sulfur dioxides (SO_2) into the atmosphere. When these chemicals go into the atmosphere and mix with atmospheric water like rain, snow, fog, hail, or dust, they can become **acid rain** and fall to Earth. This can be in wet or dry form.

Day 129

When soil or water becomes acidified because of acid deposition, there can be some environmental effects. For example, often you will see dead or dying trees in areas affected by acid rain. The soil may have higher levels of aluminum in it because acid rain can leach aluminum from the soil; this is toxic to plants and animals. In aquatic biomes, acid rain can be harmful to fish and other wildlife. The aluminum that was leached from the soil on the land may run off into the water and lead to a loss of biodiversity.

Day 130

A—Humans should try to limit the amount of noise pollution to lessen the impact on animals. The answer comes mainly from the last sentence, where the author writes: "This unintended result of human urbanization is having a dramatic effect on the animals we must coexist with, and these noise levels need to be limited."

Day 131

A point source is pollution you can point to and say, "There it is," for example, a pipe that is dumping waste into a river or a smokestack that is spewing out soot and smoke. You can literally point to it. On the flip side is nonpoint-source pollution. You can't point to any particular thing, like cars on the road. You can't point with your finger to all the cars on the road or farmers spraying pesticide on all the crops in an area.

Day 132

D—Car exhaust coming from cars on highways and city streets. This is because nonpoint-source pollution comes from many different places, and these are many different cars.

Day 133

The point of discharge is where the sewage is being dumped into the river. The dissolved oxygen begins to drop because sewage contains millions of organisms, such as fungi and bacteria, that need oxygen. This increases the biological oxygen demand (BOD) on the oxygen in the river and lowers the amount of dissolved oxygen. Usually there are very few organisms that can live in the area where the dissolved oxygen is at the lowest. However, because this is a river and the pollutant will eventually get diluted, the dissolved oxygen goes up again as you get farther downstream from the pollutant.

Day 134

Percent change is calculated as

$$\text{Percent change} = \frac{\text{New value} - \text{Old value}}{\text{Old value}} \times 100\%$$

If the result is positive, it is an increase.
If the result is negative, it is a decrease.

So $(350 \text{ NTUs} - 50 \text{ NTUs})/50 \text{ NTUs} \times 100 = 600$ percent.

Day 135

Endocrine disruptors are chemicals that can mimic hormones in organisms; they can come from a variety of things, such as pesticides, food, and pharmaceuticals. These can cause birth defects and have been linked to developmental, reproductive, neural, immune, and other problems in animals.

Day 136

A—Plant new mangrove trees along coastlines to prevent further erosion. This is because the biggest threat to wetlands and mangroves is erosion after trees are cut down. Mangroves are trees and shrubs found near the coastal zone that protect the coast from erosion and flooding and provide habitat to many organisms. These are being harmed by humans when we drain and build on the areas and pollute with trash and chemical waste.

Day 137

Nitrogen and phosphorus have entered the body of water, causing it to have too many nutrients, and these nutrients have fertilized the algae that live in the water. These nutrients are coming from agricultural runoff, homes/gardens, etc., and this causes the water to become so thick and green with algae that no light can penetrate it. The algae then die, and microbes such as bacteria and fungi that live in the water eat the algae and in so doing take up a lot of oxygen. Then there is an oxygen sag curve where there isn't enough oxygen for things like fish and other aquatic organisms to survive.

Day 138

Thermal pollution is caused by heated water being released into a body of water, usually from a nuclear power plant. This heated water is unable to hold as much dissolved oxygen as colder water. The oxygen diffuses out of the water, and therefore, organisms such as fish and other aquatic organisms may be impacted.

Day 139

POPs do not break down in the environment very quickly and can build up in the tissues and the fat of animals. This accumulation of POPs in an organism's tissues can be toxic. In addition, because they are persistent (they don't break down quickly), because animals migrate long distances, and because these chemicals can travel in wind and water very far distances, we have POPs in almost all parts of our planet.

Day 140

A—Environmental concentrations of persistent substances are responsible for hormonal disruptions of breeding birds and abnormalities in their offspring. A good hypothesis for his study would be to see if hormonal changes have occurred in the birds and to see if there are any problems with the birds' offspring. Persistent substances can work their way up the food chain to high concentrations. For example, when DDT made its way up to predatory birds such as bald eagles, the chemical interfered with the ability of the bird to make strong eggshells. The shells were so soft that they often broke during incubation, and the baby birds died. It went on for many generations with the bald eagle population, and we had entire species on the brink of extinction because of this problem.

Day 141

Chemicals such as the pesticide DDT can build up in the fatty tissues of animals because they don't break down but accumulate there. This is referred to as **bioaccumulation**. In addition, because animals eat other animals, these chemicals can magnify up the food chain; this is referred to as **biomagnification**. It occurs because top predators eat many different animals; each animal may have eaten many different organisms as well. The following figure is an illustration of how things magnify up the food chain.

Fish-eating birds
(DDT 5 ppm)

Large fish
(DDT 2 ppm)

Small fish
(DDT 0.5 ppm)

Zooplankton
(DDT 0.04 ppm)

Water
(DDT 0.003 ppm)

Day 142

B—Food scraps, yard trimmings, paper. These items are the largest amount of MSW according to the graph, making up a total of 56.9 percent (paper 31.0 percent, food scraps 12.7 percent, and yard trimmings 13.2 percent).

Day 143

Landfills—can contaminate groundwater and release gases that contribute to such things as climate change.

Incineration of the waste—can release air pollutants.

Dumping of the trash on land or into the oceans—can lead to disease, can harm wildlife, has caused floating islands of trash in the oceans.

Day 144

0.78 MW = 780 kW.

(2,800 tons × 432,000 ft^3 gas × 780 kW)/(1 million × 432,000 ft^3 gas) = 2.18 kW

Day 145

We can reduce, reuse, and recycle, including incorporating composting.

Day 146

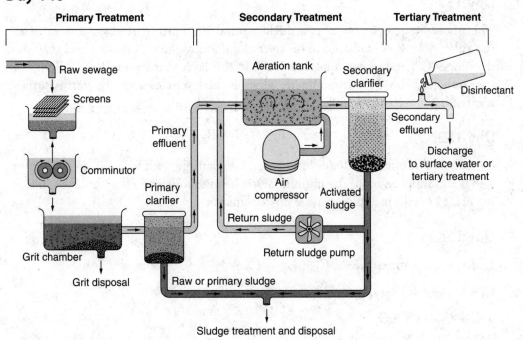

Day 147

(180 lb × 1 kg × 12,000 mg × 1 g)/(2.2 lb × 1 kg × 1,000 mg) = 981.81 grams of salt.

Day 148

About 23 mg. This is where the 50 percent response hits the dose-response curve. Find this by going across from the 50 percent, hitting the line and going down to find about 23 mg.

Day 149

Mesothelioma comes from exposure to asbestos, a heat-resistant fibrous silicate mineral that was used for panels, floor boards, ceiling tiles, etc.

Day 150

The plague is spread from fleas being carried on rats. People were living in close living quarters with poor sanitation. There was sewage and filth in the streets, and rats were everywhere. Rats often coexisted with humans, thus allowing the disease to spread quickly.

Day 151

As our climate is changing and the Earth is getting warmer, diseases from insects such as West Nile and malaria are spreading to areas where they were not seen before. In addition, many of these diseases are spread in areas that are poor and lack sanitation or clean water.

Day 152

The stratospheric ozone layer is a shield around the Earth that absorbs most of the sun's ultraviolet (UV) radiation. This layer of our atmosphere contains ozone (O_3). It is the ozone (O_3) and oxygen molecules (O_2) in this layer that absorb the UV light. The stratosphere is above the troposphere, which is the layer closest to the Earth's surface; it extends from 10 km (6 miles) to about 50 km (31 miles) into space.

Day 153

Human health effects include skin cancer, eye damage such as cataracts, premature aging, and suppression of the immune system. Environmental effects include inhibiting plant growth, including marine phytoplankton.

Day 154

$CCl_3F + UV \text{ light} \rightarrow Cl + CCl_2F$

$Cl + O_3 \rightarrow ClO + O_2$

$ClO + O \rightarrow Cl + O_2$

You could use F rather than Cl with the same explanation.

Day 155

The Montreal Protocol was a global agreement to protect the stratospheric ozone layer by phasing out the production and use of ozone-depleting substances such as chlorofluorocarbons.

Day 156

Replace things such as chlorofluorocarbons (CFCs) with hydrofluorocarbons (HFCs) or hydrochlorofluorocarbons (HCFCs) that have a lower ozone-depletion potential.

Day 157

Carbon dioxide, methane, nitrous oxide, and chlorofluorocarbons are the major greenhouse gases.

Day 158

The greenhouse effect occurs when solar radiation (infrared) from the sun is absorbed by the Earth's surface, warming the surface, and some is reflected back to space. This is important because without the greenhouse effect, it would be too cold on Earth for life.

Day 159

Chlorofluorocarbons (CFCs) have a greater global warming potential than does CO_2. In fact, CFCs have a global warming potential of 12,000 to 16,000, whereas CO_2 has a global warming potential of 1.

Day 160

- Glaciers have shrunk.
- Ice sheets are melting.
- Plant and animal ranges have shifted.
- Sea levels are rising.
- Seas expand from thermal expansion.
- Biodiversity is affected because many species depend on ice for food and for a place to live.
- Many organisms cannot move or adapt quickly enough to survive, so population numbers decrease, particularly specialist populations.

Day 161

- Insects are moving to places that used to be too cold for them, and these insects can carry disease.
- Droughts are threatening crops, wildlife, and freshwater supplies.

Day 162

As greenhouse gases trap more energy from the sun, the oceans are absorbing more heat, resulting in an increase in sea surface temperatures and rising sea level.

Day 163

According to the graph, temperatures will be about 8°+ above average.

Day 164

Temperatures have fluctuated up and down for many hundreds of thousands of years but have leveled off for the last 10,000 years and have increased sharply recently.

Day 165

Environmental consequences include rising sea levels, melting permafrost and sea ice, flooding estuaries, habitat loss of marine ecosystems, soil changes including erosion, thawing tundra, and habitat loss of polar species.

Day 166

Because of their light color, snow and ice also reflect more sunlight than open water or bare ground, so a reduction in snow cover and ice causes the Earth's surface to absorb more energy from the sun and become warmer. Polar regions have ice and snow that reflect back, leading to a positive-feedback loop.

Day 167

Corals need zooxanthellae, algae that live in the tissues of coral and capture sunlight and convert it into energy for the coral animals. When the temperature of the ocean is too warm, the zooxanthellae come under stress and can die or leave their coral host, causing the coral to die and turn white, a process known as **coral bleaching**.

Day 168

A warmer ocean can lead to loss of habitat for marine organisms, coral bleaching, metabolic and reproductive changes in marine organisms, loss of breeding grounds for fish and mammals, and stronger and more powerful tropical storms.

Day 169

Burning fossil fuels, vehicle emissions, and deforestation (because fewer trees means less absorption of CO_2) can lead to ocean acidification.

Day 170

Ocean acidification reduces the amount of carbonate, making it harder for marine organisms such as coral to form their shells.

Day 171

More acidic. This is because as the amount of carbon dioxide in the atmosphere rises, the oceans absorb it. The CO_2 reacts with seawater to form carbonic acid, increasing the acidity of the ocean.

Day 172

Three ways to control invasive species are

- Biological—using natural enemies to control the pest species. This can work, but sometimes the biological control backfires and the new species becomes a problem.
- Mechanical—mowing, hoeing, hand pulling, and more to control the pest species. This is expensive and time consuming.
- Chemical—using pesticides (such as herbicides, insecticides, and rodenticides). This can lead to the problems discussed earlier in this book on pesticides.

Day 173

A—A generalist. Invasive species tend to be generalists and r-selected species, and they become invasive because of a lack of competition, no predators, and/or abundant resources.

Day 174

A—The species is most likely an invasive species. Invasive species often spread extremely quickly, and their growth, when plotted on a graph, looks like the letter "J" or exponential growth.

Day 175

A species may become endangered for many reasons. Habitat loss, invasive species, poaching, climate change, taking too many of a species in hunting and fishing, pollution, if the animal is highly specialized (lives in a certain place, eats a certain thing), competition within or with other species, and selective pressures on the species are all reasons animals and plants might become endangered.

Day 176

Habitat destruction is one of the main reasons amphibians are more susceptible to environmental pressures. This is because they live in small ranges and don't move from habitat to habitat, so habitat fragmentation is a big problem. In addition, they are sensitive to changes in climate, and with climate change, they are being impacted more greatly than other species. In addition, there are invasive species, amphibian collection, and a fungus that is impacting amphibians.

Day 177

Critically endangered—a species facing an *extremely* high risk of extinction in the wild. Endangered—a species considered to be facing a *very high* risk of extinction in the wild. Vulnerable—a species considered to be facing a *high* risk of extinction in the wild.

Day 178

H—Habitat destruction

I—Invasive species

P—Population growth

P—Pollution

C—Climate change

O—Overexploitation

Day 179

We can prevent the loss of habitat by protecting large tracts of land so that it can't be developed, creating and enforcing legislation to protect biodiversity, preventing importation of nonnative species, creating habitat corridors so that animals can move between native areas, preventing deforestation, using sustainable farming and ranching practices, and helping to restore areas that have been harmed by human or natural disasters.

Day 180

Habitat fragmentation is defined as the process of large expanses of habitats being transformed into a number of smaller patches of smaller total area isolated from each other. This is happening when habitats are harmed by cutting down forests, by building roads, or by building human habitation in areas where there used to be large areas of open land.

NOTES

NOTES

5 Steps to Teaching AP Environmental Science

TEACHER'S MANUAL

Courtney Mayer, MEd

Thanks to Greg Jacobs, an AP Physics teacher at Woodberry Forest School in Virginia, for developing the 5-step approach used in this teaching manual.

Introduction to the Teacher's Manual

Nowadays, teachers have no shortage of resources for the AP Environmental Science class. Classes are no longer limited to just the teacher and the textbook; today's teachers can utilize online simulations, apps, computer-based homework, video lectures, and so on. Even the College Board itself provides so much material related to the AP Environmental Science exam that the typical teacher—and student—can easily become overwhelmed by an excess of teaching materials and resources.

One vital resource for you and your class is this book. It explains in straightforward language exactly what a student needs to know for the AP Environmental Science exam. It also provides a complete review for the test, including explanatory materials, questions to check student understanding, and test-like practice exams.

This teacher's manual will take you through the five steps of teaching AP Environmental Science. These five steps are:

▶ Prepare a strategic plan for the course

▶ Hold an interesting class every day

▶ Evaluate your students' progress

▶ Get students ready to take the AP exam

▶ Become a better teacher every year

I'll discuss each of these steps, providing suggestions and ideas of things that I use in my class. I present them here because over the years, I found that *they work*. You may have developed a different course strategy, teaching activities, and evaluation techniques. That's fine; different things work for different teachers. But I hope you find in this teacher's manual something that will be useful to you.

STEP 1

Prepare a Strategic Plan for the Course

The Course and Exam Description (CED) from the College Board can be found at: https://apcentral.collegeboard.org/courses/ap-environmental-science/course. It lays out a suggested scope and sequence for the AP Environmental Science class. My suggestion is to stick with the suggested scope and sequence for your first few years; the College Board has set it up in a way that topics and skills build as the year goes on.

But after you have taught the course a few times and feel comfortable with the material, you may want to move topics and units around to better meet your classroom needs. Some years I have decided to start with Unit 3 before moving on to Unit 1, because Unit 3 is something students enjoyed and got them hooked on environmental science. But I would not suggest moving Units 6, 7, 8, or 9 to the fall semester. These topics cover material that build on earlier units and also cover the bulk of the exam. Leaving these topics until the spring semester will ensure that students are ready for the advanced skills found in these units, and covering these topics closer to the exam helps make sure they are fresh in students' minds.

The following chart shows the units and the time suggested for each unit. The number of class periods is based on a typical 45-minute class. If your school follows a block schedule or other nontypical schedule, you need to adjust the pacing to fit your class needs.

TOPICS	PACING	5 STEPS TO A 5
Unit 1: The Living World: Ecosystems	14–15 class periods	Chapter 5, pp. 53–66
Unit 2: The Living World: Biodiversity	11–12 class periods	Chapter 6, pp. 67–76
Unit 3: Populations	12–13 class periods	Chapter 7, pp. 77–88
Unit 4: Earth Systems and Resources	11–12 class periods	Chapter 8, pp. 89–101
Unit 5: Sampling Distributions	18–19 class periods	Chapter 9, pp. 103–119
Unit 6: Energy Resources and Consumption	16–17 class periods	Chapter 10, pp. 121–130
Unit 7: Atmospheric Pollution	11–12 class periods	Chapter 11, pp. 131–140
Unit 8: Aquatic and Terrestrial Pollution	19–20 class periods	Chapter 12, pp. 141–154
Unit 9: Global Change	19–20 class periods	Chapter 13, pp. 155–164

As you plan your year, make sure to leave plenty of time for review. You can't assume students will remember the details of information from months ago.

I like to leave two to three weeks of dedicated review time just before the test.

STEP 2

Hold an Interesting Class Every Day

AP Environmental Science students should love coming to your class. Why? Because you should offer many opportunities and strategies to help students understand the material and internalize what they learn. I follow the same schedule daily but with different activities to keep it interesting.

▶ **Bell ringer.** I choose a released AP exam question from the topic questions found on AP Classroom and have this "Question of the Day" on the board when class begins. Students write down the question and think about it or discuss it with their classmates while I am taking roll call and getting class started. I then go over the question and the answer with them. This takes no more than five minutes per day.

▶ **Lecture/notes.** I upload my notes (I use PowerPoint) to the students' learning management system, and the students are required to download or print those notes on their own. This saves hours of time, because I can quickly address the important or often misunderstood sections of the notes, skipping over the things they can study and learn on their own. I move on quickly; I *never* lecture for more than 10 minutes a day. The AP students are capable of reading my notes and studying, and they can always come to me if they have any questions outside of class time.

▶ **Activity/lab/video.** So far we have used about 15 minutes, so I still have 30 minutes to do an interesting activity. Hands-on labs (a "cookbook" lab and using lab equipment), group activities, a movie/documentary, and so on, all fall into this category. Some units are better for labs than other units. For example, Unit 3 is all about populations; there simply are not that many labs to be done for this unit. So this unit may have more group activities and movies than other units where there are so many lab ideas that you will need to pick and choose.

The idea here is to get the students "doing" science. I have a gigantic sign in my room with a quote from Benjamin Franklin that describes my teaching philosophy: "Tell me and *I forget*. Teach me and *I remember*. Involve me and *I learn*." Involve your students in the class, and they will not only love the class but also excel on the AP exam.

If you have a classroom set of *5 Steps to a 5 AP Environmental Science*, you can assign the students the homework of reading a few pages of the book that correlate to the topics you are teaching next. You can also assign them the review questions at the end of each chapter as homework. The book covers each unit and topic in the CED, and all the review questions are aligned to the science practices. *5 Steps to a 5* can also be accessed online; see instructions on the back cover.

The labs, classroom activities, and videos/documentaries that you decide to use in your course depends on your interests, school budget, class composition, and so on. However, some activities are used in many AP Environmental Science classrooms, and these are listed by unit as follows. A quick Google search usually finds all of these activities (search for videos by title). In addition, you might consider joining the Facebook page that is specifically for AP Environmental Science teachers. If you go to Facebook and search "National APES Teachers," you can request access to this resource that contains more ideas than you could possibly do in a year! Here are some of my favorites:

UNIT	RECOMMENDED ACTIVITIES
Unit 1: The Living World: Ecosystems	▶ Chalk drawings of the different biogeochemical cycles on lab tables ▶ Biome charts in which students document characteristics of each biome ▶ *Strange Days on Planet Earth: Predator* (https://www.youtube.com/watch?v=SIXAytRvDQ0) video ▶ Ecobottles
Unit 2: The Living World: Biodiversity	▶ Simulation activity on the theory of island biogeography ▶ Cats of Borneo lesson ▶ Easter Island discussion ▶ *Cane Toads* video ▶ *Planet in Peril* (You might have to purchase this video.)

Unit 3: Populations	▶ Demographic transition activity
	▶ Duckweed population lab
	▶ Estimating population size activity
	▶ Pyramid activity (use census.gov)
	▶ Short population videos, such as:
	  ▶ https://www.youtube.com/watch?v=i4639vev1Rw
	  ▶ https://www.youtube.com/watch?v=khFjdmp9sZk
	  ▶ https://www.ted.com/talks/hans_rosling_the_best_stats_you_ve_ever_seen?language=en#t-57587
	  ▶ https://www.youtube.com/watch?v=M-qkTmHqW5k
	  ▶ https://www.ted.com/talks/hans_rosling_global_population_growth_box_by_box?language=en

Unit 4: Earth Systems and Resources	▶ Soil labs covering soil permeability, porosity, texture, and chemical analysis ▶ *El Niño/La Niña* video (https://www.youtube.com/watch?v=tyPq86yM_lc)
Unit 5: Land and Water Use	▶ Tragedy of the commons activity (Goldfish crackers) ▶ Cooking mining activity
Unit 6: Energy Resources and Consumption	▶ Energy audit ▶ *Japan's Killer Quake, Gaslands,* and *Chernobyl Heart* videos ▶ Practice energy calculations

(continued)

UNIT	RECOMMENDED ACTIVITIES
Unit 7: Atmospheric Pollution	▶ Particulate lab ▶ Acid rain lab ▶ Chart of all the air pollutants, including the pollutant, the source, and the effect (both environmental and human health) ▶ Tropospheric ozone (Schoenbein strip) lab
Unit 8: Aquatic and Terrestrial Pollution	▶ LD_{50} lab (can use plants, brine shrimp, earthworms) ▶ Thermal pollution and its effect on dissolved oxygen lab ▶ *E-Waste* video (https://www.youtube.com/watch?v=-jSbYTNAJIQ)
Unit 9: Global Change	▶ Chalk drawings of global warming and ozone depletion on lab tables ▶ Videos about the concept of global warming (there are so many) ▶ Ocean acidification lab

The *5 Steps to a 5 AP Environmental Science: Elite Edition* provides additional questions that can be used in your class. It contains 180 activities and questions that require five minutes a day or less. While they are primarily intended to be used by students studying for the test, you can use these as daily warm-ups in your course or assign them as homework or classwork/group work. To do this, you will need the following table that organizes these questions and activities by unit.

UNIT	QUESTIONS/ACTIVITIES IN THE ELITE EDITION
Unit 1: The Living World: Ecosystems	Days 1–11 (pp. 241–251)
Unit 2: The Living World: Biodiversity	Days 12–24 (pp. 252–264)
Unit 3: Populations	Days 25–46 (pp. 265–286)
Unit 4: Earth Systems and Resources	Days 47– 68 (pp. 287–308)
Unit 5: Land and Water Use	Days 69–92 (pp. 309–332)
Unit 6: Energy Resources and Consumption	Days 93–115 (pp. 333–355)
Unit 7: Atmospheric Pollution	Days 116–130 (pp. 356–370)
Unit 8: Aquatic and Terrestrial Pollution	Days 131–151 (pp. 371–391)
Unit 9: Global Change	Days 152–180 (pp. 392–420)

STEP 3

Evaluate Your Students' Progress

I recommend that you incorporate released AP questions from the College Board (found on AP Classroom) on your unit exams. You can also add additional questions from your textbook, from *5 Steps to a 5 AP Environmental Science,* or those you create yourself. However, there is no better resource than the people who write the test, and there are over a thousand questions on AP Classroom for you to use.

It is vital that you have a free-response question (FRQ) on each of your unit exams. Getting the students to practice responding to an open-ended question in the exam format is the best way to help them on the AP exam. Remember, the FRQs count as 40 percent of the student's grade on the exam, so including these on every unit exam you give is crucial.

In my classroom, I use peer/personal grading for the FRQs. Here is how the process works. The students come into class the day after the exam, and they pick up a red pen, two copies of the scoring sheet, and a copy of the scoring guidelines (the rubric) from the College Board (or if you wrote the FRQ yourself, you will need to make a rubric). You can make a Google form where they record their answers digitally, if you prefer. Here the scoring sheet that I give students:

Free-Response Question Scoring

Part A:

Points awarded: _____

Where did you get the points? Give a full explanation! _____

_____

_____

Part B:

Points awarded: _____

Where did you get the points? Give a full explanation! _____

_____

_____

Continue this for as many parts of the FRQ that there are.

Next, I hand them a copy of another student's responses, and they use the scoring guidelines/rubric to document how many points they think the student earned. This is not converted to a grade. (I grade the FRQ myself, and that is the grade that goes into my grade book!) This is just to get students seeing different responses so they can get better at writing. Then after they have scored a classmate's FRQ, they give it them, and that student repeats the process scoring their own response. After they do this, I call them up one by one and tell them what I gave them as a grade and where I gave them the points.

I know this "eats up" an entire day of class time; however, it is one of the most effective things you can do to get the students ready for the exam. The nine days (one for each unit test) you spend doing this activity will make a huge difference in the way they approach the actual AP exam's FRQ.

STEP 4

Get Students Ready to Take the AP Exam

I leave two or three weeks to dedicate to reviewing for the exam in class. This means I have covered all nine units completely and we now have time to review.

I start by giving one of the three full-length exams found on AP Classroom to the students. Since my class is only 45 minutes, it takes two days for them to take just the multiple-choice exam. (By the way, this practice exam is not something I grade; it is for diagnostic purposes only.) When they have finished, have the students score their own test and identify the questions they missed by marking in the appropriate box in the following chart. This allows the student to self-diagnose which units they need to devote the most time to. (The breakdown of questions by units in the following example comes from released Practice Test 2.)

Evaluate Your Performance

									# CORRECT	% CORRECT
Unit 1	13	27	32	40	57	60				
Unit 2	38	49	65	71	77					
Unit 3	1	2	3	14	18	28	76	79	80	
Unit 4	4	5	6	16	24	29	36	45	51	
	52	55								
Unit 5	17	25	26	50	53	56	59	62	63	
	64									
Unit 6	19	20	21	30	33	34	35	36	58	
	72	74	78							
Unit 7	15	23	37	46	47	48	55	61	73	
Unit 8	7	8	9	10	11	12	35	39		
Unit 9	6	22	31	41	42	43	44	54	66	
	67	68	69	70	75					

I set up stations in my class and allow the students to review in whatever way works best for them. Here are my stations:

▶ **Station 1: Review a chapter in *5 Steps to a 5 AP Environmental Science.*** If you have multiple copies of this book, students can use it to review. (The book can also be accessed online; see the instructions on the back cover.) This is especially important if the diagnostic test showed there was a chapter that they just didn't get the first time. The text in this book explains the subject, key terms are identified and defined, and review questions can be used to check the student's understanding.

▶ **Station 2: Make your own review card.** You know those laminated, posterlike cards they sell to students to review? They can make their own now that they know what topics they need to study. Then they walk away with a personalized study card just for them. I provide the students with a blank file folder and a variety of markers.

▶ **Station 3: Flash cards.** I have a list of 150 words they might need to know on the exam. A good place to start is the list of terms and their definitions at the beginning of each of the nine review chapters in *5 Steps to a 5 AP Environmental Science* (or the online Cross-Platform Edition of the book). The students then make flash cards on index cards of the words they need to review. An example follows:

Biome

A large region having similar climate and plant life, determined mostly by temperature and precipitation

▶ **Station 4: Taboo.** Here I've made a Taboo-type game for them to play. The game has cards a player draws with a word that they need to get their partner to say, but they can't use the taboo words. The following card provides an example:

Eutrophication
▶ Nutrients
▶ Algae
▶ Phosphates
▶ Many

They are trying to get their partner to say the word *eutrophication*, but they can't use the words *nutrients, algae, phosphates,* or *many* when they are describing it to their partner. Both partners need to know the definitions. I also have a textbook sitting next to this station in case they need to look up a definition.

▶ **Station 5: FRQs.** I have every single released FRQ printed on one side with the scoring rubrics on the other side (you can get this from the AP Classroom). The students can pair up or work on their own reviewing the question, thinking about or actually composing a response, and then checking their work with the scoring guideline to see if they would have received each point.

▶ **Station 6: Released multiple-choice questions.** Just like it sounds, I printed every single multiple-choice question that has ever been asked and I sorted them by unit. There is an envelope that says "Unit 1" on it and inside are all the questions ever asked that relate to Unit 1. Students draw a card, read the question on it, see if they know the answer, and then flip it over where I have written the answer on the back. This is something you could also do digitally if you wanted to. Students can focus on the units they found they need the most help with from their diagnostic exam.

▶ **Station 7: Practice math.** One of the FRQs students have to respond to involves math. This is usually math that is best done using dimensional analysis. If students know that math is not their strong point, they can spend time at this station, where I have lots of math practice problems for them to do. Most of these come from released math FRQs. My colleague Elisa McCracken developed a four-page math review sheet that I love to use with my students. It shows the important formulas and gives some examples of math problems they may see on the exam. I have included these four pages at the end of this teacher's manual. Making sure to practice math with your students is critical, and using this four-page sheet can really help them.

▶ **Station 8: AP Classroom videos.** At this station, I have a computer or iPads, and the students can simply log into their own AP Classroom and watch the videos that correspond to the units and topics they found from their diagnostic exam that they needed the most help on. You can set this station up with headphones so they don't disturb others.

▶ **Station 9: Take a practice exam.** You can have a station where students can practice taking the test using the released tests found in the AP Classroom. If students have access to *5 Steps to a 5 AP Environmental Science*, they can take the two full-length practice exams found at the end of the book and score themselves (see instructions for accessing the Cross-Platform Edition on the back cover). Taking the diagnostic test found in Chapter 3 of this book is especially useful for students. A chart in the book, similar to the one provided earlier, allows them to reassess their weaknesses, showing the progress they've made and the areas they still need to study. Since taking the test requires three or four days of class time, a good option is to have the students do it at home and use the class time to evaluate their progress.

I'm sure you can come up with other stations to add to these, but these can help you get started. My philosophy is the that students know what they need and are mature enough to use this time wisely. I am also around to help with any individual questions they may have and to do a mini review over any topic they want my help with.

STEP 5

Become a Better Teacher Every Year

A good AP teacher tries to do better, regardless of how they measure success. If there is anything that didn't work as well as you had hoped this year, there's always next year to try something different. The message is the same whether you are a novice at the AP exam or a veteran: your goal is to become a better teacher every year.

A qualifying score is considered a 3 or better. I tell teachers that a 3 or better means "college done." They earned a score that, at most universities, will mean they get the college credit and they do not have to take the class again. However, what about a 2? I say a 2 is "college ready." This means that the student that earns a 2 is ready to do very well in this course when they take it in college. They have the background knowledge, and with just a little more time and practice, they will be ready to earn that A in their college environmental science class. Keep this in mind when you receive the score reports in July; you can be proud of those students who earned a qualifying score but also celebrate those students who are college ready!

How do you judge success? There is no right or wrong answer to this. We all teach at different schools with different students. A few students come to you with strong science and math skills and, let's be honest, could probably pass the exam on day 1 with or without you. Most students may lack some of the skills or knowledge that is needed to do well on the AP exam. These students are the ones who need us most, and when they succeed, it is because of their effort and our support.

For all AP teachers, both new and experienced, the best thing you can do to improve is to use the Instructional Planning Report you will receive after student scores are calculated. You can access this document in your AP Classroom. You will get a breakdown of scores by unit, by question type (multiple choice and FRQ), and so on. This information is what you need to adjust your course for the next school year. If you notice that students as a whole struggled with a particular unit, this is where you make changes. Perhaps you'll spend a little extra time on this unit or maybe you'll find new activities to use during class. Maybe you'll review this unit in class before next year's AP exam. What if students did really well on the multiple choice but not the FRQs? How can you get some additional professional learning to better teach them how to write? It may take a few years to see results, but with attention to the Instructional Planning Reports and with continuous adjustments to your class, your scores will soar!

It is also very important to attend an AP Summer Institute (APSI), both as you begin to teach the course and also every few years as you continue. To get new ideas and insights, I recommend that you attend summer institutes by different instructors. I also encourage all AP teachers to apply to be a reader for the AP exam after they have three years of teaching the AP class under their belts. The AP reading is the best professional learning experience you can receive. You can apply online through the College Board's website.

Additional Resources for Teachers

Make sure to always use the College Board's CED for the course that is found at: https://apcentral.collegeboard.org/courses/ap-environmental-science/course. If the topic is in the CED, it will be on the AP test. If the topic is not in the CED, it is out of the scope for the course and will not be tested.

Videos

I have organized these by units. There are many more, but these are some of my favorites. Also, do not forget that AP Classroom has videos for every topic.

Unit 1

Strange Days on Planet Earth: Predator— https://youtu.be/SIXAytRvDQ0

Strange Days on Planet Earth: Troubled Waters— https://www.youtube.com/watch?v=eVKlt3DLzso

Unit 2

Cane Toads (I like the older one)— https://www.youtube.com/watch?v=6SBLf1tsoaw

Planet in Peril (Anderson Cooper from CNN)

Unit 3

Miniature Earth— https://www.youtube.com/watch?v=i4639vev1Rw

World in the Balance— https://www.pbs.org/wgbh/nova/transcripts/3108_worldbal.html

Population Dot— https://www.youtube.com/watch?v=khFjdmp9sZk

TED Talk Bubbles— https://www.ted.com/talks/hans_rosling_the_best_stats_you_ve_ever_seen?language=en#t-57587

60 Minutes: "Miracle" Food Saves Lives—https://www.youtube.com/watch?v=M-qkTmHqW5k

TED Talk Boxes— https://www.ted.com/talks/hans_rosling_global_population_growth_box_by_box?language=en

Unit 4

Your Yard Is Evil: John Green— https://www.youtube.com/watch?v=-enGOMQgdvg

Unit 5

Dirt! The Movie—http://www.dirtthemovie.org/

Unit 6

Japan's Killer Quake—https://www.pbs.org/wgbh/nova/video/japans-killer-quake/

Chernobyl Heart— https://topdocumentaryfilms.com/chernobyl-heart/

Unit 8

60 Minutes: E-Waste— https://www.youtube.com/watch?v=-jSbYTNAJIQ

Strange Days on Planet Earth: Dirty Secrets— https://www.youtube.com/watch?v=eVKlt3DLzso

Unit 9

6 Degrees Could Change the World— https://www.youtube.com/watch?v=EU5tUY3W3WI

An Inconvenient Truth (there is the old one and a new one, but you have to buy or order)

Strange Days on Planet Earth: The One Degree Factor— https://www.dailymotion.com/video/x35hl34

Websites

I have broken down a few websites for each unit that might be useful for you. Some of these might be good to use with students, and others are good for you as the teacher as a reference.

Unit 1

Science World: What Is a Biome?— https://www.scienceworld.ca/resource/what-biome/

Khan Academy: Biogeochemical Cycles—
https://www.khanacademy.org/science/
biology/ecology/biogeochemical-cycles/a/
introduction-to-biogeochemical-cycles

Unit 2

Biodiversity Hotspots—
https://www.conservation.org/priorities/
biodiversity-hotspots

Unit 3

World Population Clock—
https://www.census.gov/popclock/

US Census Data—https://data.census.gov/cedsci/

Population Reference Bureau—https://www.prb.org/

CIA World Factbook—
https://www.cia.gov/the-world-factbook/

Unit 4

Online Meteorology—
https://www.youtube.com/watch?v=5QX8O1vq31k

Coriolis Effect—
https://www.youtube.com/watch?v=OT7O_1MdFKc

NOAA Weather Maps—
https://www.nws.noaa.gov/outlook_tab.php

Unit 5

The 1988 Forest Fires of Yellowstone National Park:
https://www.x98ruhf.net/yellowstone/fire.htm

Unit 6

Timeline of Nuclear Waste—
https://www.pbs.org/wgbh/americanexperience/
features/three-nuclear-technology/

Energy Audit Activity—
https://securemedia.collegeboard.org/apc/ap03_
apes_homeenergy__29565.pdf

Unit 7

Air Quality Index—
https://www.airnow.gov/aqi/aqi-basics/
EPA: Air Topics—
https://www.epa.gov/environmental-topics/air-topics

Unit 8

EPA: Ecosystems and Air Quality—
https://www.epa.gov/eco-research/
ecosystems-and-air-quality

Unit 9

Greenhouse Effect 101—
https://www.nrdc.org/stories/greenhouse-effect-101

National Geographic: Greenhouse Effect—
https://www.nationalgeographic.org/encyclopedia/
greenhouse-effect/

NOAA Ocean Acidification:
https://www.noaa.gov/education/
resource-collections/ocean-coasts/ocean-acidification

National Geographic Stratospheric Ozone Depletion:
https://www.nationalgeographic.com/environment/
article/ozone-depletion

EPA Climate Change:
https://www.epa.gov/climate-change

AP Environmental Science Math Review, Page 1

Things to Know
Million = 10^6
Billion = 10^9

Mega = 10^6 (example: 1,000,000 BTU 1 MBTU)
Kilo = 10^3 (example: 1000 watts/ 1 kW)

Half-Life
1 1/2 1/4 1/8 1/16 1/32 1/64

pH or Richter Scales
These scales are both logarithmic scales, meaning that an **increase or decrease of a natural number changes the concentration by tenfold**. For example, a pH of 3 is ten times more acidic than a pH of 4. Likewise, a pH of 3 is one hundred times more acidic than a pH of 5.

Percent
Percent is the part divided by the whole times 100
$$\text{Percent Change} = \frac{N - O}{O}$$
N = new (the newest number or year),
O = old (the oldest number or year)

Population Stuff
Approximate population for:
The world: 7.5 billion
China: 1.3 billion
India: 1.3 billion
The US: 325 million

Per Capita = Per Person

Population Math
Population Density
Number of individuals/area

Growth Rate as a %
B-D/population size times 100

Rule of 70
DT = 70/GR

Energy
KWh = kilowatts times hours
Efficiency can be solved using ratios

Show your work!
Numbers must be labeled in the setup (use dimensional analysis).
Don't forget to always put your unit labels! A number means nothing without a label to go with it.
Your numbers must be neat.
If you can't use scientific notation, count your zeroes when you multiply and reduce them when you divide. Double check.
Always make sure your answer makes sense!
Label and identify your answers clearly!

AP Environmental Science Math Review, Page 2

Dimensional Analysis

1. Determine what unit is given and what unit you are seeking in the answer.

2. The given unit will be in the top of your chart (numerator).

3. Write the unit you are seeking at the right margin of your paper. This unit will not cancel and will be in the top of your chart (numerator).

4. Determine the conversion factors you need to go from the given to the answer unit. (Conversion factors are relationships between numbers.)

5. To cancel out the original unit, place that same unit in the conversion factor's denominator.

6. Continue this procedure until the last remaining unit is the actual unit you are seeking in your answer. When you arrive at the final unit, circle it.

Example Problem

It is estimated that the world loses 12,614,400 forested hectares per year based on an estimate of 1 acre of forest cleared per second.

Determine whether the state of New Jersey, Virginia, or Texas is closest in size to 12,614,400 hectares. You will need the following information to solve this problem:

▶ Approximately 2.5 acres = 1 hectares (ha)

▶ 1 square mile = 640 acres

▶ New Jersey is 8,721 square miles

▶ Virginia is 42,774 square miles

▶ Texas is 268,581 square miles

New Jersey

$$(8,700 \ mi^2) \times \left(\frac{640 \ acres}{mi^2} \right)$$
$$= 5,568,000 \ total \ acres \ in \ New \ Jersey$$
$$5,568,000 \ acres \times \left(\frac{1 \ ha}{2.5 \ acres} \right)$$
$$= 2,227,200 \ ha \ in \ New \ Jersey$$

Answer

Virginia is 10,932,200 hectares, which is closer in size to 12,614,400 hectares than the other two states.

Note: When confronted with a math problem that includes "messy numbers" and does not require a precise answer, as in this situation or in many multiple-choice questions on the exam, the solution will be easier to find if you round the numbers first.

AP Environmental Science Math Review, Page 3

Ratios/Proportions

Remember, a proportion is set up in the form $\dfrac{A}{B} = \dfrac{C}{D}$.

Example 1: If a car can travel 325 miles on 15 gallons of gasoline, how many gallons will it take to drive 800 miles?

To set up this proportion, the first fraction should be the information that we know and that is directly related to each other. In this case, it's "325 miles on 15 gallons." I usually put the first number on top and the second one on the bottom, but it doesn't matter. <u>What's important is that if we put miles on top in the first fraction, we must put miles on top in the second fraction as well</u>. This is why the labeling is important.

So, where does the 800 go? _____

$$\frac{325 \text{ miles}}{15 \text{ gallons}} = \frac{\text{miles}}{\text{gallons}}$$

Since the problem asks "how many gallons," then the "gallons" is our variable. You can use any variable you want, but mathematicians usually just use "x." Again, notice that since "gallons" is on the bottom in the first fraction, it must be on the bottom in the second fraction. So, here's what we should have:

$$\frac{325 \text{ miles}}{15 \text{ gallons}} = \frac{800 \text{ miles}}{x \text{ gallons}}$$

Once we have our numbers, we can drop the labels for the actual work of solving for "x":

$$\frac{325}{15} = \frac{800}{x} \leftarrow \text{Cross multiply!}$$

Answer: 37 gallons

AP Environmental Science Math Review, Page 4

Percent Change

To calculate the percent change:

▶ First, work out the difference (increase) between the two numbers you are comparing.

▶ Increase = new number − original number

▶ Then divide the increase by the original number and multiply the answer by 100.

▶ % increase = increase ÷ original number × 100

▶ If your answer is a negative number, then this is a percentage decrease.

Example Problem 1

Global Iron and Steel Data

1.6 billion tons of iron ore are used yearly to make pig iron.

1.2 billion tons of pig iron are produced each year.

Iron ore reserves are estimated to be 800 billion tons.

95% of iron ore that is mined is used in steel production.

Calculate the weight (in tons) of pig iron that could be produced if all of the estimated global iron ore reserves were used for pig iron production.

$$\frac{1.2}{1.6} = \frac{x}{800} = 600 \text{ billion}$$

Example Problem 2

A typical home in the northern United States might require 120 MBTUs of heat for the average winter. If this heat were supplied by a natural gas furnace operating at 60 percent efficiency, how many MBTUs are needed?

$$\frac{60}{100} = \frac{120}{x}$$

x = 200 MBTUs will be needed to heat the house